AMAZING TENNESSEE

AMAZING STORIES, HISTORICAL ODDITIES AND FASCINATING TIDBITS ABOUT THE VOLUNTEER STATE

T. Jensen Lacey

T. Jensen Lacey

ISBN: 978-0-9978344-8-2

Cover by Michael Ilaqua
www.Cyber-Theorist.com
FV-16
Printed in the United States

WWW.MOONHOWLERPUBLISHING.COM
PO BOX 1175, FAIRHOPE, AL 36533

MOON HOWLER PUBLISHING, LLC

AMAZING TENNESSEE: AMAZING STORIES, HISTORICAL ODDITIES AND FASCINATING TIDBITS ABOUT THE VOLUNTEER STATE

T. Jensen Lacey

FOREWORD BY THE GOVERNOR

When Tennessee celebrated its bicentennial not long ago, one fact became clear: our state owes its progress and promise to its people. Some of the stories are captured here.

T. Jensen Lacey offers an entertaining collection of facts, oddities of history, and tales both true and tall.

-From the Governor's Office
The Capitol, Nashville, Tennessee

T. Jensen Lacey

PREFACE

SOME TIPS ON HOW BEST TO ENJOY THIS BOOK

I love researching and writing history, and I enjoy telling folks where to see more about virtually any event (such as museums or historical homes). Thus, at the end of this book you will find a section titled "Virtual Tennessee," which gives websites for places mentioned in each chapter's stories. If you have AMAZING TENNESSEE in e-book form, you can easily tap on a hyperlink I've added in the "Virtual" section and go to websites that offer more information about tour-able places in the Volunteer State.

Thanks for getting a copy of AMAZING TENNESSEE!

T. Jensen Lacey

ACKNOWLEDGMENTS

Just like the saying goes, "It takes a village to raise a child," to paraphrase that and apply it to a work such as this, "It takes many people to write a book." In this, the republication of AMAZING TENNESSEE, I met, interviewed and spoke with many people who were, in their own unique way, a huge help to me. These include:

The staff of the Office of the Governor of Tennessee, Bill Lee, and a special thanks to Gov. Lee for writing the Foreword. The staff of Tennessee Department of Archives and History, as well as Fay Hicks and Jill Kilgore at the Tennessee Department of Tourism, a huge thanks for all your help.

Shout-out goes to Sutton and Deb Flynt, who put me up when I was around the Nashville area. National Park Service Ranger Emma Murphy was helpful in giving me information about the Andrew Johnson National Historic Site, as well as other places in Tennessee that are under the auspices of the National Park Service. Thanks to Mayor Doris Hensley of Erwin for the (positive!) update on the story of Mary the Elephant.

Debbie Coplen, Traci Smith and Mary Kellogg (owner) were all a great help with the story on the Titanic Museum Attraction. I appreciate the extra information from Stacey Allen McGee of Tennessee Ghost Walkers. Thanks to Marleitta and Dan Cooper, along with Mary Lynne Bell of the Sam Houston Historic Schoolhouse who were so pleasant and forthcoming in their information on early education in Tennessee, and I thank them for that.

Tim Yates with the East Tennessee Historical Society was a font of information and help with things all related to that area of the Volunteer State. Another big thank-you goes out to the staff of The Museum of Appalachia in Norris (Natalie Lay and Jan Marshall), and to President Elaine Irwin Meyer, who were so helpful to me with the updates on the museum.

Special thanks to Laura Beaver, Managing Director of the Casey Jones Village, and to CEO Clark Shaw for their updates on the newly expanded and improved Casey Jones Village, and new photos. I appreciate the information and photos from Sue Bell and George Zepp of Historic Rugby Living Heritage Museum. Elaine Turner of Heritage Tours, I owe you a big "thank you" for the information on the Underground Railroad (Slave Haven) and the W. C. Handy Boyhood Home.

Interpretive Director Carol Borneman of Cumberland Gap National Historic Park was very helpful with my story about updates on the park and its newest amenities. Ruby Fall's Lara Caughman was a gem to help me out with the information on the newest amenities found there. A big thanks goes to Keith Wimberly of Old Stone Fort Archaeological State Park for an update on that story.

And to all the other dozens of folks who were helpful and friendly, I thank you.

AMAZING TENNESSEE

AMAZING STORIES, HISTORICAL ODDITIES AND FASCINATING TIDBITS ABOUT THE VOLUNTEER STATE

T. Jensen Lacey

CHAPTER ONE

Truly Bizarre Events and Notorious Tennesseans

"I Got This Six Point with my Chevy Pickup": The Road Kill Bill

In 1999 Representative Tommy Head (D-Clarksville) and Senator Tim Burchett (R-Knoxville) sponsored the "Road Kill Bill" in the state house and senate. The bill proposed to make legal the keeping and consuming of wild game, such as deer and bear, accidentally killed by motorists. The house passed it, 95-0; in the senate, there was only one dissenting vote, and Governor Don Sundquist allowed it to pass without his signature.

This legislation was the topic of many comedy talk shows, such as The Tonight Show with Jay Leno, but the politicians themselves were not without a sense of humor. For example, when asked his opinion of the legislation, Senator Steve Cohen was quoted in The Tennessean as saying, "This is really a Jewish

Mother's bill. 'There are people in Europe who are starving. Eat it.'"

The Road Kill Bill gives a new meaning to the term "bumper crop."

Notorious Tennesseans

Tennessee has more than its share of colorful, notorious folks. Here are just a few.

The Harpe Brothers: Micajah ("Big Harpe") and Wiley ("Little Harpe") were bloodthirsty thieves and their story is a grim one. They started out stealing stock from their neighbors in Beaver Creek around 1797, but they went on to robbing travelers, often murdering them in the most gruesome ways. For example, one man named Johnson was robbed and killed, then the brothers cut open Johnson's body, filled it with stones, and tossed it in the Holston River.

Big Harpe made his fatal mistake in 1799 when he killed the wife and baby of a man named Moses Stegall. Stegall rounded up a posse and caught Big Harpe in Kentucky. Enraged with grief, Stegall reportedly decapitated Big Harpe with a butcher knife—while he was still conscious. His head was hung on a stake at a crossroads (called after that Harpe's Head) in Highland Lick, Kentucky.

Little Harpe didn't learn a lesson from this, for he continued to rob travelers along the Natchez Trace. He was caught and hanged at Gallow's Field in 1804, near the Trace. Although the Harpe brothers are long gone, they are hardly forgotten: in March of 2017, an ezine known as The Vintage News ran a story about the Harpe brothers, proclaiming them as "the first recorded serial killers in the United States."

John Andrews Murrell: This amoral outlaw with an air of gentility was launched into crime at an early age by his mother, a hotel owner near Columbia, who taught John and his siblings how to rob from their guests. He grew up to become a horse thief, robber, slave stealer, and murderer. The most infamous of his acts, though, was a regional slave rebellion he tried to arrange in 1835 whereby on a set day the slaves were to turn on their owners and kill them. It wasn't that he was sympathetic to the plight of slavery; he hoped the resulting chaos would make his looting easier. The plot was discovered and more than fifty white men and an unknown number of black men were banished, hanged, or beaten. Murrell was tried and convicted of this despicable act and sentenced to nine years of hard labor in the Tennessee State Penitentiary in Nashville. He died in 1844 in Pikeville, shortly after his release from prison.

William Walker: Born in Nashville in 1824, Walker was a brilliant man, academically. He was one of the youngest graduates from the University of Nashville in 1838, and then he earned his MD degree at the University of Pennsylvania in 1843. He also studied in Edinburgh, Scotland, and became a lawyer.

Then he decided he wanted to rule a country. In 1853 he went to California, formed a small army, and attempted to conquer Lower California and Sonora in Mexico. This failed and the U.S. government arrested him for violating neutrality laws. Soon freed, he invaded Nicaragua and became its President in 1856–57. Then he was forced to leave. He tried to gain control of Honduras, but he was captured and executed. History calls him "The Grey-Eyed Man of Destiny."

Edward Zane Carroll Judson ("Ned Buntline"): Using the nom de plume Ned Buntline, Judson edited and published in numerous Nashville publications, including the South-Western Literary Journal. Accused of having an illicit relationship with a married woman named Mary Porterfield, he killed her husband, William, in "an altercation" on March 11, 1844. When William's family came to lynch Judson, he jumped from the City Hotel's third floor to escape them, and ultimately left Nashville.

This man became known as "the King of the Dime Novelists" and also launched the show business career of Buffalo Bill Cody.

"Colonel" James Russell Davis: Born in 1840, this colorful character is said to have been a member of a Confederate guerrilla group that operated independently during the Civil War. Davis once tried to enter a cross-country car race but couldn't renew his driver's license because he was 108 years old. Davis claimed to be Cole Younger, a member of the James Gang, and he appeared with J. Frank Dalton, who claimed to be the real Jesse James, on the TV show "We the People" in 1950. He died two months after this appearance.

Annie Cook: After the Civil War, this attractive woman of German descent opened a brothel in Memphis, called Mansion House, one of eighteen in the city. When the yellow fever epidemic hit in 1873, she dismissed her "working girls" and turned Mansion House into a hospital. In 1878, when the fever gripped the city again, she repeated this charitable act and earned praise from Christian ladies' organizations. Unfortunately, Cook herself became a victim of the disease and when she died, the Memphis Commercial Appeal gave her this editorial eulogy: "Out of sin, the woman, in all the tenderness and fullness of her womanhood, merged, transfigured and purified, to become the healer." Cook's work inspired some of her "girls" to take up nursing as their new profession.

George Maledon: It's always good when people like the line of work they're in, but George Maledon was especially devoted to his. He was an executioner, who personally hanged sixty of the eighty-eight men sentenced to death by Judge Isaac Parker, the famous "hanging judge" of Fort Smith, Arkansas. At times he sprang the trap of as many as six people at once!

Along with his twenty-one years (1875–96) of professional executing, he is credited with killing five would-be prison escapees.

After Maledon retired, he was a colorful storyteller in the Federal Soldiers' Home in Johnson City. He took pride in doing his job right the first time, for he liked to say, "I never hanged a man who came back to have the job done over." He died in 1911 and is buried in Johnson City (Washington County). You can see his grave at Mountain Home National Cemetery, plot E, row 5, grave 1.

Kid Curry and Annie Rogers: Harvey Logan, known to history as Kid Curry, and Delia Moore, really Annie Rogers, were members of the Wild Bunch. Their leaders were Butch Cassidy and the Sundance Kid. Kid Curry was captured in 1901 after a shoot-out with Knoxville police. Annie got into trouble when she tried to exchange five hundred dollars in stolen Montana bank notes at the Fourth National Bank in Nashville that same year, but Curry helped get her acquitted, saying he gave her the money. He then escaped from the Knoxville jail in 1903, tried to join Cassidy and Sundance in South America, but failed. He fled to Colorado, where he finally shot himself and saved the legal system the trouble of executing him for his misdeeds. Annie's fate remains a mystery.

Night Riders: For several months in 1908, masked riders wreaked their own form of justice on people affiliated with the West Tennessee Land Company. The Night Riders, composed of men and women who lived in the area, had always taken much of their subsistence from Reelfoot Lake, but the land company had secretly bought it and planned to drain at least part of it and turn it into cotton fields. Most of the public sympathized with the Night Riders, seeing the terrorism as a form of self-defense. On the night of October 19, 1908, some of the Night Riders kidnapped two of the company's officers, Quinton Rankin and R. Z. Taylor, from Ward's Hotel in Walnut Log. Rankin was murdered; Taylor escaped into swampland and was rescued the next day.

Governor Malcolm Patterson called in the Tennessee National Guard to quell the violence and identify and capture the Night Riders. By the end of October, almost one hundred alleged members of the group were assembled in a makeshift camp. Six of them were convicted and sentenced to death, but their conviction was overturned by the Tennessee Supreme Court in 1909.

The Tennessee Historical Society recorded this infamous event as one of the most polarizing ones of West Tennessee, with neighbor pitted against neighbor in the region of Reelfoot Lake. As a result of the West Tennessee Land Company's greed and the subsequent Night Riders' violence, the state of Tennessee acquired the land in 1914, returning it to the people.

Today, Reelfoot Lake is one of Tennessee's premier State Parks, with cabins, a campground, an RV park, and the lake itself is full of largemouth bass, bream, and catfish. Also located at Reelfoot Lake is the lovely Blue Bank Resort, which offers hunting, fishing and nature packages. See "Virtual Tennessee" for websites.

J. Frank Dalton: Also known as "Happy Jack," this man's real identity remains a mystery. While working at a carnival, he met Frank James, and Dalton appeared at the Tennessee State Fair in 1948 as Jesse James himself. His claims were supported by "Colonel" James Russell Davis. Debunked by some as a weaver of fantasy, Dalton circulated the story of the Confederate Underground, a group also known as the Knights of the Golden Circle, who reputedly were plotting for a second Civil War from their headquarters on Fatherland Street in Nashville. Dalton died in 1951.

Did You Know?

The "battle of Athens" was a peacetime battle, fought by post–World War II veterans against a corrupt political ring believed to be attempting to rig the election of 1946. To force the sheriff, Pat Mansfield, to return confiscated ballot boxes, the veterans broke into the National Guard Armory, took weapons and ammunition, and, when the boxes were still not returned, opened fire on the deputies and blew up the front of the jail with dynamite. Although this was an embarrassment to many because of the negative national press it got, the battle of Athens came to be a source of pride among those who, returning home, found themselves fighting for their freedoms on their home turf.

Jacob Franklin "Jake" Butcher: With his brother Cecil Butcher Jr., Jake amassed a multibillion-dollar empire in the banking business in the 1970s and early 1980s, taking over

Hamilton National Bank in Knoxville, whose name he changed to United American Bank. Federal bank examiners began to suspect that the Butchers were moving their assets from one bank to another, making it seem as though they had more money than they did. The investigation proved the examiners right: they discovered a paper pyramid of bank fraud, unsecured loans, and forged documentation.

Jake Butcher, who had been a strong contender in a gubernatorial race, pleaded guilty to bank fraud charges in 1985. Although he was sentenced to twenty years' prison time, he only served seven and was released on parole in 1992.

A Tragedy within a Tragedy: When a Murder Victim's Family Pleaded for the Accused

Martin Luther King Jr. stood on the balcony of the Lorraine Motel in Memphis, waving to the people below. It was April 4, 1968, at the height of the Memphis sanitation strike, and he was there to support it as part of his Poor People's Campaign. He felt a sense of change in the air, but also of violence. Only the night before he had said, "I may not get there with you, but we as a people will make it to the Promised Land."

His words were eerily prophetic. A gunshot sounded and onlookers watched in horror as King fell dead, the victim of an assassin's bullet. Charged with the slaying was James Earl Ray, who was soon afterward arrested in London, England. He pleaded guilty to the shooting and was sentenced to ninety-nine years in prison. Until recently, that would have been the end of the story.

The Lorraine Motel in Memphis, where Dr. Martin Luther King Jr. was assassinated, was reopened as the National Civil Rights Museum in 1994. (Courtesy Memphis Convention & Visitors Bureau)

Ray, however, began to recant his guilty plea. First, he told people he pleaded guilty because he had been framed with overwhelming evidence against him. He felt his family was threatened and feared for the death penalty. As the years dragged on, his incarceration seemed interminable. Then, when Ray fell ill from liver disease, his pleas for a new trial and justice began to reach more and more people.

Some of those people included the family of Martin Luther King Jr., especially one of King's sons, who went to see Ray. In an extraordinary conversation in the Tennessee State Prison, Dexter King asked Ray, "Did you kill my father?"

Ray was near death and in need of a liver transplant. People in that kind of situation usually have little to hide. He looked King in the eyes and responded, "No, no, I didn't. No."

King's amazing response was, "I believe you and my family believes you. And we will do everything in our power to see you prevail."

Since then, Jerry Ray (James Earl Ray's brother), Dexter King, and Coretta Scott King (King's widow) have tried to have

James Earl Ray continued to protest his innocence, even when he was near death, and the family of his "victim," Martin Luther King Jr., agreed to fight for his retrial. This photo was taken in prison, shortly before his death. (Courtesy Jerry Ray)

the case reopened and a more in-depth investigation done of the clues surrounding the assassination, including a more sophisticated ballistics test of the alleged murder weapon. The Reverend James Lawson, minister and stalwart civil rights leader who had invited King to come to Memphis to support the strike, asked for donations to pay for Ray's liver transplant. If he stayed alive, the case would remain open. For a time, it seemed justice, or at least further investigation, had a chance.

In 1998 Attorney General Janet Reno ordered a limited investigation into allegations of a conspiracy in the King murder case. On April 23, 1998, James Earl Ray died of liver failure in Nashville Memorial Hospital, making a reopening of the case moot. It was thirty years and a few days after the death of Martin Luther King, Jr.

In a poignant postscript, in December 1999 the Associated Press reported, "A jury hearing a lawsuit filed by [King's family] found that the civil rights leader was the victim of a vast murder conspiracy, not a lone assassin." On hearing this, Mike Gabriel, Ray's friend who was at his deathbed, said, "Dexter [King] has said this will rewrite history."

While we may never know the real truth behind King's assassination, this is one of the few times in American history that the family of a murder victim went to such great lengths to help the accused murderer attain justice.

The Alcatraz of Tennessee, or, "Murder, Mayhem and Moonshine"

In the town of Petros (Morgan County), is a place that people used to dread going: Historic Brushy Mountain State Penitentiary. It closed its doors as a prison back in 2009, but it is now open as a tourist destination.

Brushy Mountain State Penitentiary has held many famous and infamous inmates, including James Earl Ray. It also has a museum located on the grounds that is open by appointment. One of the artifacts is a ladder used by Ray for an escape attempt—said to have precipitated the largest manhunt ever in Tennessee. In 2009, the prison which inmates called "The End of the Line" closed its doors as a penitentiary but is now re-purposed. Today, the former penitentiary offers tours, including paranormal tours. These tours are limited to no more than 25 people, and those wishing to take these tours must sign legal waivers before taking part.

Also, within this former maximum-security prison is a distillery. Using local grains and water obtained from nearby mountain springs, the spirit they dubbed "End of the Line Tennessee Moonshine" currently is offered in nine different flavors. My favorite is "Scared Straight."

The former prison also has a restaurant (The Warden's Table), a liquor distillery which offers "End of the Line Moonshine," and live concerts. See "Virtual Tennessee" for website information.

Another jail I enjoyed touring is the Old Jail Museum, located in Winchester (Franklin County), with exhibits of Native American artifacts found in the area, Civil War memorabilia, and items from World Wars I and II. Capable of holding sixteen prisoners, the jail operated as such until the 1970s, with the sheriff and his family living upstairs. Kids love having their pictures made as they stand inside one of the actual cells. See "Virtual Tennessee" for websites.

The Infamous James Gang: A Few Odd Facts

Jesse Woodson James: During the 1870s a man calling himself John David Howard lived alternately in Nashville and in Humphreys County. When it was revealed that he was Jesse James, he fled the state with his brother Frank and their families. One story that portrays him and his brother as folk heroes claims they gave local African Americans the proceeds from a bank robbery to start a school.

Alexander Franklin "Frank" James: Lawrence County historical documents indicate that Frank James, Jesse's brother, settled in that county after the Civil War. They also point to the existence of a secret underground in post–Civil War Lawrence County that included over twenty-five hundred Confederate soldiers who did not surrender; Frank James was involved in this group's furtive activities. It's said he also taught school and lived a quiet, private life. Another story says, however, that Frank left Tennessee and joined Thomas Coleman Younger in an ill-fated attempt at a Wild West show. Either way, the people in Lawrenceburg can show you the (contested) grave site of Frank James.

Thomas Coleman Younger: Younger and Frank James went into partnership to produce a show like Buffalo Bill's highly successful one. Unfortunately, the James-Younger Wild West Show was a failure, and the crew never seemed to stay out of trouble. Younger is buried in Lee's Summit, Missouri.

Jesse Edwards James: Born in Nashville to outlaw Jesse and Zee James, Jesse Edwards James's story may be the most colorful of all the James Gang. His parents never told him his real name (his own alias was Tim Howard and sometimes Charlie) until after his father's death in 1882. He wrote the book *Jesse James, My Father* in 1899, became a lawyer, and starred in a silent movie in 1920 entitled "Jesse James under the Black Flag." He portrayed his own father in the film.

William Ryan and James Andrew "Dick" Liddil: Ryan and Liddil were lesser-known members of the James Gang. Ryan was captured after the gang robbed trains in Missouri and Tennessee. He served time in prison (1881–89), then disappeared into obscurity following his release. Dick Liddil surrendered to legal agents in 1882, was pardoned, then worked as a tavern-keeper with Bob Ford, who took the credit for killing Jesse James.

A Mummy Story

Finis L. Bates was a lawyer in Memphis in the 1870s when he met a man in Texas who claimed to be Abraham Lincoln's assassin, John Wilkes Booth. Bates later identified a suicide victim in 1903 as the same man, although the man had been an actor going by the name of David E. George. Bates had the body

embalmed, stored it in his garage in Memphis, and wrote a book, *The Escape and Suicide of John Wilkes Booth*, which sold seventy thousand copies when it came out in 1907.

After Bates's death in 1923, the "mummy" became a sideshow exhibit in a carnival and was last seen at a fair in New Hope, Pennsylvania, in 1975. Since its disappearance, a Memphis man named Ken Hawkes has been avidly searching for the mummy to settle once and for all the question of its identity.

This quirky bit of history has become legendary and has been featured on NBC's Unsolved Mysteries and ABC's 20/20. Publications such as Life, The Saturday Evening Post, and Rolling Stone have run stories about the mystery as well. Even as recently as 2015, an article about the so-called "mummy mystery" appeared in an issue of Memphis: The City Magazine, so there is still a fascination with the phenomenon.

The mummy's whereabouts are currently unknown, but if you find it, please call Ken.

When the Fish Hits the Pan, or Gentlemen, Start Your Fins

Every April at the annual World's Largest Fish Fry in Paris, Tennessee, an unusual racing event is held. On the lawn of the Paris courthouse, using a fifteen-foot-long Plexiglas trough of water for a track, the Parisians hold a catfish race.

I still don't know: does the winning fish get to choose whether it's deep-fat or pan fried?

Where Lawyers, Politicians, and Preachers Can't Compete!

The Middle Tennessee town of Dickson has its own special event, and it's located in a rather weird spot. Since 1959, every April they have a Liar's Contest in the building formerly known as the Grand Ole Hatchery. The hatchery was once the nation's fifth largest chicken hatchery, but it now is devoted to music, comedy, and other entertainment, when it's not filled with liars.

Trying to maintain an amateur character, the Liar's Contest bars politicians, lawyers, and preachers. Otherwise there are no rules. One of the locals put it this way: "We do have some standards, but over the years we have gotten rid of most of them."

An Elephant Who Was Executed

Once upon a time an execution in the Volunteer State was of elephantine proportions: the hanging of an elephant called "Murderous Mary."

Mary was owned by the Sparks Brothers Circus, who had come to perform in the East Tennessee town of Kingsport. She was proclaimed to be "the largest living land animal on earth" and was said to weigh more than five tons. Mary was being attended by her temporary trainer, Walter Eldridge, when she made a lunge for the lemonade stand. When Eldridge made an attempt to restrain the pachyderm by hitting her with his club, Mary lost her temper, picked up the hapless trainer, and killed him. Some accounts say she trampled him; others say she dashed him on the ground. Either way, Eldridge was dead.

The people of Kingsport felt they had to avenge Eldridge's death, and according to one account, some kind of trial was held. The circus owner agreed to the death penalty; apparently, he was nearby when Mary grabbed her victim, and it could have been him. First, they tried to shoot her, but no bullet could pierce Mary's tough hide; so she was taken to nearby Erwin, the headquarters of Clinchfield Railroad, to be hanged from a railroad derrick.

After her weight broke the first chain around her neck, the handlers were successful with a stronger one, and Mary hung by the neck until she was dead, witnessed by between two hundred and five thousand people, depending on which account you read. A steam shovel was used to dig Mary's grave and bury her on the spot. Accounts of the hanging were published in such magazines as Tennessee Conservationist, Argosy, Popular Mechanics, and Ripley's Believe It or Not. Whether or not there was a trial, the hanging remains the most bizarre one ever to have occurred in the United States.

After killing her trainer, Mary the elephant was hanged from a railroad derrick in Erwin. (Courtesy the Erwin Record)

A postscript to this story is of a town that was, in the words of a National Public Radio (NPR) segment, "eager to redeem itself." Some high school students in nearby Elizabethtown heard about NPR's first-ever "Student Podcast Challenge," made an eleven-minute podcast about Mary, and their piece won the high school category. One Erwin citizen, Jamie Rice, formed an organization, RISE Erwin, in an effort to help the town get over the "black eye" the city had because of the incident.

Eager to get past the stigma of a town that hanged an elephant that was probably being abused by her trainer, the town now embraces and celebrates elephants. The first year of the celebration was in 2016, which marked the 100th anniversary of Mary's hanging. Rice also called The Elephant Sanctuary in Hohenwald, Tennessee, and asked for their cooperation (see their story in the chapter on Flora and Fauna). That first year, the town held a weeklong series of events to celebrate elephants. Local artists painted more than a half-dozen fiberglass elephants, which were auctioned off as a fundraiser, the proceeds of which went toward The Elephant Sanctuary.

I caught up with Erwin's Mayor, Doris Hensley, who told me, "For over a century, Erwin, Tennessee has been known throughout the world as the town that hung an elephant. We have been criticized severely for allowing the execution to have taken place in the Erwin railyard.

"In 2016, one hundred years after Mary's death, RISE Erwin came up with a plan to try to remove the stigma that Erwin is a cruel, animal hating, barbaric community. The Elephant Revival was a month-long event that memorialized Mary. The event consisted of festivals, a farmers' market, a parade and an auction. The town purchased 8 fiberglass elephants, had sponsors adopt the elephants, artists to paint them and displayed the whimsical elephants in downtown during summer months. In October the elephants were auctioned, and each year since 2016 a new "herd" of elephants arrives in Erwin. This year (2019) we have a 'herd' of 20 elephants. Funds received from the auction and during the festivities are donated to the Elephant Sanctuary in Hohenwald,

Tennessee. To date, the Town of Erwin has donated over $20,000 to the sanctuary."

Mayor Hensley added, "The whimsical elephants have

Every year, the town of Erwin shows their love for all things elephant with parades, a celebration and an elephant art competition. This, a whimsical tribute to Dr. Seuss, was one of the 2020 winners. Photo courtesy City of Erwin.

become a beloved addition to our town. We want the world to see that Erwin, Tennessee is a caring, humane, friendly town." Now, thanks to some forward-thinking citizens, the town of Erwin is being thought of as the town that LOVES elephants.

Q&A

Q. Into what animal-related partnership did Jesse James enter with a member of his gang, Edward Miller?

A. They bought a racehorse named Jim Malone. (It is suspected that James murdered his partner in an argument over the horse in the summer of 1880.)

Q. In Memphis in 1879, an ordinance was pending that prohibited the smoking of what particular substance?

A. Opium. (The editor of the Memphis Public Ledger wrote a protest in response.)

Q. Who was the original Grand Wizard and chief officer of the Ku Klux Klan?

A. General Nathan Bedford Forrest.

Q. What bizarre item did Jeremiah George Harris bring back as a gift to the Tennessee Historical Society when he returned from his travels with the U.S. Navy in 1860?

A. A mummy from Egypt. The mummy is still on display in the Tennessee State Museum, Nashville.

Q. What actor, who later committed a heinous murder, gave a benefit performance in Nashville in 1864?

A. John Wilkes Booth. (Ironically, his final performance was on February 12, the birthday of the president he assassinated fourteen months later.)

CHAPTER TWO

Politics, Military and Transportation Tales

Politics Makes Strange Bedfellows

Tennessee politicians have always had a special air about them, something that sets them apart from politicians in the rest of the country. They have the swagger of what has been called a "frontier democrat," showing, with flannel shirt sleeves rolled up, that they are just one of the people. In the gubernatorial race of 1886, two of Tennessee's more flamboyant politicians who ran against each other happened to be brothers.

Robert Love Taylor (born 1850) and Alf Taylor (born 1848) were born and raised in Happy Valley in Carter County. They enjoyed the rough-and-tumble antics and friendly fights any other brothers might have had, and then some, because they learned early on how to be at odds by their parents' example. Their father, Nathaniel G. Taylor, had been affiliated with the

Brothers Bob (left) and Alf Taylor Competed against each other in the 1886 race for the office of governor.
Courtesy Tennessee State Museum

Whigs in northeastern Tennessee. Their mother, Emmeline Hayes Taylor, had a brother (Landon C. Hayes), who'd served as senator from Tennessee in the Congress of the Confederate States of America. To her, most likely, the War of Northern Aggression and Southern Rebellion was not really ended. Thus was the home environment in which Bob and Alf Taylor were raised.

Alf grew up to become affiliated with the Republican Party; Bob went with the Democrats. When each decided to run for Governor in 1886, the situation attracted the imaginations of the people and the media.

Naming their political competition the "War of the Roses" after the fifteenth-century struggle for the English crown, Alf Taylor's Republicans wore red roses and Bob's Democratic supporters, white. Their political stumping was amicable for the most part: they oftentimes shared not only a hotel room but the bed, as well. And, like so many politicians who are of a musical bent, Bob and Alf even got into a fiddling contest during their campaign of 1886.

When it came voting time, Bob won by a landslide victory of more than thirteen thousand votes. Undaunted, however, Alf persisted—and became governor when he was seventy-two, in the gubernatorial election of 1921.

Today Bob and Alf Taylor, the brothers who once shared a hotel room and bed while campaigning against each other, share a burial plot in Elizabethtown, Carter County, in front of the Franklin Club. You can see more about their life and times at the Tipton-Haynes State Historic Site in Johnson City. The site has steady visiting hours in the months of March through the end of October; it is recommended you call for hours November through February. See "Virtual Tennessee" for the website.

The "Unsinkable" in Pigeon Forge

"Mother, are we all going to die?" It was in April of 1912 that the 15-year-old Lucille Polk Carter stood with her siblings and parents and watched the horrifying drama around them unfold. They were standing on the boat deck of the R.M.S. Titanic. Everywhere they looked, hundreds of panicked people were trying to save themselves and their families in the aftermath of the great ship's having struck an iceberg. The Titanic was said to be what was then, at that time, the world's most opulent and luxuriously appointed liner in the world, the jewel in the crown of the White Star Line.

It was also said to be unsinkable, yet here she was, on her maiden voyage, with perhaps an hour remaining before she went below the waves of the Atlantic, never to be seen above water again.

A relative of Tennessee native and former U.S. President James Polk, Lucille had led what people call a "charmed life": she was born into an affluent family, enjoyed travel and private schools. She and her family had been touring Europe; her father had initially wanted them to travel back to the states on a different ship, but changed plans when he learned of the opportunity to be a "part of history," as passengers aboard the R.M.S. Titanic, and bought boarding passes for himself, his family and their three servants. He would soon learn how prophetic his words would be.

That tragic night of April 14, 1912, Lucille and her family survived (they were first class passengers). Around the world, newspaper accounts of the sinking of Titanic, and of the rescue by the Carpathia, sent shock waves throughout the civilized world.

Today, you and your family can experience Titanic for yourselves, and you can do so at Pigeon Forge, in the heart of the Smoky Mountains. When you first enter the White Star Line office to get your ticket, employees dressed in period costume will hand you a boarding pass with the name of an actual passenger of the ill-fated cruise. The outside of the ship is 1:2 scale of the original, but the interior is full-scale, including first-class rooms that are luxuriously appointed (as they might have been in 1912). Outside, you can see that the ship floats in a large pool of water, with an iceberg on its starboard side.

Inside, the grand staircase is a view not to be missed. The museum holds more than 400 artifacts, many of which were brought from the floor of the Atlantic Ocean, while others were found in the pockets of or on the bodies of those who did not survive. From greeters at the doors to docents who dress and take on the personae of their Titanic passenger (the "unsinkable" Molly Brown is one), you will feel as though you are stepping back in time to another era.

The Promenade deck is another favorite with tourists, as is the "Crow's Nest," where you can see the same view that the sailors did who initially saw the deadly iceberg. There is one room where you can actually touch a real iceberg!

The Titanic Museum in Pigeon Forge is a "must-see" for you and your family. See "Virtual Tennessee" for websites.

Bare-Faced Honest (along with everything else)

In 1966 a Knoxville panel consisting of three federal judges ruled a certain state law unconstitutional. The law was challenged by the American Sunbathing Association and the Tennessee Outdoor Club, because it tried to do away with nudist camps in Tennessee. Thus, nudist camps are still legal in Tennessee.

When in 2019 I checked on the status of these, there were three such camps, including a "family-friendly" one, and a nudist club in Knoxville. See "Virtual Tennessee" to see websites—it's the naked truth!

Sam Houston, Tennessee's Renaissance Man

"Johnny Smith, please rise and read from page 10 of our Grammar Primer." These words, or something similar to them, might have reverberated against the hand-carved log walls of the little one-room schoolhouse in Maryville, circa 1812. They were said by whom I consider to be Tennessee's very own "Renaissance Man," Sam Houston.

Sam Houston

Samuel Houston was not originally a Tennessean. Born near Lexington, Virginia, in 1793, Sam was the middle child of nine. After his father's death and the sale of their Virginia home, his mother took her large brood to a farm near Maryville, Tennessee.

Houston was impatient to learn all he could about everything and was an avid reader. To help support his family, he worked a while in a store in Maryville owned by a Mr. Weber, but he couldn't take being indoors.

Leaving with only some food, his books, and a musket, Houston ran away. For three years he lived with the Cherokee in their village on Hiwassee Island (in the middle of the

Hiwassee River), and there he learned to live in the natural rhythms of the native people. After some time with them, he could run twenty-five miles in a day alongside the best braves and hunt with a bow and arrow. Finally, the chief of the village gave Sam Houston an Indian name: Co-lon-eh, meaning "the Raven," one of the Cherokees' favorite birds.

After his three years with the Cherokee People, Houston returned to Maryville, and for a short time was a schoolmaster for the local children. You may know the rest of Houston's story: he became a self-taught attorney, then after Jackson became U.S. President, Houston became his envoy to the Indians. He also sided with Andrew Jackson's Tennessee Regulars and, in the 1848 Battle of Horseshoe Bend, was wounded. After marrying Margaret Lea of Marion, Alabama, Houston had eight children with her. He became one of the U.S. Senators to Texas, then later, Governor of Texas in 1859. He died in 1863, still opposing cessation and the Civil War.

His days as a teacher in Maryville are not forgotten. Mary Lynne Bell is Director of the Sam Houston Historic Schoolhouse in Maryville, and she told me that the schoolhouse has been lovingly restored, complete with hand-carved logs. Serving as the schoolhouse's "school-marm," Marleitta Cooper offers classes to school children, giving lessons as they might have been offered in Houston's day. Her husband Dan Cooper gives regular demonstrations on how to grind corn, taking visitors back to the early 19th century.

See "Virtual Tennessee" for websites relating to Sam Houston and his years living as Tennessee's own "Renaissance Man."

Death for Defending First Amendment Rights

Alone at the end of the workday in his newspaper office, Edward Carmack toyed with the handle of his Smith and Wesson as he contemplated the possibility of his own death. Little did he realize on the afternoon of November 9, 1908, that this would be one of the last thoughts he would ever entertain.

Born in 1858 in Sumner County, Carmack had always been outspoken, sometimes even vindictive, self-righteous, and passionate in his beliefs. With this attitude, he began to have troubles early on. He was suspended from the highly acclaimed Webb School in Bell Buckle for taunting a fellow student in a religious dispute; Carmack then took up the study of law instead of the classics that had been taught at his former alma mater.

Edward Carmack, editor of the Nashville Tennessean

Growing up during the strife between the North and the South, Carmack witnessed much of the Civil War and Reconstruction and began to keep a journal. This journalistic bent would stay with him the rest of his tragically brief life.

Edward Carmack had a number of interests. He established a law practice in Columbia, and for a time was editor and chief of both the *Nashville Democrat* and the *Memphis Commercial*

Appeal, as well as other smaller newspapers. He also served in the state legislature, the U.S. House of Representatives, and the U.S. Senate. He had high hopes to be chosen as the Democratic gubernatorial candidate during its 1907 convention, but to his dismay, Malcolm Patterson, someone with whom he politically disagreed, won the nod. Ultimately, his passions for both politics and journalism would lead to his death.

While Patterson was campaigning for governor of Tennessee in 1907, Carmack was editor of the Nashville Tennessean. Using his newspaper as a forum, Carmack voiced negative opinions about a future Patterson administration with its ties to a political machine, and denounced saloons and the use of liquor in any form.

As governor, Patterson had an enemy in Carmack, but the governor had an ally named Colonel Duncan Cooper, who had plans to defeat the proposed prohibition of liquor. The colonel and his son Robin threatened to harm Carmack if he wrote any further editorials against Patterson, his cronies, and the liquor trade.

Although he didn't want to believe the Coopers would do any real violence to him, Carmack nonetheless began carrying his Smith and Wesson revolver. One day he found himself in need of it.

After he left his office and headed for home on November 9, 1908, he stopped near the intersection of Seventh Avenue and Union Street to chat with two ladies of his acquaintance. The Coopers accosted him, and the moment Carmack had feared was upon him. There was no time to aim and shoot carefully. Four shots rang out, the women screamed, and Robin Cooper walked away, slightly wounded, with his father's help.

The outspoken editor of the Tennessean was dead with three bullets in his body.

Edward Carmack now lies buried in a cemetery in Columbia, but his statue stands on the capitol grounds. Both Coopers, father and son, were tried, found guilty of murder, and each sentenced to twenty years in prison. Through appellate procedures, the duo was later freed: Robin, on a technicality, and Duncan, by a pardon from Governor Patterson. Colonel Cooper died in his bed in 1922; his son Robin, however, was murdered in 1919 by unknown killer(s).

Carmack died exercising his right of freedom of the press under the First Amendment to the Constitution. Editors who wrote his eulogies, however, while praising him for his high and unbending standards, agreed with what the Memphis Commercial Appeal wrote: "His pen was too often steeped in bitterness . . ."

Today, you can see a statue of Carmack as he might have looked in his mature years. The statue stands outside the state capitol building in Nashville.

The question still has gone unanswered: Did Carmack die defending the First Amendment? Or did he ultimately die by his own "poisoned pen"?

Strange... but True!

One Bad Editor and One Worse Marksman

In Knoxville on March 11, 1882, an encounter similar to Carmack's occurred, but with results much less tragic—in fact, it was nearly comical. James Walker, editor of the Knoxville

Tribune, encountered his rival, William Rule, editor of the Knoxville Chronicle, near the corner of Gay and Church Streets. Walker had, as they say, "a bone to pick."

He demanded to know if it was true that Rule had written something insulting about him, and Rule replied yes, he had. "I demand an apology!" Walker announced. Instead, Rule began to strike Walker with his cane. Drawing his revolver, Walker shot at Rule, who first fell to the ground, then got up and fled to a nearby apothecary.

Walker sought out the sheriff and gave himself up. When he was released on bond, he discovered that his bullets hadn't even struck Rule; the editor had merely suffered from powder burns. You can see more about these unusual Tennessee stories at the Tennessee State Museum in Nashville, which opened in spring of 2019.

Tennessee and the Perfect Thirty-six

Anne Dallas Dudley (Mrs. Guilford Dudley) was the envy of every socially ambitious woman in Nashville. Prominent, respected, and wealthy, Anne Dudley was also one of Tennessee's first suffragettes. In the summer of 1920 she was actively campaigning for women's right to vote.

The nation's attention was totally riveted on Tennessee that year. Thirty-five states had already ratified what would become the Nineteenth Amendment, and ratification by only one more state was needed for it to become law. The Tennessee General Assembly was in session to consider having the state become "the perfect thirty-six."

Anne Dudley was right in the middle of things: she traveled throughout Tennessee, speaking to people about her vision of when "a woman's home will be the whole world" and urged Tennessee congressmen to vote for the amendment. She was scoffed at and ridiculed by the press and much of the public... that is, until her cause became more popular and even women who had no interest in voting began to support their choice to do so.

Another "War of the Roses" broke out in Tennessee that hot summer. Women who were for the amendment wore yellow roses and ribbons, and those who opposed it wore red. As time passed, more young ladies' and matrons' blouses were decorated with yellow than scarlet. Due in large part to Anne Dallas Dudley's efforts, Tennessee ratified the Nineteenth Amendment in August 1920, making women's suffrage the law of the land and furthering American women in their battle for equality of the sexes.

Today, you can visit the Women's Suffrage Memorial in Knoxville, Tennessee. Sculpted out of bronze by artist Alan LeQuire, it stands in Market Square, where it was first erected in 2006. There is also a Tennessee Woman Suffrage Monument in Nashville's Centennial Park, which was also created by LeQuire and unveiled in 2016. Both of these artistic works honor the women, including Anne Dudley, who campaigned for the state to ratify the 19th Amendment.

Due in large part to Anne Dallas Dudley's efforts, Tennessee ratified the Nineteenth Amendment in August 1920, making women's suffrage the law of the land and furthering American women in their battle for equality of the sexes.

Did You Know?

The first black man to hold judicial posts in the city of Nashville, and the first to hold the position of Supreme Court Justice of Tennessee, was Adolpho A. Birch. He was Nashville's first black assistant attorney general (1966), was the first black judge appointed to be in charge of General Sessions Court in the city (1969) and was named criminal court judge by Governor Ray Blanton (1978). He was appointed to the Tennessee Supreme Court in 1993.

Why Lamar Alexander Was Sworn in Early

January 7, 1979, was cold, dreary, and wet. Lamar Alexander and his wife, Honey, were preparing to move from their home in the Green Hills section of Nashville. Half of their possessions would go to their retreat in East Tennessee; the rest were being moved to the governor's mansion. Lamar Alexander was scheduled to be inaugurated January 10.

But Alexander would be sworn in early as Tennessee's governor. As Alexander sat writing his inaugural address, U.S. Attorney Hal Hardin telephoned him and came right to the point. Outgoing Governor Ray Blanton was about to release prisoners from the state penitentiary and Hardin suspected they had bought their freedom. To stop this from happening, Alexander had to take office immediately.

Alexander suggested that Hardin confer with some state leaders, including Lieutenant Governor John Wilder and State House Speaker Ned Ray McWherter, to get their thoughts on what was essentially a takeover. Although Wilder disapproved, saying the early swearing-in was unconstitutional, the general consensus was for Alexander to be inaugurated right away nonetheless.

Several hours later, wearing borrowed clothes because everything they owned had been moved during the day, Lamar, Honey, and their children were ready for the impromptu inauguration.

They piled into state trooper Herschel Winstead's unmarked car with their friend Tom Ingram and drove to the basement parking garage of the Supreme Court Building. Exiting an elevator, the Alexander family was enveloped by swarms of reporters, friends, and staff members. No one had been told what was going to happen; they had just been told to come.

Lamar Alexander took the oath of office surrounded by his friends and family. As he had written in his notes following Hardin's fateful call, he took office early because it was "in the best interests of the people of Tennessee."

Former Governor Ray Blanton was eventually convicted on charges relating to his unscrupulous activities and was imprisoned at Maxwell Air Force Base for twenty-two months. He died on November 22, 1996. The Tennessee State Museum, which opened its doors in the spring of 2019, has many exhibits offering more information on this time in Tennessee history. See "Virtual Tennessee" in the back of this book.

Hail to the (Vertically Challenged) Chief!

The tune "Hail to the Chief" was first played at the inauguration ceremony of Martin Van Buren in 1837. Sarah Childress Polk, however, is said to be the person responsible for the tune being played every time the president enters a room. She started this during the presidency of her husband, James K. Polk, the Tennessean who served from 1845 to 1849.

President Polk was only five feet, six inches tall. As a result, his entry often went unnoticed, and this annoyed Sarah. She had the White House band play "Hail to the Chief" so everyone in the room would know when President Polk arrived.

Every president since then (vertically challenged or not) has continued this musical tradition. The song itself has an interesting history. James Sanderson, an English composer, set the words from Sir Walter Scott's 1810 poem "The Lady of the Lake" to a traditional Scottish tune; he published the song in the United States in 1812. Here are the words so you can sing along:

Hail to the Chief
Hail to the Chief we have chosen for the nation,
Hail to the Chief! We salute him, one and all.
Hail to the Chief, as we pledge cooperation
In proud fulfillment of a great, noble call.
Yours is the aim to make this country grander,
This you will do, that's our strong, firm belief.
Hail to the one we selected as commander, Hail to the
President! Hail to the Chief!

(Words by Sir Walter Scott, music by James Sanders)

Incidentally, you can learn more about the life of James K. Polk, and his determined wife, by touring the President James K. Polk Home and Museum in Columbia, Tennessee. See "Virtual Tennessee" at the back of this book.

Lawrence County: Home of Aviation's Pioneer?

Soon after the Civil War, James Jackson Pennington of Henryville began making sketches of his "flying machine." His aeronautical wonder consisted of a balloon under which was suspended a fan, which drew air into a chamber and expelled it though a narrow opening, causing the machine to fly. In a letter to a friend, Pennington claimed, "My aerial bird had the power to... cross the briny deepe [sic] and plane the North Pole and conquer the world and will stop all Wars."

Originally his flying machine was about the size of a mouse trap, but Pennington continued to tinker with his machine, making it ever larger, until it could carry a book weighing several pounds. He patented it through the U.S. Patent Office in 1877. Still trying to convince the general public of the reality of air transportation, he exhibited his "aerial bird" at the Columbia Exposition in Louisville, Kentucky, in 1883 and was offered money for his invention by two mysterious unidentified men. Pennington would not sell it to them.

After his death in 1885, two mysterious unidentified men came to Henryville and visited with Pennington's widow. After she died, the Pennington daughters sought to find their father's plans of the "aerial bird," but although they located the patent in the U.S. Patent Office, the plans themselves were missing.

The family believes that Mrs. Pennington sold the plans to those two well-dressed, mysterious visitors. It was in 1903 that a plane did get constructed and take flight, but it wasn't in Lawrence County, or even in Tennessee. Two brothers by the name of Orville and Wilbur Wright made their historic flight in North Carolina.

Had the Wright brothers purchased those plans from Mrs. Pennington? Or were her two visitors aviation pioneers from Paris, France, as some suggested? It remains an unsolved mystery, but whatever the truth is in regard to Pennington and his plans, Pennington Field, the airfield in Henryville, carries his name in honor of his contribution to aviation.

You can see more about Pennington, and Tennessee's contributions to air travel, at the Tennessee Museum of Aviation in Sevierville. Also in Sevierville is the Tennessee Aviation Hall of Fame. One more museum well worth the trip is in Tullahoma, where you can tour the Beechcraft Heritage Museum and see pristinely restored aircraft. These three venues also have events such as "fly-ins" throughout the year (and, in the fall, the Beechcraft Heritage Museum hosts a "Beech Party"). See "Virtual Tennessee" for websites.

Strange... but True!

Shape Is Everything

Warren County, originally comprising nine hundred square miles, found itself shrinking as counties were formed around it. When the Tennessee State Constitution of 1834 ruled on boundaries and county seats, Warren County took on a distinctive shape.

The ruling said that when a new county was formed, the county seat had to be at least twelve miles from the county seat of the existing county. Therefore, with the creation of Grundy, Van Buren, Cannon, Coffee, and DeKalb Counties, Warren County became nearly perfectly round. It still has the nickname, "the Round County." You can learn more about Warren County's history and people by visiting the Warren County

Heritage Center and Museum in McMinnville. See "Virtual Tennessee" for website information.

For Railroad Buffs

Billed as "The Largest Operating Historic Railroad in the South," the Tennessee Valley Railroad Museum is located in Chattanooga. It was started in 1959 as a way to preserve the era of steam locomotion and passenger trains. The museum consists of an active restoration workshop where engines dating back to the 1900s and beyond are repaired and restored. In the train yard itself there is a working turntable, train depot (the East Chattanooga Station), and the museum inside the terminal. Regular six-mile train rides and special excursions (such as "The Polar Express" at Christmastime) are offered throughout the year.

Trains of the Tennessee Valley Railroad offer daily rides from Chattanooga, some with a dining car luncheon onboard. (Courtesy Tennessee Valley Railroad; photo by Steven R. Freer)

Roughly 99 miles from Nashville, you will find the Cowan Railroad Museum. It is housed in the original 1904-era wooden frame depot; exhibits include a steam locomotive, a caboose and other train cars, and inside the depot it is furnished much like it would have been more than 100 years ago, including uniformed telegraph operator (a mannequin) at his post.

Another interesting museum is located in Jackson, Tennessee: Casey Jones Village, which is dedicated to the courage and memory of "the brave engineer." Check out his story in Chapter 4, "Famous Tennesseans." See websites for both these places in "Virtual Tennessee" at the back of this book.

The Building of "the World's Steepest Passenger Railway"

In the latter part of the nineteenth century, people liked to come to Chattanooga in the summer months to enjoy the mountain elevation and the relatively cool climate it offered. For some alert entrepreneurs in Chattanooga, easy access to Lookout Mountain for these visitors would mean increased revenues for themselves and the city.

Two attempts at maintaining and establishing rail service to the top of Lookout Mountain had not gone well. Then a Chattanooga resident by the name of John T. Crass came up with the idea of an incline railway that would take passengers directly to the summit from a station at the base of the mountain. He formed the Lookout Mountain Incline Railway Company and set out to build the steepest, most direct route up the mountainside.

The first car ascended on November 16, 1895; today, the Incline Railway claims to be the steepest passenger railway in the world, with a grade of 72.7 percent at its steepest point. Named both a National Historic Site and a National Historic Mechanical Engineering Landmark, for over one hundred years it has taken millions of visitors up and down one of the most famous mountains in the world.

Hey this is Tennessee!
There has to be a section on trucks!

In Chattanooga in 1998, a group identified as "Friends of Towing" opened the International Towing and Recovery Museum. Why Chattanooga? Because the world's first tow truck was made there in 1916. The museum has over 20 antique

Antique tow trucks can be seen at the International Towing and Recovery Museum in Chattanooga. (Courtesy International Towing and Recovery Museum; photo by Mark Martin)

tow trucks and its hall of fame immortalizes manufacturers of tow trucks, more than 170 tow-truck drivers, and others who have had an international impact on the industry.

Strange... but True!

The "Impossible" Tunnel

When there was a desire to offer rail service between Nashville and Chattanooga, the problem was how to get over the imposing Cumberland Plateau. Then Gerald Troost, Tennessee's first geologist, made a suggestion: if the railroad engineers couldn't see a way over the mountain, why not bore a hole through it? He suggested a tunnel through the portion of the rocky ridge of the Cumberland Mountains located near Cowan, Tennessee. In 1848 the N&C engineers decided his idea was worth a try.

It was an arduous and dangerous process. First, they made five simultaneous digs on the top of the mountain, chiseling three shafts from the mountain top down to tunnel level 170 feet below. The workers hacked away at the mountain, aided only by the light from torches, using picks, shovels, hand drills, and sledgehammers. Every day for three years, using round-the-clock laborers, the work progressed until the three shafts had reached tunnel level. Then the workers divided into two crews, fanning out in opposite directions, and dug and hacked their way until they saw sunlight. The tunnel was completed in 1852. It was 2,228 feet long.

Incorporated in 1845, the N&C was the first successful railroad line completed in Tennessee, reaching Chattanooga by 1854. The N&C Railroad became the nucleus for the Nashville, Chattanooga and St. Louis line, which formed in 1873 and is today part of the CSX line.

The ride up the steep grade is a thrilling one, and the view at the top is breathtaking. See "Virtual Tennessee" for the website.

Did You Know?

At one time, the Louisville and Nashville Railroad had competition for its use of Union Station in Nashville. The Tennessee Central Railroad, founded by Jere Baxter, built a line that reached into previously inaccessible areas of Tennessee. The line was the major link to the outside world for many because of Baxter's efforts—but he failed in his attempts to wrest total control of Union Station from the L&N.

Something to see in McKenzie: The Browning Museum

On the fourth of July, people across America celebrate our nation's anniversary. In the little town of McKenzie, Tennessee, there's a wonderful museum that celebrates governors of the Volunteer State. It's in a rather nondescript building that used to be a post office on the town square in downtown McKenzie. Named after Gordon Browning, who governed during 1937-1939 (and again from 1949 to 1953), the museum houses an amazing array of gubernatorial memorabilia, family histories, priceless artifacts and genealogical records. So extensive are their records, in fact, that many people come here to research their family histories.

Browning, who was born and raised not far from where the museum stands, is well-chronicled in his namesake museum, as he was a deeply rooted Tennessee statesman. One display I particularly liked was the World War II exhibit, complete with all kinds of uniforms, weapons and tools dating back to the 1940s.

Salute to the Military in Nashville

An addition to the Tennessee State Museum, the Military Branch is inside the War Memorial building. The entrance is near the Vietnam War Memorial and admission is free. Inside are displays and interactive exhibits that have to do with conflicts as far back as the Spanish-American War to today.

Tennessee War Memorial building

Q & A

Q. How did Brownsville-born adventurer and author Richard Halliburton die in 1939?
A. In a storm while trying to cross the Pacific Ocean in his Chinese junk, the Sea Dragon.

Q. What was Tennessee's first official road?
A. Walton Road, named for William Walton, from Knoxville through Kingston to Nashville.

Q. What is Walton Road's highway designation today?
A. U.S. 70.

Q. In 1787 what delayed construction of Walton Road?
A. Indian fighting by the militia that had been called out to cut the wagon road.

Q. Where did the first section of interstate open in Tennessee in November 1958?
A. Ardmore, in Giles County, at the interchange of the Alabama border.

Q. In what city was the first scheduled airline stop in Tennessee?
A. Chattanooga, on December 1, 1925, on the Atlanta-to-Evansville route.

Q. During World War II, Camp Tyson, near Paris, performed what unique function?
A. It was the nation's sole training center for operators of barrage balloons employed for aerial defense of the coasts.

Q. The administration of what governor, the first to die in office, created the Department of Highways and Public Works that paved many miles of roads?
A. Austin Peay.

Q. More than fifty wind-tunnels test the aerodynamics of everything from car engines to space rocket models at what center near Tullahoma?
A. Arnold Engineering Development Center, which performs tests to simulate flight conditions—even to speeds of Mach 20. The B-2 Spirit Stealth Bomber was researched and developed at the AEDC. (Next time you watch a space vehicle's well-timed re-entry, remember that the wind tunnel project helped bring it to earth safely.)

Q. Who is the first Tennessee governor to serve two consecutive four-year terms of office?
A. Lamar Alexander.

Q. In 1920 Kingsport passed what bill to clean up the streets—literally?
A. The city's first antipollution ordinance, by which pigs were forbidden to roam the streets and were to be "removed from backyards."

Q. What colonel in the Confederate States of America and member of the Tennessee General Assembly and U.S. Congress was instrumental in removing federal troops from the beleaguered South and is buried in Henry County?
A. John DeWitt Clinton Atkins, 1825–1908.

Q. What Reconstruction-era governor of Tennessee was by trade a Methodist circuit rider and editor of the Knoxville Whig?

A. William G. "Parson" Brownlow.
Q. What trapper, soldier, and explorer served in the Tennessee General Assembly and the U.S. House of Representatives before dying at the Alamo in 1836?
A. David Crockett.

Q. On what day was the city of Nashville founded?
A. Christmas Day, 1779.

Q. What man, known for his oratory skills, built a home in Clarksville known as Emerald Hill, served in the Tennessee and Kentucky legislatures, and was a senator in the Congress of the Confederate States?
A. Gustavus Adolphus Henry, the "Eagle Orator of Tennessee." Incidentally, Emerald Hill is open to the public for tours, and is well worth the visit.

Q. What antebellum home near Nashville was built by the seventh president of the United States, who is buried on its grounds?
A. The Hermitage, home of Andrew Jackson. The Hermitage is also open for tours.

Q. As a result of the elections of 1966, what U.S. senator was the first popularly elected GOP senator in Tennessee's history and the first Republican to win a statewide election since 1920?
A. Howard H. Baker Jr.

Q. Senator Howard Baker Sr. refused to sign what racist document, which protested the U.S. Supreme Court's decision in the case Brown v. Board of Education (1954)?
A. The "Southern Manifesto."

Q. Because of his role in founding the United Nations, what Tennessee-born former U.S. senator and secretary of state received the Nobel Peace Prize in 1945?
A. Cordell Hull.

Q. What Tennessean was the first U.S. President to be impeached?
A. Andrew Johnson.

Q. Before turning to politics, Andrew Johnson followed what business?
A. Tailoring. (His first shop was in Rutledge, Grainger County.)

Q. In what town is the Andrew Johnson Homestead?
A. It is located in Greeneville, but the President Andrew Johnson Museum and Library is located in the town of Tusculum. See "Virtual Tennessee" for websites.

Q. Who was the first African American to serve in the Tennessee General Assembly, but whose first form of livelihood was as a barber?
A. Sampson W. Keeble. Incidentally, there is a bronze bust of Keeble, created by Roy Butler, inside the Tennessee State Museum in Nashville.

Q. In 1973 what object did Congressman Dan Kuykendall (R-Tenn.) hold up to dramatize his entreaty against the U.S. House of Representatives' rushing to begin impeachment proceedings against President Richard M. Nixon?
A. A hangman's noose, warning them not to become a "legislative lynch mob."

Q. During the fight for women's suffrage, the groups both for and against it stayed at what famous Nashville hotel?

A. Hermitage Hotel. Incidentally, this historic hotel, Nashville's first hotel, continues to operate and is a luxury, five-star hotel today!

Q. Between what state and what nation was the Treaty of Dumplin County signed in Sevier County in 1785?
A. The State of Franklin, represented by Major Hugh Henry, and the Cherokee Nation, represented by Ancoo, chief of the Chota, allowing settlement in the area between the Holston and French Broad Rivers.

Q. By what dramatic action did Lamar Alexander campaign for governor in 1978?
A. Walking across the state—1,022 miles.

Q. Who was the first African American surgeon in the Southeast and the first African American woman elected to the Tennessee General Assembly?
A. Dorothy Lavinia Brown. You can see more about her life and times at the Tennessee State Museum, Nashville.

Q. In 1958 what environmentally conscious U.S. senator from Tennessee recommended to President Dwight D. Eisenhower that he stop exploding nuclear weapons in the atmosphere for three years?
A. Al Gore Sr., father of Vice President Al Gore Jr.

Q. Who was the first African American to run for governor of Tennessee?
A. William Francis Yardley, in 1876.

Q. During the Civil War the U.S. Army Medical Corps legalized what controversial social practice?

A. Prostitution, to protect soldiers from disease, by legalizing and then regulating the "trade."

Q. In 1869 "Radical Republican" state senator Philip Nelson introduced a bill to allow women to wear what type of clothing?
A. Pants, for more freedom of movement. (The bill states: "Be it enacted, etc., that the costume now worn by female citizens of Tennessee be changed from petticoats to pants...")

Q. What three U.S. presidents came from Tennessee?
A. Andrew Jackson, Andrew Johnson, and James K. Polk. Incidentally, all three presidents' homes are open to the public (Jackson's is The Hermitage in Nashville; Johnson's is a National Historic Site in Greenville; and Polk's home is in Columbia).

Q. In 1772 James Robertson and John Sevier established what self-governing community in eastern Tennessee?
A. Watauga Settlers Association.

Q. In 1839 how many Cherokee were in Tennessee when their infamous forced march to Oklahoma began?
A. Around fifteen thousand men, women, and children (around four thousand died along "the Trail of Tears").

Q. Who was the first governor of Tennessee?
A. John Sevier. His historic home in Knox County is known as Marble Springs and is open to the public.

Q. In 1682 Tennessee was claimed for what country?
A. France, by Pierre Cavelier, Sieur de La Salle.

Q. What is the smallest county in Tennessee?

A. Trousdale, in northern Middle Tennessee, nicknamed "the runt of the state." A living history museum in Hartsville is open for a tour, if you call the Chamber of Commerce.

Q. How many Republican governors has Tennessee had between 1900 and 2019?
A. Seven (Ben Hooper, Alfred Taylor, Winfield Dunn, Lamar Alexander, Don Sundquist, Bill Haslam and Bill Lee). The latter began serving in 2018.

Q. William Carroll served how many terms as governor of Tennessee?
A. Six (it's a record).

Q. The first "dark-horse" candidate to win a presidential nomination was which Tennessean?
A. James K. Polk.

Q. What Tennessee commissioner of education from 1963 to 1971, who was known as a "bare-knuckled political brawler," dominated Lewis County politics during his lifetime?
A. John Howard Warf (1904–1996).

Q. What were President Andrew Jackson's last words?
A. "We shall all meet in heaven."

CHAPTER THREE

Prehistoric Tennessee

Did you know?

Dinosaurs once roamed Tennessee!

Until about 75 million years ago, the part of the North American continent that was destined to become Tennessee was underwater. There are many museums throughout the Volunteer State that have prehistoric exhibits of corals, mollusks, and starfish. In addition to ancient marine invertebrate fossils, Tennessee was also home to prehistoric mammals dating back to the Cretaceous period.

These include animals such as the Duck-Billed Dinosaur, the fossils of which have been excavated in the sedimentary rock of Tennessee. Camels, which most people believe originated in the Middle East, originally evolved in North America; one such fossil is known as the "Camelops," which roamed the state between 12 million to 12,000 years ago. Two mastodon skeletons were found in Williamson County, Tennessee (in what is called the Coats-Hines Site) as well as parts of prehistoric animals in other areas of the state.

In present-day Tennessee, Washington County is home to what is known as the Gray Fossil Site. The ancient remains of mammals from this site include prehistoric elephants and saber-toothed tigers! The Gray Fossil Site, located in the town of Gray, is an active prehistoric (Pliocene-era) dig site and is open to visitors. Archeologists say that the site was an underground limestone cave that, when it collapsed long ago, created a sinkhole, leaving a huge fossil deposit dating back to about 5 million years. Admission to the Gray Fossil Site is currently included in the Hands On! Discovery Center Museum. In addition, the Gray Fossil Site hosts a summer camp for young, would-be archeologists. See "Virtual Tennessee" for websites.

The Ancient Peoples of Tennessee

Long before the time of recorded history, ancient people lived, cultivated and hunted in what would eventually become Tennessee. Modern-day scientists know this due to extensive excavations they have done throughout the state.

You can see more about the ancient people who lived in what is now the Volunteer State at many museums around Tennessee. One notable museum is the McClung Museum of Natural History & Culture. The museum is on the campus of the University of Tennessee in Knoxville. Admission is free and they welcome groups such as school groups to visit. The museum hosts birthday parties and offers special events and workshops throughout the year.

This museum displays the Duck River Cache, which contains the largest collection of ceremonial flint-knapped items ever found in one cache in the United States.

Mound Bottom, near Dickson, associated with Montgomery Bell Park, is the largest Mississippian mound site in Tennessee. According to Kevin Smith of the Tennessee Historical Society, Mound Bottom is now a State Archaeological Area. In The Online Encyclopedia of Tennessee, Smith wrote, "Mound Bottom served prehistoric people as a sacred ceremonial center. Within the confines of the site are at least 29 earthen pyramids and burial mounds."

In Memphis, one must-see place is the C. H. Nash Museum at the Prehistoric Chucalissa Archaeological Site. When the Civilian Conservation Corps (CCC) discovered this important Mississippian period archaeological site in Memphis in the 1930s, the Memphis Press-Scimitar reported the workers as being "ankle-deep in crumbling bones, bricks, and ancient pottery."

Listed as a National Historic Landmark, visitors can wander the trails that meander through Chucalissa's arboretum, which is awash with plants that were indigenous to the area many years ago and learn how prehistoric people used them. On the grounds is a Mississippian-era, fully furnished replica of an ancient dwelling, to give visitors an idea of the way those ancient people might have lived. Inside the museum itself is a wonderful gallery (that is like walking through a prehistoric time capsule), a hands-on archaeology laboratory, and a gift shop. Like the McClung Museum, the Chucalissa Archaeological Site also hosts events through the year. See "Virtual Tennessee" for websites.

Other Interesting Archaeological Sites in Tennessee

Fort Watauga: Located in the Sycamore Shoals State Historical Area at Elizabethton is the site where, in 1772, the first American-born settlers formed a free and independent community called the Watauga Settlers Association.

John and Landon Carter Mansion: On the other side of Elizabethton is the oldest frame structure in Tennessee, built in 1780. Elizabethton itself is named after John Carter's wife, Elizabeth. The house that John Carter and his son Landon built is located at a site formerly occupied by prehistoric people, as evidenced by artifacts uncovered by archaeologists.

Last Capital of the Cherokee: In the town of Cleveland lies Red Clay, the Cherokee's last capital before their forced march on the Trail of Tears. Red Clay State Park now hosts many events throughout the year, including the Cherokee Cultural Celebration held the first weekend in August.

Pinson Mounds State Archaeological Area: Just outside of Jackson is one of the largest Middle Woodland period archaeological sites in the Southeast.

Did you know?

Tennessee is home to the oldest cave and rock art in the entire United States. According to a 2013 article first published in the journal Antiquity (and later that year, in Indian Country Today), "at more than 6,000 years old, prehistoric cave and rock art found in what is today Tennessee is easily the oldest discovered yet within the United States." President Emeritus and Distinguished Professor of Science Jan Simek at the University of Tennessee said in an interview with the publication Discovery News that, "The discoveries tell us that prehistoric peoples in the Cumberland Plateau used this...distinctive upland environment for a variety of purposes and that religion was part of that broader sense of place."

You can see petroglyphs and other prehistoric art in various places throughout the cave-rich state of Tennessee. One of them is Mud Glyph Cave, which was first discovered in 1979 by amateur spelunkers and is currently a protected site in the Cumberland Plateau. But there are plenty of other places you can go and see prehistoric art for yourself.

In Clarksville, Dunbar Cave is the site of some charcoal pictographs; it is open to the public and cave tours are provided, for a nominal fee.

Professor Simek wrote of prehistoric people apparently taking risks to make petroglyphs in unusual and dangerous places. One such place can be found in bluffs overlooking the Narrows of the Harpeth River, and May's Mace Rock Art Site. I myself have usually viewed the Harpeth petroglyphs from a relatively comfortable seat in a canoe as I floated downstream. Many of those petroglyphs seem impossible to get to, especially without all the modern-day accoutrements rock-climbers have access to today. Mace Bluff itself overlooks the Harpeth River and the Mound Bottom complex. Unlike the petroglyphs at the bluffs of the Narrows of the Harpeth, there is now a relatively well-worn trail to this area, and although it is a protected archaeological site, it is showing signs of disrespectful vandalism.

But Simek and his team are continuing to find and explore caves and cave art in Tennessee; Albert Bender, who is a Cherokee and a board advisor for the group Native American Indian Association of Tennessee (based in Nashville), said in an interview with Reuters News Service (in 2013), that the examples of cave art that have been discovered "shows the sophistication of Native American society in the South going back thousands of years."

Besides the C. H. Nash Museum and the McClung Museum of History & Culture, another place where you can see more examples of ancient artifacts is at the Wyatt Archaeological Museum in Cornersville, Tennessee.

The Mystery of the Old Stone Fort

In Manchester, Old Stone Fort Archaeological State Park has what you might expect to find: campgrounds, hiking trails, and picnic areas. But this has all been built around a "fort," which archaeologists say was built sometime between 80 and 550 A.D., in the heyday of the Woodland Indians.

According to Park Manager Keith Wimberly, the area was painstakingly built by many hands. He says construction on the site was begun approximately two thousand years ago and had most of its mound circumference in place before A.D. 200. The one-and-one-quarter-mile circumference of long mound walls and cliffs lying between the Big Duck and Little Duck Rivers set a limit or boundary to a special or ritual use area—not a controlling barrier, but a demarcating fence designating a special place.

Because few artifacts have been unearthed, it is believed that no one ever actually lived at this fifty-acre "hilltop enclosure" mound site. Archaeologists believe it was used as a purely ceremonial site. But for what types of ceremonies? No one knows for certain, although one hypothesis says it may have been used as a kind of celestial observatory.

This is a section of Old Stone Fort, a fifty-acre "hilltop enclosure" mound site in Manchester, that was begun approximately two thousand years ago. Archaeologists are still uncertain of its original purpose. (Courtesy Tennessee Division of Archaeology)

One legend says that the Old Stone Fort is an ancient place of power and that spirits the Cherokee Indians called sungnawyee edda-hee, or "night goers," wander here. Years ago, a professor of mythology and legend at Salem University in Massachusetts by the name of Dr. Geoffrey Moorehead, came to Manchester to investigate this spirit legend—and disappeared without a trace. Circumstances surrounding his fate remain a mystery.

Old Stone Fort harbors this and other enigmas. Experts have only been able to make educated guesses as to the religious practices of the Woodland Indians and their specific use for Old Stone Fort. The site is off the Manchester exit of I-24. It is accessible by foot and is surrounded by bluffs and rushing waters. Standing in the center of the flat meadow within the boundaries of the fort, maybe you'll feel a sense of mysticism yourself and gain some understanding of a place whose origins and purpose may forever remain unknown. See "Virtual Tennessee" for website information.

Did You Know?

Tennessee's oldest community is not Chattanooga, Knoxville, Memphis, or even Nashville. While Jonesborough is Tennessee's oldest incorporated town, it's not Tennessee's oldest community. There are places that have been inhabited by Native Americans, but not continually.

Formerly known as Trade Gap, tiny Trade, which lies between Mountain City, Tennessee, and Boone, North Carolina, claims the honor of being Tennessee's oldest community, with the longest continuous history of settlement. Trade is part of the old trail west, and this path was used by Creek, Yuchi, Shawnee, and Cherokee peoples. Artifacts in the area are estimated to be at least one thousand years old. Later, of course, pioneers such as Daniel Boone and early settlers traveled through and stopped in Trade to rest and exchange goods with the Indians. The area first appeared in maps made in 1749 by Peter Jefferson, Thomas Jefferson's father.

You can learn more about Trade and its history by visiting Butler Museum in Butler, Tennessee, and the Trade Community Center and Gristmill Park. See "Virtual Tennessee) for website

Trade, Tennessee's oldest city

CHAPTER FOUR

The Early Days Of Tennessee

The Dogs Have Their Day at Fort Nashborough

The winter of 1781, as Tennessee winters go, was a hard one, with rain, snow, sleet, and bitter cold. The handful of settlers, who'd established Fort Nashborough two years earlier along the banks of the Cumberland River, were unprepared for such a hard season. The winter seemed interminable as their food and ammunition supplies dwindled.

At first their relationship with the local Cherokee people had been amicable, but they were on the western front in the Revolutionary War and both the British and the Spanish were encouraging the Indians to harass these newest settlers. The Cherokees began ambushing settlers who ventured out of the fort to hunt. Their horses and cows, which would determine the settlers' survival, were constantly being depleted by marauding bands of warriors. The fort's leader, Captain James Robertson, gave his followers hope with his unwavering bravery, but it was his wife's quick thinking that would ultimately save lives.

By April 1781, some settlers had been killed, others had died of disease, and others had simply left. Early one morning, some Cherokee warriors approached the fort, fired their guns, and left. It was a "cross this line" kind of tactic, and it worked. About twenty settlers went out after the Cherokee. Too late, the pioneers found themselves in an ambush. All around them were Indians firing upon them. Terrified of the gunfire, the settlers' horses reared, throwing their hapless riders, and bolted away.

Just then, the Captain's wife, Charlotte, known as "Mama Robertson," unleashed the fort dogs. There were about fifty of the fierce canines, who quickly came to their masters' aid. With bloodcurdling growls and snapping jaws, they leaped upon the warriors, allowing most of the settlers to hurry back to the protection of the fort. Some of the men who had been ambushed gave chase to the Cherokee warriors and defeated them in a skirmish near what is now Nickajack Dam.

Today, a replica of the old Fort Nashborough is open for tours, after the former replica was demolished in 2015. The old fort has been rebuilt as the original one had been, by frontier settler and architect James Robertson. It reopened in 2017 and is a great way to get a glimpse of what life was like in the frontier days of Tennessee.

When I interviewed "Lori," who works at the park, she said that, yes, dogs are still allowed at Fort Nashborough...but on a leash.

There is a saying, "Every dog has his day." On that day in 1781, about fifty dogs had theirs, all at once.

Town Names, Now and Then

Many cities in Tennessee have gone through more than one name change. Jackson used to be known as Alexandria; Clinton was formerly called Burrville. Bolivar was originally Hatchie, and before Nashville was called Nashborough (after the fort), it was known as Bluff Station.

Bristol was called Sapling Grove in its early days, and Hartsville's east side had the name of Damascus. Before it was known as Kingsport, the town went by the name of Boat Yard. Finally, Knoxville used to be known as White's Fort.

The Story of "Beloved Woman"

Born in 1738, Nancy Ward, whose Cherokee name was Nanye-hi or "One Who Goes About," was first called "Beloved Woman" by her people because of her valor on the battlefield when she fought alongside her husband against the Creek.

When her husband was killed in battle in 1755, she rallied the remaining warriors to victory. The Cherokee leaders often came to her for advice after this because they believed that the Great Spirit spoke through Beloved Woman.

She was friends with early frontiersmen James Robertson and John Sevier and once saved Lydia Bean (wife of William Bean, the area's first recorded white settler in 1768) from being burned at the stake by Indians. She saved other settlers from Indian massacres as well, and from her friendship with white settlers, she learned of and introduced the Cherokee to dairy farming.

In helping to negotiate a treaty in July 1781 on the Long Island of the Holston River, Ward pleaded for peace on behalf of both white and Indian women. She also interceded in other treaty negotiations, again on behalf of the women and children on both sides. Because of this, she could be regarded as the first "feminist" in Tennessee.

Nancy Ward died in 1822; a monument at her grave site near Benton (near the Polk-McMinn County line) is a lasting tribute to the one the Cherokee called "Beloved Woman." There is also a historical marker near her grave, and the site is now part of the Cherokee Heritage Trail.

The Battle of Kings Mountain

During the American Revolution, men west of the Appalachian Mountains were, as one author put it, "just sitting out the War." Then in 1780 a British officer sent word to them, saying that if any of them did try to assist their rebellious eastern neighbors, he would "lay their country to waste with fire and sword."

That did it. Inspired by a fiery sermon given by Reverend Samuel Doak, nine hundred "Overmountain Men" under Colonel William Campbell destroyed a force of eleven hundred Loyalists under Major Patrick Ferguson at the important Battle of Kings Mountain in South Carolina. The victory demoralized the British and bolstered the cause for the Revolutionary Army. Today, you can tour the Overmountain Valley National Historic Trail, which runs through Tennessee, North Carolina and South Carolina, and learn more about the battle that turned the tide of the American Revolution.

"Lost" Counties of Tennessee

Two counties organized in Tennessee's earlier days later disappeared: Tennessee County, formed in 1788 in what is now Middle Tennessee, under the auspices of the state of North Carolina; and James County, created in 1871 in what is now southeastern Tennessee. Tennessee County was divided and pretty much absorbed by Robertson County in 1796; James County was dissolved in 1890 to later became parts of Bradley and Hamilton Counties.

Two Unusual Mansion Tales

The Love Story That Built a House

Historic Sites Director David Stieghan related to me the tale of how Rippavilla Plantation in Spring Hill was built because of a love story. It began with a man named Nathaniel Cheairs, who had ten children, the youngest one named after the father. In 1841 the younger Nathaniel fell in love with a girl named Susan McKissack and wanted to marry her, but his father was against

Every single brick in Rippavilla mansion was made in William McKissack's kiln as a wedding present to his daughter. (Courtesy Rippavilla Plantation)

it. One day the father and son had "the talk." It went something like this:

"Why don't you want me to marry Susan? What's wrong with her?" "Nothing's wrong with her; it's just her name."

"Her name?"

"Yes, son. You see, I married a girl named Sarah, just as my father did, and his father before him, and his father before him, and his father before him." The elder Nathaniel looked at his son. "Can't you find a Sarah who'll do just as well?"

The young man thought for a minute. "No, father. I love Susan." There was a dramatic pause, then, "Son, I'll give you five thousand dollars in gold if you agree not to marry Susan. It'll be breaking a family tradition."

The son was again silent for a moment. "Father, Susan's father is William McKissack and he owns a brick kiln. He's one of the richest men in the county, and his slaves are skilled brick masons and carpenters. Surely, she'll bring more than five thousand dollars into this marriage."

The younger Nathaniel had his way. He married his Susan, and ten years later they started building Rippavilla mansion. Susan's father gave them something special as a wedding present: every single brick in the mansion, which still stands in Spring Hill, was made in the McKissack kiln as a wedding present to the young couple. Incidentally, young Nathaniel wasn't disowned by his father. On the contrary, upon his father's death the youngest child in the family got the lion's share of the estate, including the fifteen-hundred-acre plantation!

Today, you can tour this memento to true love. Rippavilla Mansion is open for tours most days of the year and is available for special events such as weddings. See "Virtual Tennessee" for website information.

Rattle and Snap: A Gambler's Tale (or, Your Tax Dollars at Work!)

It was 1792 and Tennessee was still part of North Carolina. William Polk, a Revolutionary War hero, and his friend Alexander Martin, the governor of North Carolina, were involved in a gambling game played with dice (though some say dried beans). Legend has it they were sitting in the halls of the North Carolina legislature.

Martin had recently come into nearly six thousand acres of land from General Nathanael Greene, who had fallen on hard times. He had paid the taxes on the land in what is now Maury County and had taken title to it. When the betting got heavy, Martin put up his land, and with a fateful roll of the dice (or a throw of the beans), William Polk won it.

One of Polk's sons built a house on the land and named it after the game, Rattle and Snap. In early 2004, Rattle and Snap was purchased at auction by Michael and Roberta Kaslow, who moved to the area from Santa Barbara, California. The couple now owns the home heralded by architectural scholars as one of the finest examples of Greek Revival architecture in the country.

Located in Columbia, Rattle and Snap is open for tours and special events (perhaps, except for gambling, for obvious reasons). See "Virtual Tennessee" for website(s).

Historic Homes and Sites You Can Visit

This list, provided by the Tennessee Historical Commission, is divided into the three "Grand Divisions" of the state. Not all of the sites were built before the war.

West Tennessee

Alex Haley House Museum (Henning) Ames Plantation (Grand Junction) Arlington Historic Post Office

The Buford Pusser Home and Museum (near Savannah)

Casey Jones Home and Railroad Museum (Jackson)

Chucalissa Archaeological Museum (Memphis)

Church Park (Memphis)

Collierville Town Square and Railroad Cars

David Crockett Cabin (Morristown)

Davies Manor (Brunswick)

Elmwood Cemetery (Memphis)

Fort Pillow State Historic Area (near Garland)

Freed House (Memphis)

Gotten House (north of Memphis)

Hannum-Rhea House (Somerville)

The Little Courthouse Museum (Bolivar)

Magevney House (Memphis)

Mallory-Neely House (Memphis)

The Pillars (Bolivar)

Pinson Mounds State Archaeological Area (near Jackson)

Reelfoot Lake Resort Park (Tiptonville)

Shiloh National Military Park Woodruff-Fontaine House (Memphis)

Middle Tennessee

The Athenaeum (Columbia)

Belle Meade Plantation (Nashville)

Belmont Mansion (Nashville)

Bowen Plantation House (Nashville)

Carnton Plantation (Franklin)

Carter House (Franklin)

Cookeville Depot Museum

Cordell Hull Birthplace and Museum (near Byrdstown)

Cragfont (near Gallatin)

Cravens House (Chattanooga)

Fort Donelson National Battlefield (Dover)

Fort Nashborough (Nashville) (see story in this chapter)

The Hermitage (Nashville)

Hohenwald Depot

The Homeplace 1850 (near Dover)

James K. Polk Home (Columbia)

Natchez Trace Parkway and Meriwether Lewis Monument (near Hohenwald)

Oaklands Historic House Museum (Murfreesboro)

The Parthenon (Nashville)

Rock Castle (near Hendersonville)

Sam Davis Home (near Smyrna)

Sergeant York Home (Jamestown)

Smith-Trahern Mansion (Clarksville)

Sparta Rock House

Stones River National Battlefield (near Murfreesboro)

Tennessee State Capitol (Nashville)

Travellers' Rest (Nashville)

Trousdale Place (Hartsville)

Tulip Grove (between Nashville and Lebanon)

Wynnewood (outside Gallatin)

East Tennessee

Andrew Johnson National Historic Site (Greeneville)

Armstrong-Lockett House (Crescent Bend)

Beck Cultural Exchange Center (Knoxville)

Blount Mansion (Knoxville)

Burra Burra Mine Site (Ducktown)

Cades Cove (near Gatlinburg)

Davy Crockett Birthplace State Park (near Jonesborough)

Etowah L&N Depot

The Exchange Place (Kingsport)

Fort Loudon State Historic Area (near Madisonville)

James White Fort (outside Knoxville)

Mabry-Hazen House (Knoxville)

Marble Springs (near Sevierville)

The Netherland Inn (Kingsport)

Old Roane County Courthouse (near Lenoir City)

President Andrew Johnson Museum Library (near Greeneville)

Ramsey House (Knoxville)

Red Clay State Historic Park (Cleveland)

Rhea County Courthouse and Scopes Trial Museum (Dayton)

Rocky Mount (Elizabethton)

Sam Houston Schoolhouse (Maryville)

Samuel Doak House (Greeneville)

Tipton-Haynes Historic Site (Johnson City)

Did you know?

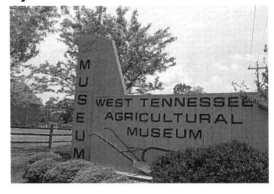

If you'd like to learn more about the early farming days in the Volunteer State, then look no further than the Tennessee Agricultural Museum in downtown Nashville. Here you will find a plethora of farming implements as well as an 1800s-era threshing machine and a tractor from the 1920s. The museum itself is housed in an historic barn. This museum offers educational tours for schoolchildren, farm-to-table dinners, musical concerts and more. See "Virtual Tennessee" for website information.

Q&A

Q. What county is known as the Antebellum Homes Capital of Tennessee?
A. Maury. Among its many antebellum homes are the four Polk family homes: the James K. Polk Ancestral Home, Hamilton Place (Lucius Polk's Palladian manor), St. John's at Ashwood, and Rattle and Snap.

Q. When it was governed by William Blount, what was Tennessee's original name before statehood?
A. The Territory of the United States South of the River Ohio.

Q. By defeating what Indian nation at the Battle of Horseshoe Bend in 1814 did Andrew Jackson add twenty-three million acres of land in present-day Georgia and Alabama to the United States?
A. Creek.

Q. Land now occupied by Jackson, Tennessee, was acquired from what Native American tribe?
A. Chickasaw.

Q. What pioneer was hired to head a group of woodsmen to improve and connect existing Indian trails to form the famous Wilderness Road through the Cumberland Gap to help the westward expansion of the American nation?
A. Daniel Boone.

Q. What invention made cities on the water such as Memphis and Nashville major trading centers in the nineteenth century?
A. The steamboat.

Q. The first of several such groups, the Cumberland Agricultural Society was formed in 1819 in what county to help farmers improve farming techniques?
A. Davidson.

Q. To aid him in his fight against the British during the battle of New Orleans, Andrew Jackson allied himself with what Louisiana-based pirate?
A. Jean Laffite.

Q. What small town in West Tennessee has more than one hundred buildings on the National Register of Historic Places?
A. Bolivar.

Q. What is the total area of the state of Tennessee?
A. 42,144 square miles, including 989 square miles of inland water.

Q. On what day did Congress approve admission of Tennessee as the sixteenth state?
A. June 1, 1796.

Q. The name Tennessee comes from what Indian word?
A. Tanasi, a Yuchi word meaning "old town"; the Native Americans used this word for a village and gave the same name to the Little Tennessee and Tennessee Rivers.

Q. How many ships were constructed at the navy yard in Memphis between 1844 and 1857?
A. One, the USS Allegheny.

Q. In 1540 what Spaniard led the first European expedition into Tennessee territory?
A. Hernando de Soto.

Q. What five major Indian tribes originally inhabited the Tennessee region?
A. Cherokee, Chickasaw, Creek, Chickamauga, and Choctaw.

Q. In 1819 what three Tennesseans bought five thousand acres from the U.S. government and organized a settlement on the Mississippi River which they named Memphis?
A. General Andrew Jackson, Judge John Overton, and General James Winchester.

Q. What Tennessee county was named after a Revolutionary War hero and the first governor of Kentucky?
A. Shelby, whose county seat is Memphis, after Isaac Shelby.

Q. An unsuccessful plan to create a canal between the Hatchie and Tennessee Rivers was attempted by what colorful early Tennessean?
A. David Crockett.

Q. In 1835 Newton Cannon became what party's first governor of Tennessee?
A. Whig.

Q. What four Tennessee towns have served as the state capital?
A. Knoxville, Kingston (for one day), Murfreesboro, and Nashville.

Q. Why was Kingston the state capital for only one day, September 21, 1807?

A. To satisfy a treaty requirement with the Cherokee.

Q. What gunboat fired the first shot of the Spanish-American War?
A. USS Nashville.

Q. Captain William Atkinson mustered fifty-seven volunteers from what county for the war against Mexico?
A. Hamblen. (Because so many Tennesseans volunteered to fight in the Mexican War, Tennessee became known as "the Volunteer State.")

Q. What small Indian boy, orphaned during the Creek War, did Andrew Jackson bring home to raise as his own?
A. Lincoya

CHAPTER FIVE

Famous Tennesseans in Education, Arts, Science and Literature

The Story of Casey Jones

Jonathan Luther "Casey" Jones was an engineer for the Illinois Central rail line when he had his fateful crash the night of April 29, 1900. More than two hundred songs have been written and published about him and his tragic end.

A substitute for the regular engineer for this route, Jones had taken out Engine Number 382, the Cannonball, when he realized that the switch at Vaughan, Mississippi, was blocked. Knowing his train would crash into the oncoming train, he stayed at the controls to apply the hand brake, telling the fireman to jump to safety. All the passengers survived the crash; Casey Jones was the single fatality.

The first person to compose verses about Jones's self-sacrifice was Wallace Saunders, an African American engine-wiper and friend of Casey Jones. Saunders wrote the original song, "Casey Jones, the Brave Engineer." Jones has been immortalized in hundreds of songs, in literature, and with a museum in his honor in Jackson, Tennessee, where he made his home.

Incidentally, I was able to interview Ms. Laura Beaver, Managing Director of the Casey Jones Home and Railroad Museum, and she added more to the story about the song. "That year—1900—135 train engineers lost their lives on the job," she said, "but there were 40 of those 135 engineers killed in the line of duty in the month of April. Jones's story would never have been known had it not been for Saunders's song, which has been popular since it was first published." So, here are the lyrics!

Casey Jones, the Brave Engineer

Come all you rounders if you want to hear A story about a brave Engineer. Casey Jones was the Rounder's name,
On a six eight-wheeler, boys, he won his fame.
The caller called Casey at half-past four.
He kissed his wife at the station door.

He mounted to the Cabin with his orders in his hand
And he took his farewell trip to that Promised Land.

(Chorus)

Casey Jones, mounted to the cabin, Casey Jones, with his orders in his hand,
Casey Jones, mounted to the cabin, And he took his farewell trip to the Promised Land

"Put in your water and shovel in your coal,
Put your head out the window, watch them drivers roll. I'll run her till she leaves the rail

'Cause I'm eight hours late with that western mail."
He looked at his watch and his watch was slow,
He looked at the water and the water was low,
He turned to the Fireman and then he said,
"We're goin' to reach Canton but we'll all be dead." (Chorus)

Casey Jones, going to reach Canton, Casey Jones, but we'll all be dead, Casey Jones, going to reach Canton, "We're going to reach Canton, but we'll all be dead."

Casey pulled up that Southern Hill. He tooted for the crossing with an awful shrill. The switchmen know by the engine's moan That the man at the throttle was Casey Jones. He pulled up within two miles of the place. Number One stared him right in the face.

He turned to the Fireman and said, "Sir, you'd better jump, 'Cause there's two locomotives that's a-goin' to bump."

(Chorus)
Casey Jones, two locomotives, Casey Jones, that's a-goin' to bump,
Casey Jones, two locomotives, "There's two locomotives that's a-goin' to bump."

Headaches and heartaches and all kinds of pain

Are not apart from a railroad train
Tales that are earnest, noble and grand
Belong to the life of a railroad man.

Mrs. Jones sat on her bed a-sighin',
Just received a message that Casey was dying.
Said, "Go to bed, children, and hush your crying
'Cause your Daddy's now ridin' on that heavenly line."

Today, you can spend a delightful day (or more) at the Casey Jones Village. It offers many things to please children of all ages. There's the Casey Jones Home and Museum, an old country store, a recreation of an 1890s-era ice cream parlor, a café which offers country-style dining, a circa-1905 village chapel, and more. See their website in the "Virtual Tennessee" section to learn more.

Alvin York, Education's Agent

You know Alvin York was the most decorated soldier of World War I. What you may not know is what York did for education in Tennessee after he came home.

Born in 1887 in Pall Mall, Tennessee, York was one of eleven children whose father was a subsistence farmer. In his early days York enjoyed shooting his gun and fighting, and he had little education and few skills. Some said then he'd never amount to much.

In 1914 he was, as southerners say, "born again," when he went to a revival of the Church of Christ in Christian Union, a small religious sect with followers in Tennessee, Ohio, and Kentucky. While attending church there, he met his future wife, Gracie Williams.

York's church held firm convictions against violence in general and war in particular, so when he received his draft card, he scrawled on it, "Dont [sic] want to fight." His stand as a conscientious objector was short-lived, however.

The local and state review boards denied him that status because his church was not recognized as a "legitimate Christian sect."

Once York became a company soldier his company commander had several talks with him and convinced the young man war could be morally right when it was necessary to fight. The rest, as they say, is history. In a skirmish in October 1918, with only the

Alvin York, the most decorated soldier of World War I, was drafted despite his stance as a conscientious objector. He later established the York Institute in Fentress County. (Courtesy Tennessee State Museum Photographic Archives)

aid of a few men, York silenced the enemy's machine guns, capturing 132 prisoners. He was a national hero but still felt dissatisfied. He'd never felt comfortable with his lack of education, so upon his return home he worked to establish a school in Jamestown, Fentress County. He was so dedicated to his vision that in the lean years he even paid teachers' salaries and purchased buses.

Today the York Institute is said to be the world's largest high school campus — more than fourteen thousand acres. It became a public high school when it was transferred to the state of Tennessee in 1937. It is the only secondary school in the nation that is financed and operated by the state government.

The campus is also designated as a Wildlife Resources Agency, which includes a working farm with a herd of cattle, and five ponds for aquaculture and bird sanctuaries. The jewel in the campus's crown is the Alvin C. York Agricultural Institute Historic District, which is on the National Register of Historic Places. The building, once badly in need of repairs, was restored and reopened in 2010. On the grounds, there is a statue of York as he might have appeared in his World War I uniform. See "Virtual Tennessee" for website(s).

The "Unsinkable" Kathy Bates

Born Kathleen Doyle Bates in Memphis in 1948, this woman who played the role of Margaret "Molly" Brown in James Cameron's blockbuster movie "Titanic" almost didn't take the part. She'd already committed to doing two other movies, but then one fell through and rehearsals for the other clashed with Bates's schedule.

She admits she was "made" for the role: "If you ever see a picture of Molly Brown, I look just like her," she told a Washington Post interviewer during shooting for the film.

This "unsinkable" Tennessean keeps a frenetic pace: after all the grueling work required to make Titanic, her schedule kept her from attending the movie's premiere.

Bates went later, with some friends, and bought her own ticket. And unlike many enthusiastic Titanic fans, that was the only time she saw it in a theater.

"Steamboatin' Tom" Ryman: Not Your Everyday Romantic Type

You probably know the Ryman Auditorium, the long-time home of the Grand Ole Opry, was built by Tom Ryman as a religious tabernacle after his conversion (read more about this part of his life in the chapter on Religion and Utopian Communities). Nashville-born Ryman, known as "Steamboatin' Tom," was probably the most successful steamboating man plying the Tennessee, Ohio and Cumberland Rivers. At the height of his steamboating career in the 1870s, he had a fleet of 35 such vessels.

When Ryman married Mary Elizabeth Baugh of Franklin, the wedding was attended by some of the best-known riverboat captains on the river. The week-long "wedding cruise" from Nashville to Evansville, Indiana, was aboard his first vessel, The Alpha, with thirty-five guests on board.

Tom Ryman

It was on the return voyage, when they were off the Ohio River and back on the Cumberland, that Steamboatin' Tom had all his honeymoon dreams realized. He was in a race against another steamboat, The Tyrone, and Steamboatin' Tom came close to losing the contest until he harangued his engineer and workmen to accelerate to the highest possible speed.

The Alpha overtook and passed The Tyrone as the honeymoon party cheered and waved at the defeated crew. You can learn more about the life and times of Tom Ryman at the Ryman Auditorium in downtown Nashville. The Ryman, which was originally a place of worship (see its story about that in the chapter on Religion and Utopian Communities), has been made into a music venue, and guided tours are offered daily. See "Virtual Tennessee" for website(s).

Luke Lee Soldier, Newspaperman, Senator – and Kidnapper?

It was New Year's Day 1919. The Armistice had been signed two months before, and while waiting to be shipped back home, Colonel Luke Lea, commander of the 114th Field Artillery (National Guard) Unit, brooded in Luxembourg. He was dissatisfied because the person responsible for the destruction and misery caused by the war, the German kaiser, had been granted asylum and was currently living in the castle of Count Bentinck in Holland. Lea thought the kaiser should go to Paris to be tried for war crimes, instead of allowing his people to suffer severe war reparations for his deeds.

Therefore, Lea decided if the kaiser wouldn't go of his own volition, then Lea would see that he went. Lea rounded up a handful of his fellow Tennesseans, telling them they were going on a secret mission. He got passes for them, and they headed out that same day. Their mission: kidnap the kaiser and bring him to justice!

Lea was accustomed to getting his own way. Founder of the newspaper The Nashville Tennessean, former U.S. senator, and forceful in his opinions, he didn't let a washed-out bridge on the Rhine or being stopped at two borders deter him from his mission. The group bluffed its way past everyone who stopped them, saying they were on official business for their country.

Once inside the castle and face to face with Count Bentinck, Lea repeatedly requested an audience with the kaiser; it was just as many times denied. With no kaiser forthcoming and German soldiers all around the chateau, Lea abandoned his mission. He and his men returned to Luxembourg and from there, home to the United States.

Lea received an "official" reprimand from his commander in chief, General Pershing. After the incident, Pershing was reported to have said, "I'd have given a year's pay to have been able to take Lea's trip into Holland, and to have entered the castle of Count Bentinck without invitation."

Incidentally, there is a wonderful exhibit of the heroes (and heroines) of World War I at the Museum of East Tennessee History in Knoxville. See "Virtual Tennessee" for websites.

Martha Ingram: The "Cultured" Pearl of Music City

All good mothers try to offer the best for their children. In Nashville, one mother not only created a cultural environment for her children but was instrumental in making Nashville into a cultural Mecca.

This woman with the effervescent smile and down-to-earth personality was born Martha Robinson Rivers in Charleston, South Carolina. Although she had a good childhood, it was when she went to Vassar that she was first exposed to the performing arts. In New York City on a blind date she met Erskine Bronson Ingram. This was one blind date that went well, for they married and had four children. They moved to Nashville, where Martha Ingram wanted her children to have the same love of the fine arts that she had experienced. The only way to do this was to create that environment herself. She became determined to make Music City a more cultured city.

In 1973 she and a handful of other dedicated philanthropists were able to build the Tennessee Performing Arts Center (TPAC). That was only the beginning of what she was to do.

When her husband died in 1995, he was Tennessee's only billionaire. His business, Ingram Industries, was ranked by Forbes magazine as number 14 of the top 500 privately held corporations in the United States. Ingram Industries, of which Martha Ingram is now CEO, includes a barge transportation business, a large book distribution company, a software distribution company, and an insurance company. With intellect, enthusiasm, and commitment, Ingram continued to turn her good fortune toward a higher purpose. In April 1998, this woman whom Forbes named the wealthiest businesswoman in the country, kicked off a fundraising campaign she called "Symphony 2000." Its main goal was to fund an endowment to elevate the Nashville Symphony to a level of national prominence.

Next time you attend a ballet, an opera, or a symphony performance in Nashville, send a mental note of thanks to the Pearl of Music City, Martha Ingram.

Guess Who?

These two African American civil rights activists helped found the National Association for the Advancement of Colored People (NAACP). She got her start in journalism after being forcibly removed from a first-class ladies' coach in Memphis because of her color, after which she wrote of

that experience under the pen name lola. He was a graduate of Fisk University in Nashville who joined forces with her in efforts to increase racial equality and protest violence against African Americans, especially lynching. They began the National Negro Conference, which grew into the NAACP.

Who are they? Ida B. Wells-Barnett and W. E. B. DuBois. Read more about Tennessee native DuBois in the chapter, "From Civil Wrongs to Civil Rights."

Ernest P. Worrell: "Know What I Mean, Vern?"

Now you know this man who played up his "red neck ways" as the guy with the bill cap who did commercials for a variety of products all over the country. In many of these he addressed his unseen friend, "Vern," and the commercials became so popular that Tennesseans took to using his expression, "Know what I mean, Vern?" in conversations when they wanted to make sure they were understood.

Although he died February 11, 2000, Ernest P. Worrell (a.k.a. Jim Varney) has left us a treasure trove of belly-laughing films. They include Ernest: Scared Stupid (1992), Ernest Saves Christmas (1989), Ernest Goes to Camp (1987), Ernest Goes to Jail (1990), Ernest Goes to School (1994), Ernest in the Army (1998), Ernest Rides Again (1994), and Slam Dunk Ernest (1995), in which he shared the spotlight with Kareem Abdul-Jabar.

This just goes to show what any Tennessean with feistiness, a pleasantly skewed sense of humor, and a bill cap can do.

Know what I mean?

Dolly Parton, the Creative Dreamer of East Tennessee

As a student growing up in sight of the Pigeon River in East Tennessee, Dolly Parton was assigned to give a book report to the class. She was an avid reader, so this was no problem. But Dolly was a dreamer, too, with a mischievous spark in her, and she loved to make things up. She rose to the challenge of the

book report. When the time came for her to give her report, she stood up and fabricated the entire "book," including a fictitious author's name, title of the book, and subject matter.

Today Dolly Parton is a successful singer, actress, and the owner of Dollywood and other attractions in Pigeon Forge. When she recalled those school days, she admitted she's sure her teacher realized her fabrication, but never said a thing about it. She went on to write stories and songs, but when it came time for her to write her autobiography, "that was the hardest thing," she stated in her book My Life and Other Unfinished Business. "I had to tell the truth."

Dolly Parton's creative dreaming allowed her to come up from incredibly poor beginnings and make her dreams realities.

Some of those realities include the world-famous Dollywood, her DreamMore Resort and Spa, Dollywood's Smoky Mountain Cabins, and Dollywood Splash Country. Her Imagination Library has helped fight illiteracy (and foster a love of reading) by gifting books to 78 million children around the world!

Walking Tall: Buford Pusser

Born in Adamsville in 1937, Buford Pusser went to high school in Oklahoma, then joined the Marines but took a medical discharge because of an asthmatic condition. Back in Adamsville, he became a semipro wrestler and met his future wife, Pauline Mullins. They married in 1959 and moved to Chicago, where he worked as a die-cutter, until destiny called for his return to Adamsville.

There he finally found his calling. Incensed over the locally rampant illicit whiskey trade, Pusser ran against the incumbent constable and won in an upset victory by more than one hundred votes. Then he ran against the McNairy County sheriff, James Dickey, who was involved with a moonshine ring operating illegally at the borders of the Tennessee and Mississippi state lines. Dickey was a dyed-in-the-wool Democrat in a county of the same leanings; Pusser was a Republican. When Dickey was killed in an automobile accident before election day, Pusser's position as sheriff was assured.

T. Jensen Lacey

The members of the moonshine ring came after Pusser. Ambushes against him began in November 1964. Despite being stabbed seven times, shot eight times, and run over by a car, Pusser persisted in his war on the illegal whiskey trade. The first year on the job, he arrested seventy-five moonshiners and raided forty-two stills. In later years, he took on illegal gambling houses and prostitution rings. When his wife was killed in a 1967 ambush meant for him, Pusser became even more determined to root out the criminals.

In 1969 he was recognized for his one-man anticrime crusade by the Tennessee General Assembly, which made him an honorary sergeant of arms. His law enforcement days ended in 1970, but three movies were made of his life. The first one, Walking Tall, was a box-office success in 1973, and millions of Americans came to know Pusser as the no-nonsense sheriff who meant business. Unfortunately, Pusser would never see the other films of his life (Walking Tall II in 1976, Walking Tall III: The Final Chapter in 1977, and Walking Tall, the new version in 2004). He died in a car wreck in 1974.

Today, you can go learn more about this no-nonsense, by-the-book sheriff. His life and times have been immortalized at the Buford Pusser Home and Museum in Adamsville. Their website reads in part, "[The museum] stands as a monument in time," and is dedicated to honor his memory. The combination home and museum is open most days of the week, and this fascinating place takes about an hour to tour. Learn more about the museum by checking out their website in the chapter on "Virtual Tennessee."

A Tennessee Senator with Hollywood Credits

Prior to his 2002 retirement as a senator, Fred Thompson of Tennessee had amassed twenty-seven professional acting credits—eighteen films, six made-for TV movies, and four appearances on television series.

Films:

Marie (1985), with Sissy Spacek,

No Way Out (1987), with Kevin Costner and Gene Hackman Feds (1988), with Rebecca DeMornay

Fat Man and Little Boy (1989), with Paul Newman

Hunt for Red October (1990), with Sean Connery

Die Hard II (1990), with Bruce Willis

Days of Thunder (1990), with Tom Cruise

Flight of the Intruder (1990), with Danny Glover and Willem Dafoe

Class Action (1991), with Gene Hackman

Necessary Roughness (1991), with Scott Bakula

Curly Sue (1991), with Jim Belushi

Cape Fear (1991), with Robert DeNiro

Thunderheart (1992), with Val Kilmer

White Sands (1992), with Mickey Rourke and Willem Dafoe

Aces: Iron Eagle III (1992), with Lou Gossett Jr.

Born Yesterday (1993), with Melanie Griffith and Don Johnson

In the Line of Fire (1993), with Clint Eastwood

Baby's Day Out (1994), with Joe Mantegna

Television Movies:

Unholy Matrimony (1988), with Patrick Duffy

Bed of Light (1992), with Susan Dey

Stay the Night (1992), with Jane Alexander

Keep the Change (1992), with William Peterson

Dayo (1992), with Delta Burke

Barbarians at the Gate (1993), with James Garner

Television Series:

Matlock (1986)

China Beach (1988)

Roseanne (1988)

Wiseguy (1987)

The Audition That Gave Her the Name

Frances Rose Shore sat waiting in the studio of radio station WNEW in New York City. She had sold everything she owned to come to the city to make it as a singer. This, her first audition, had to be the best performance of her young life. As she waited for her name to be called, she thought about what she really wanted for a stage name. Nothing came immediately to mind.

Born in 1917 in Winchester, Tennessee, Fannie Rose was accustomed to fighting against odds. Stricken with polio when she was eighteen months old, she was left with a crippled leg, requiring her to relearn how to walk. If it hadn't been for her mother, who pushed her to keep exercising in such sports as tennis, Fannie Rose might never have recovered as fully as she did.

The family moved to Nashville where Fannie Rose went to Hume Fogg High School and was active in theatricals. Her biggest obstacle in her dream to be a professional singer was her father. When he found out she was really serious about a singing career, he cut off her charge accounts and her allowance. By keeping her broke, her dad thought he could keep Fannie Rose at home.

The determined young girl got a job singing on a local radio station and finished college at Vanderbilt University; then she sold everything she owned to raise funds to go to New York.

Finally it came time for her to audition and she was told to sing the song "Dinah." She was hired and the folks at the studio began calling her "Dinah," the name she adopted. Multitalented Dinah Shore went on to enjoy fabulous success as a recording artist; a radio, TV, and movie entertainer; and a cookbook author.

She was a star of the first magnitude—spunky, cheerful, with a wide trademark smile, and a kiss to the audience at the end of every TV show. Dinah Shore continued to perform until she died in 1994. In her hometown of Winchester, the townspeople honored her by calling a boulevard by the name she chose after her audition: Dinah Shore.

Today, you can learn more about her life at two places: The Old Jail Museum in Winchester, which houses many artifacts about the city's "hometown girl"; and in Brooklyn, NY, which features her in an exhibit in their Russian-American Museum. See "Virtual Tennessee" for websites.

Did You Know?

This Mississippi-born girl once approached a famous singer as she was stepping from her limousine and told her she had no money and was without a place to stay. The singer gave her one hundred dollars and the girl used it for hotel accommodations.

The girl?

Oprah Winfrey, who came to live in Nashville when she was thirteen. She later attended Tennessee State University and was a news reporter for radio station WVOL and the CBS television station in Nashville. The Chicago-based Oprah Winfrey Show was America's top-rated talk show until its final airing in 2011. She went on to host other TV shows, such as Super Soul Sunday, and produces the hit magazine O.

Patricia Neal: Because of a Fly…

You may know that Patricia Neal was born in Kentucky in 1926 but was raised in Knoxville, where she began to develop her career in the performing arts. You may know she performed in Lillian Hellman's drama The Little Foxes, then signed a contract with Warner Brothers in 1947. You may recall her roles in The Fountainhead and The Hasty Heart, her ill-fated romance

with Gary Cooper, or her doomed marriage to author Roald Dahl. You may remember she was Tennessee's Woman of the Year in 1962 and starred in Tennessee Williams's play Cat on a Hot Tin Roof and in the Broadway production of The Miracle Worker.

But you may not know about the strange thing that happened on the set of the 1963 movie Hud, which led Neal to give her most "natural" performance. The director had yelled, "All quiet on the set!" and "Action!" then something happened that wasn't in the script. "I was standing on the front porch and I was making cheese," Neal recalled in a phone interview with me (back in 1999), "and Paul [Newman] was about to come in. Just then, a fly came on the screen of the window, and instinctively I slapped at it with my towel. I was just acting normally. We continued on with the scene, and the director decided to keep on filming." She paused and quipped, "I don't think flies take direction, do you?"

After the director viewed the footage, the "fly scene" remained in the movie; in 1963 Neal won the Academy Award for Best Actress for her role in Hud. "The fly won it for me," she said.

Neal passed away in 2010, but the Patricia Neal Rehabilitation Center in Knoxville is named in her honor.

Samuel L. Jackson

Samuel Leroy Jackson was born in Washington, DC, in 1948 and raised in Chattanooga. He's a successful actor now, but an incident during his college years nearly put an end to his promising beginnings.

In 1969, Jackson was a junior at Atlanta's Morehouse College. He and other students were protesting the skewed ratio of black-to-white trustees at the predominantly African American college and were demanding a curriculum of African American Studies. Trying to force the issue and gain media attention, Jackson and his friends took members of the college's board of trustees hostage, locking them in a building on campus. One of those held hostage was Martin Luther King, Sr., father of the slain Civil Rights leader.

Jackson and the other students held the hostages for two days. The students were expelled, then reinstated. Jackson graduated in 1972 with a degree in Theater Arts, but his big break came when he played the role of "Gator" in the movie "Jungle Fever" (1991), which won him the New York Film Critics

Circle Award for Best Supporting Actor at the Cannes Film Festival.

Jackson has been in more than thirty films; he's probably best known for the character Jules, the hit man in Quentin Tarantino's Pulp Fiction (1994), for which he got an Academy Award for Best Supporting Actor. Incidentally, director Tarantino is also a Tennessee native.

Jackson has a philanthropic side to his character: In 2008, for example, he spearheaded the refurbishing and renovating of what used to be known as The Lorraine Motel in Memphis, but is now the site of the National Civil Rights Museum, as part of a program called "Save a Landmark."

In 2013, visitors to the newly opened Chattanooga History Center were thrilled to hear the voice of Jackson doing the voice-over narration of the introductory film. See "Virtual Tennessee" for websites.

More Claims to Fame

Here is a short list of other actors and actresses from Tennessee:

Cybill Shepherd: Named after her grandfather (Cy) and her father (Bill), Cybill Shepherd won a Golden Globe Award for best actress in the TV sit-com Cybill and maintains a home in Memphis.

Cherry Jones: A native of Paris, Tennessee, Cherry Jones starred in the 1999 made-for-TV movie Murder in a Small Town. She also starred as Liz Hammond (opposite Robert Redford) in the 1998 movie The Horse Whisperer.

Dixie Carter: Born in McLemoresville and a graduate of Memphis's Rhodes College, this soft-spoken epitome of traditional Tennessee womanhood is known for the sit-com Designing Women and for commercials advertising General Foods' International Coffees and the Yellow Pages.

Morgan Freeman: Memphis-born Morgan Freeman almost quit acting out of frustration and considered becoming a taxi driver instead. Ironically, his most famous role was that of Hoke Colburn, the chauffeur for Jessica Tandy's character in the hit movie Driving Miss Daisy, for which he received an Oscar nomination.

Oh, to What Heights They Will Go!

You may know that Tennessee's highest mountain is named for the mountain climber and U.S. senator Thomas Lanier Clingman, but there's an unusual story about how Clingman's Dome got its name. It started with a dispute between Clingman and a University of North Carolina professor, Elisha Mitchell, as to what peak in the Appalachian Mountains was the highest. Mitchell claimed Black Dome in North Carolina and Clingman said it was Tennessee's Smoky Dome.

While doing altitude checks of Black Dome, Mitchell accidentally drowned in a stream. Clingman then hired Arnold Guyot, a Swiss-born geographer, to make a study of the mountains. At 6,643 feet, Smoky Dome (now Clingman's Dome) is the highest point in Tennessee, but Black Dome (now Mount Mitchell) won the debate, at 6,684 feet.

Inner Vision

Francis Joseph Campbell was born in Franklin County in 1832 and attended school in Nashville. He was a quick learner, became a teacher, was cofounder of a college in England, and was knighted by King Edward VII in 1909. He also became something of a mountain climber, and even ascended Mount Blanc in the Alps.

None of this is especially noteworthy until you know the rest of the story. For Francis Campbell had been blind since the age of four and is the only blind person ever to climb Mount Blanc. The school he cofounded was the Royal College for the Blind in London.

The First Man-Made Tunnel in the United States

Tennessee's first capitalist and industrialist, Montgomery Bell, came from Pennsylvania's iron-producing country and in

Montgomery Bell

1804 purchased Cumberland Furnace from "the Father of Tennessee," James Robertson. This was the beginning of his empire. Bell then bought some land located on the Narrows of the Harpeth River, so called because it flows within a couple of hundred feet of itself, twisting around the base of a bluff. Bell became inspired by what the power of water could do for a furnace, and he had his slaves work for three years, boring a three-hundred-foot-long, fifteen-foot-wide tunnel through the base of the bluff. This diverted some of the water to flow through the tunnel, and the seventeen-foot drop on the other side turned wheels to provide power for Bell's furnace, which he called Pattison Forge or (Petterson Forge), after his mother.

Bell's tunnel is believed to be the first man-made tunnel in the United States, and his forge provided the cannon balls used by Andrew Jackson's men in the Battle of New Orleans. The land on which this historic tunnel was made has been turned into a state park, with an inn, cabins, trails for hiking and horseback riding, and lakes for canoeing and fishing. You can canoe the Narrows of the Harpeth River and see where the furnace used to be. See "Virtual Tennessee" for websites.

An Accident Leads to an Invention

A boy named George was born in eastern Tennessee around 1760. His mother was Wurtah, daughter of a prominent Cherokee family, and his father was Nathaniel Gist (or Guess), a fur trader from Virginia. One day while George was hunting, he had an accident and was forced into a period of inactivity. During this time, he became fascinated with the marks white people made on paper. He called the papers "talking leaves" because he saw how people could communicate using their written language.

George Gist, better known as Sequoyah, invented the Cherokee Syllabary

105

George then decided he would create a written language for his people.

After twelve years of work, in 1821 he had devised an eighty-five-character syllabary, which was adopted by the Cherokee nation. It was used to publish newspapers and books, and thousands learned to read and write the language, preserving an entire culture. Sequoyah, as he is known to history, was part of the forced removal of the Cherokee to Indian Territory. However, his statue today represents Oklahoma in Statuary Hall in the U.S. Capitol. There is more about his life and contributions at the Tennessee State Museum in Nashville. You can also tour the Sequoyah Birthplace Museum in Vonore. See "Virtual Tennessee" for website information.

Guess Who?

This debutante attended Nashville's Harpeth Hall, an all-girls' high school, and, after reading about a call for extras for a film, wound up with the lead in the movie, The Man in the Moon (1991). She went on to star in such blockbuster movies as Legally Blonde, and Sweet Home Alabama. She wrote a book, Whiskey in a Teacup, and has been host to the TV show, "Shine On." Give up yet?

She's Reese Witherspoon.

Q&A

Q. What popular home medical guide, first published in 1830 in Knoxville, became so popular with frontier and rural families that it remained in print until the 1920s and Mark Twain and John Steinbeck quoted from it in their novels (Huckleberry Finn and East of Eden)?
A. Gunn's Domestic Medicine, by Dr. John C. Gunn.

Q. What Jackson-born actor appeared in such movies such as The Steel Helmet and Walking Tall and the popular TV series My Friend Flicka?
A. Gene Evans.

Q. The character of Sergeant Carter in the TV show Gomer Pyle was played by what Clarksville native?
A. Frank Spencer Sutton.

Q. Andrew Jackson's wife, Rachel, had what "bad" habit?
A. Smoking cigars.

Q. Besides being Tennesseans, what do singer Dinah Shore, Olympic track gold medalist Wilma Rudolph, and Grand Ole Opry harmonica virtuoso Deford Bailey have in common?
A. Being stricken with polio at a young age.

Q. In 1937 what Nashvillian sculptor was the first African American to have a one-man exhibit at the Museum of Modern Art in New York?
A. William Edmondson.

Q. What Columbia native developed a serum to prevent cholera in hogs and also implemented the meat inspection program for the U.S. Department of Agriculture?
A. Marion Dorset (1872–1935).

Q. For what reason did the Memphis draft board grant Elvis Presley an extension before he had to report for army service?
A. To complete filming the movie King Creole.

Q. Tom Schulman, a former teacher at a private school in Nashville, won an Oscar for what screenplay starring Robin Williams as a teacher in a private school?
A. Dead Poets Society.

Q. Born in Humphreys County, U.S. Navy Captain William Robert Anderson was the first to accomplish what feat in 1958?
A. Commanded the nuclear-powered Nautilus, the first submarine to sail under the ice at the North Pole.

Q. Where did scientist Persa Raymond Bell pioneer a scanner that, when used with ingested radioactive substances, helped diagnose cancers and other diseases without surgical intervention?
A. Oak Ridge National Laboratory.

Q. What advocate of the use of quinine in the treatment of malaria wrote the first medical book to be published west of the Mississippi River?
A. Nashville physician Dr. John Sappington, who published his Theory and Treatment of Fevers in 1844.

Q. Greene County physician John Harvey Girdner is best known for being the first to successfully perform what surgical procedure?

A. Grafting a dead person's skin onto a living person.

Q. In 1816 what noted artist from the Northeast came to the Hermitage to paint Andrew Jackson's portrait, married Rachel Jackson's niece, and lived the rest of his life in Nashville?
A. Ralph E. W. Earl.

Q. At the turn of the twentieth century, a Montgomery County native pioneered the lovelorn, or advice, column in the New Orleans Picayune using what pseudonym?
A. Dorothy Dix.

Q. Murfreesboro author Mary Noailles Murfree wrote many novels using Tennessee mountain settings, including The Frontiersman, In the Tennessee Mountains, and In the Clouds, using what male pen name?
A. Charles E. Craddock.

Q. In 1986 what writer, raised in Clarksville, became the first poet laureate of the United States?
A. Robert Penn Warren.

CHAPTER SIX

From the Hills of East Tennessee

The Scopes Trial: A Publicity Stunt That Backfired

One of the most famous legal proceedings in American history had its beginning in the 1925 signing of the so-called "Anti-Evolution Bill." The trial which resulted from this legislation, often referred to as "the Scopes Monkey Trial," was really a public relations stunt that backfired.

In Dayton, Tennessee, soon after the signing of the bill, some of the locals were sitting in Robinson's Drug Store discussing the new law and their town's ailing economy. Two of the men were Earle Robinson, known afterward as the "Hustlin' Druggist," and George Rappleyea, the superintendent of Dayton Coal and Iron Company.

Rappleyea convinced Robinson and others to test the Anti-Evolution statute right in their own town, and they sent for the public-school teacher John Thomas Scopes. He'd taught many things, biology among them, but he wasn't sure if he had ever taught evolution. Nevertheless, he agreed to be a part of a test case that would put their town in the media limelight. Scopes taught evolution, was arrested for this, and his trial, which lasted eight days, drew more than ten thousand journalists,

Joe Mendi, the chimpanzee who visited Dayton for the Scopes trial and contributed to the circus atmosphere, enjoys a cool drink at the table in Robinson's Drug Store where the publicity stunt was first planned. With him are his trainer, Gertrude Baumen; Earle Robinson, known as the "Hustlin' Druggist"; and Frances and Wallace Robinson. (Courtesy Bryan College)

politicians, and the simply curious to the Rhea County Courthouse during one of the hottest and driest summers in Tennessee history.

Adding to national and international interest were the leaders of the opposing legal teams. Clarence S. Darrow, the nation's most famous criminal lawyer, led the defense; William Jennings Bryan, a well-known orator and former presidential candidate, appeared for the prosecution.

Even though some of the legal team members on both sides tried to retain a sense of dignity and keep people mindful of the serious nature of the case, the trial was punctuated by comic interludes and showmanship. For example, outside the courthouse there were monkey souvenirs for sale, and one trainer brought his chimpanzee named Joe Mendi. The carnival atmosphere drew a record number of reporters, including the famous H. L. Mencken. The event was also the first American trial to be broadcast live on radio, aired by Chicago's station WGN.

Ultimately, Scopes was convicted, but the Tennessee Supreme Court overturned the conviction on the technicality that the jury and not the judge should have established the fine Scopes was to pay.

According to historian Richard Cornelius, the publicity stunt backfired because "Dayton was made to look like a center for morons, anti-intellectuals, backwards thinkers, and bigots. The men who started the trial wanted publicity which would encourage investors in Dayton's potential, but this unfavorable publicity scared the fish away."

At any rate, their actions certainly put Dayton on the map. Even now, whenever the debate of evolution versus creationism comes up, Dayton, Tennessee, and the "Monkey Trial" are a part of the conversation.

Today, you can go to Dayton and learn more about the Scopes Trial. You can see more about the original trial at the Scopes Trial Museum and Rhea County Courthouse. Every mid-July, the town has a three-day festival celebrating the trial. The Scopes Trial Festival includes a re-enactment, musical entertainment, food, a quilting exhibit, and more. See "Virtual Tennessee" for websites.

"You Might Want to Do Something with This"

In the misty hollows outside Oak Ridge, this young boy loved to sit at his grandparents' feet and listen to their stories. They'd tell him tales of all kinds: pioneer stories, stories about their grandparents, and ancient folklore as they sat surrounded by the forests of the low-lying mountains of East Tennessee. Sometimes they'd give him something old: a book, a farming implement, something that anyone else might have thrown away. "You might want to do something with this," they'd tell little John Rice.

From those beginnings, John Rice Irwin created the world-famous Museum of Appalachia in Norris. His collection of implements of pioneer life has grown to over a quarter of a million pieces, exhibited in a sixty-acre working farm and turn-of-the-century Appalachian village consisting of more than thirty log structures. The Museum of Appalachia has received accolades from such publications as Reader's Digest, Southern Living, and Smithsonian. According to the Tennessee Blue Book, the Museum of Appalachia is "the most authentic and complete replica of pioneer Appalachian life in the world."

Today, the Museum of Appalachia is open daily (except for major holidays) for self-guided tours. They have events throughout the year, such as a days-long Fall Festival in

October, with music, food and living exhibits of pioneer life. The museum is also a Smithsonian Affiliate Museum. The Museum is a great site for family and corporate gatherings,

John Rice Irwin, founder of the Museum of Appalachia, gathered log cabins and buildings dating from the 1700s to early 1900s to form a village. Mark Twain was conceived in this cabin from Possum Trot, Tennessee (his family moved to Missouri before he was born). (Courtesy Museum of Appalachia)

weddings, and banquets. They've recently added a restaurant on the premises, which offers a delectable array of country dishes. The Museum is located in Norris; see "Virtual Tennessee" for web information.

The Incredible in East Tennessee

Gatlinburg has many interesting museums which contain oddities, record-breaking items, and interesting facts. One of what is (to me) the most interesting is the Guinness World Records Museum; another of my favorites is the Ripley's Believe It or Not Museum. Ripley's (of Believe It or Not! Fame) has added several museum and attractions, which includes Haunted Adventures, a 5-D Theatre, a Mirror Maze, an Aquarium with everything from eels to sharks to penguins among its exhibits, and a mini-golf course.

Some of the exhibits in the Guinness World Records Museum include people and things native to Tennessee, such as:

- **Most flying hours for a woman pilot**: Evelyn Bryan Johnson of Morristown achieved the record with 54,600 hours.

- **Youngest to graduate college:** This record is claimed by Michael Kearney of Murfreesboro, who received his B.A. in anthropology from the University of South Alabama at the age of ten years, four months.

- **World's shortest fire engine:** Owned by Fire Chief Henry Preston of Lebanon, "Little Squirt," as the engine is called, measures 118 inches long but is built to scale, and everything on it from sirens to lights and hoses works.

- **Fastest rocket powered street luge:** Current record holder was built by Billy Copeland of Ashland City and could reach a speed of seventy miles an hour.

Did You Know?

Pigeon Forge is so named because of the huge flocks of passenger pigeons that would flock to the river, attracted to the many beech trees along the banks. Some said the flocks of birds flying overhead would darken the sky at times (years before Alfred Hitchcock's movie The Birds!).

Later, the river served to provide power for an ironworks built by Isaac Love, which operated until the 1930s. The river and town are named for both the birds and the forge.

For History Buffs and Nostalgia Seekers

For those who love to step back into time or love history, the beautiful and amazing Great Smoky Mountain Heritage Center in Townsend is for you. This re-creation of an East Tennessee settlement, as it might have looked in the early 1900s, is a must-see. The village includes a visitor center, a gift shop, and cabins and outbuildings (such as a blacksmith's shop and even a moonshine still) from days of old. Since it opened its doors in 2006, the Center is near the entrance to Great Smoky Mountains National Park and welcomes visitors of all ages.

For "old-timers" who enjoy looking at ancient farming implements or cabins furnished and decorated as they might have been "back in the day," a visit here is a trip down memory lane. I heard many a visitor remark on stories they'd heard from their grandparents' experiences during this time. Throughout the year, there are special events, such as model train exhibits, country fairs and more. Regularly occurring events included guided tours of the center and cabins and tours of Cades Cove. See "Virtual Tennessee" for website information.

The Tragedy at Mecklenburg

It's always a tragedy when books are destroyed. We usually think of this as happening in other cultures, but unfortunately, it's also happened in ours. Mecklenburg is one example.

Mecklenburg was the home of Dr. James Gettys McGready Ramsey. And, prior to the Civil War, it was a place of peace, beauty, and stability. The antebellum mansion between the

French Broad and Holston Rivers was not just Ramsey's home; it also served to store the archives of the East Tennessee Historical Society, of which Dr. Ramsey was perpetual recording secretary. Within its bookshelves lay precious one-of-a-kind documents from Tennessee founders such as William Blount, Samuel Wear, John Sevier, and Alexander Outlaw.

Dr. James Gettys McGready Ramsey.

Dr. Ramsey had always been a states' rights advocate, and when the Union Army occupied Knoxville, his stance led to tragedy. He lost a son in battle and spent the rest of the war in exile. When Union soldiers came to Mecklenburg and realized it was not only the home of the outspoken Confederate leader but also served as the library and museum for East Tennessee history, they burned Mecklenburg.

Dr. Ramsey witnessed firsthand how war destroys much more than lives and property. He watched, helpless and brokenhearted, as the torch was put to more than four thousand volumes of irreplaceable historical documents, books, and letters.

Although those records, books and artifacts were destroyed, the Historic Ramsey House in Knoxville is open for tours 4 days a week, excluding major holidays. The 18th-century home is furnished and decorated as it might have been during Dr. Ramsey's time there. Listed with the National Register of Historic Places, the home hosts events during special times of the year, such as Christmas, and is also available for weddings. See "Virtual Tennessee" for websites

A World War II Tale

The U.S. Army colonel dressed in civilian clothes was on a top-secret mission when he walked into the office of Edgar Sengier in New York City. It was June 1942, a time of desperation for the Allied effort. The colonel was searching for uranium ore, the essential element in the making of atomic bombs. He knew it was a long shot that anyone there could give him a clue to help him obtain uranium, but he thought he'd ask this particular mining operator.

The colonel, whose identity is still unknown, was stunned to find the answer to his search right in Sengier's office. Within hours the military man had his uranium—one thousand tons of it!

This is the story of how the uranium vital to the success of Oak Ridge's atomic bomb project, called the Manhattan Project, was purchased from a Belgian mine operator, who had been secretly hoarding the uranium in New York City. A staunch anti-Nazi, Edgar Sengier was President of Union Minière in the Belgian Congo when he learned that scientists of the Third Reich were trying to develop an atomic bomb. If the Nazis got the technical know-how to make the bombs, he realized, they would soon be invading the Belgian Congo, where there was a wealth of uranium.

Unknown to anyone in Union Minière or in the Belgian government, from his mining operation Sengier began hoarding uranium, an ingredient found in the mineral pitchblende. He sent it in barrels to a warehouse in New York and notified some U.S. officials about his cache, but his message got lost in the mountains of government paperwork.

The colonel accidentally stumbled upon what he was looking for. The uranium became property of the U.S. government that very day, and the rest, as they say, is history. The Manhattan Project culminated in the dropping of the bombs in the Japanese cities of Hiroshima and Nagasaki, bringing an end to World War II.

In 2015, the city of Oak Ridge opened its museum related to this time in history. The Manhattan Project National Historic Park, one of three such parks (the other two in New Mexico and Washington), reveals much about this previously top-secret project. See "Virtual Tennessee" for websites

Itching for Justice

In Sevierville's early days, the town had no courthouse or other civic buildings. For lack of any other place in which to hold their judiciary proceedings, the people of Sevierville gathered in a stable. The stable had one big problem, however: it was heavily infested with fleas! Many trials were hastily performed as a result. One person wrote, "Perhaps nowhere else in Tennessee did the accused receive quicker versions of the speedy trials due them." The infestation got so bad that some of the attorneys finally burned the courthouse to the ground.

The Sevier County Courthouse, built during 1895–96, has not reported such infestations. Incidentally, people who are "itching" to see a lovely example of great Victorian architecture thoroughly enjoy visiting this courthouse. You can see the dome from a long way off, and the mountains in the backdrop make for impressive photography. See "Virtual Tennessee" for website information.

Strange... but True

The Weapon That's Been Used for a Musical Instrument

Long ago in East Tennessee there was a weapon that was also used to make music in times of lighthearted fun. It was the bow part of a bow and arrow, and it was the only "stringed instrument" in American in pre-Columbian times.

The late Carlock Stooksbury has played his "mouth bow" for Tipper Gore and for audiences in Japan. He claimed to be the only mouth bow player in the world. (Courtesy Carlock Stooksbury)

Some enterprising Native American had found that by placing one end of the bow against his mouth and opening and closing his mouth while simultaneously plucking the string, he could get different tones. This music-making technique was passed on to the American settlers.

A Moonshine Story

East Tennessee has its own style of entrepreneurs—folks in the mountains who participate in the illicit production of whiskey, called moonshine. Cocke County was, at one time, the

The person who rendered this diagram of a still claims to have no first-hand knowledge of liquor making, yet declined to be identified. (Courtesy Museum of Appalachia)

moonshine capital of the world, and in the Big South Fork National River and Recreation Area, the park service once estimated there was one still for every 116 acres of what is now park land.

The making of moonshine oftentimes has been a family

The first step in the making of moonshine is building a still. The illegal production of whiskey has often been a family tradition in the mountains of East Tennessee. (Courtesy East Tennessee State University Archives)

tradition since the first settlers came to the mountains. After the Revolutionary War, veterans were given certificates allowing them to make and sell whiskey. Then their children took up the vocation, and so on. Some people believe that the exemptions their forefathers enjoyed were passed down to them, along with their hair and eye color. Making moonshine, they claimed, doesn't clash with their being upstanding, God-fearing citizens; they consider the making of moonshine a right that is uniquely theirs. Today, you can take a tour of "Ole Smoky," a distillery that is the first in East Tennessee history to receive a federal license. Located in Gatlinburg, Ole Smoky Moonshine offers tours and tastings. See "Virtual Tennessee" for websites

Moonshine Glossary

My dear departed friend Carlock Stooksbury of the Museum of Appalachia in Norris defines the terms used by moonshiners—and the misspellings are all on purpose:

Backins: when the proof drops below 70.

Bead: the bubbles that appear when you shake the "likker."

Beading oil: used by amateur makers of cheap likker, a high-grade cooking oil used to put false beads on low-proof likker.

Beer: first stage of making likker, also called "mash" or "slop."

Branch: a source of water, a good place to set up a still so you will have plenty of cold water to cool the worm, or condenser

.

Burner iron: iron pipe, one and one-half to two inches, with gashes sawed about one inch apart to let the flames come out and make a circle inside the core.

Cap: the part that catches the alcohol vapors that come out of the still.

Cap arm: the arm on the cap that connects to the horse's head, which goes from the cap to the thump post.

Cape: the part the cap fits in.

Case: six gallons of likker in one-gallon glass jugs, or twelve half-gallon jars. (Anyone who puts likker in plastic milk jugs shows their likker is not worth a damn.)

Condenser: same function as a worm, turns steam into liquid.

Core: goes through the lower two-thirds of the pot to put the burner iron and generator through.

Feints: removing leftover liquid in the thump keg, washing it, then replacing with fresh backins before the next run.

Flake stand: also called a cooling tub; what the worm or condenser sits in, with cold water piped to the bottom to push the hot water off the top to keep it cool.

Generator: a curved pipe made out of one-quarter-inch black iron pipe, which must become hot before the fuel will start generating; works like a Coleman gas stove.

High shots: likker that first comes out of the worm, 180 proof.

Malt: may be made out of corn, barley, or rye that is sprouted, dried, and ground to break down the carbohydrates in the grain and turn them into sugar. (Modern-day moonshiners don't go to the extra work and expense. They throw yeast in.)

Pot: main part of a stilling outfit.

Pressure tank: fuel tank usually made out of an old hot water tank, into which is poured the fuel, half gas and half kerosene; connects to a gauge measure air pressure pushing fuel to the generator; also equipped with a tire valve to pump the tank with.

Proof: the amount of alcohol in your likker.

Tempering likker: occurs when the proof is cut down by adding water or backins.

Thump keg: gives likker a second distilling on one run, like a filter to catch any water or fusel oil (an oil present in the grain, mainly com-posed of amyl alcohols) to keep it from getting in the likker.

Thump post: a pipe that goes down in the thump keg with a notch cut out to let the steam through.

Worm: a copper coil, usually forty-eight feet long, that will hold anywhere from three hundred to six hundred gallons.

Worm connection: a pipe that goes from the thump keg to the worm or condenser.

You can see and learn more about the history of making moonshine at several places in Tennessee. The Museum of East Tennessee History in Knoxville is one, and three others are Ole Smoky Moonshine in Gatlinburg, The Louvin Brother's Museum at The Smoke House in Monteagle, and Tennessee Whiskey Tours in Nashville. See "Virtual Tennessee" for websites.

Jonesborough: Where Lyin is a Tradition

Remember how when you were growing up and told a story, your parents punished you and called you a liar? Well, if you come to Jonesborough you might be rewarded with applause and called a storyteller. For three days the first full weekend of every October, the town is filled with ghost stories, outlandish tales, and unbelievable lore, in what has become the National Storytelling Festival.

It all started in 1973 when this, the oldest incorporated town in Tennessee, wanted to begin a celebration or festival that would not only help preserve oral histories and traditions but would also help bring in tourist dollars. A teacher by the name of Jimmy Neil Smith suggested a storytelling festival, and in an entrepreneurial stroke of genius, they named it the

National Storytelling Festival, thereby assuring it media attention and future success.

Visitors listen to a storyteller at the National Storytelling Festival in Jonesborough (Courtesy Storytelling Foundation International; photo by Tom Raymond)

Now listed as one of the "Top 100 events in North America" (and it is a Smithsonian Affiliate), The National Storytelling Festival has achieved international fame and is attended by all types of writers and tall-tale-tellers. The organization that produces the festival, Storytelling Foundation International, is located in the historic Chester Inn. Chester Inn itself is now, as their website says, "The newest museum in Tennessee's oldest town." The inn is now known as Chester Inn State Historic Site and Museum and is a wonderful place to spend some time immersing yourself in the history of the area. The museum also has a gift shop with various publications, DVDs, artwork and more for sale. See "Virtual Tennessee" for websites.

Jonesborough in October: it's the place to go to hear tales you might have told when you were a kid! No lie.

The Melungeons

A mysterious group of people whose origin is unknown live in East Tennessee. They are called Melungeons, a term, some say, deriving from the Turkish melun can, which translates roughly as "cursed soul" or "one who has been abandoned by God." The Turkish term has its roots in the Arabic "melon jinn."

Others say the term can be traced to the French melange, or "mixture," referring to a mixed breed. Despite these linguistic suggestions, no one really knows from whom these people are descended.

The Melungeon people were first written about when explorers James Needham and Gabriel Arthur traveled to a region now a part of Hancock County, which was one of the earliest areas to be settled in Tennessee. In 1673 they reported seeing "white people which have long beards and whiskers." When exploring the same area in 1784, John Sevier and his party also came upon the strange group, described as having olive, or sometimes copper-colored, skin and wavy black hair.

A Melungeon Family

The Melungeons lost their considerable land holdings to the incoming Scots-Irish settlers when in the early 1800s the government of Tennessee declared the Melungeons to be "free persons of color." As noncitizens with their lands gone and with no possibility of gaining them back by legal means, the Melungeons withdrew into some of the more isolated parts of the mountainous regions of Tennessee.

Although some experts say it's possible the group is a "lost Native American tribe" or people with a combination of African American and Native American blood, the Melungeons maintain they are descended from Mediterranean people. In January 1999 in Sneedville, the Tennessee Commission on Indian Affairs met to discuss loosening its requirements on who could claim Native American ancestry. Melungeon historian Scott Collins of Sneedville was there and declared, "We have worked for generations to discover who we are . . . we know Melungeons are not Native Americans."

Genetic research is ongoing to unearth more information on the origins of the Melungeons and how they came to be in Tennessee. With an international team conducting studies at Clinch Valley College in Virginia, perhaps more information on their mysterious beginnings will be discovered in the next millennium.

In the meantime, the Children's Museum in Oak Ridge has a number of exhibits relating to the Melungeons. See "Virtual Tennessee" for websites

The Road to Nowhere

Near the quiet village of Townsend, Tennessee, just north of Bryson City, North Carolina, deep in the woods bordering Fontana Lake, is a road. You can travel this road until it ends abruptly at a long tunnel that goes underground for several hundred yards.

Its official name is Lakeview Drive, but the locals know it as the Road to Nowhere. Begun in the late 1950s as a combined project of the U.S. Department of the Interior, the Tennessee Valley Authority, and Swain County (North Carolina), it would have brought more visitors to Fontana Lake and connected travelers with a more straightforward route from Bryson to Townsend. Because of a lack of foresight, however, a few problems got in the way of the road's completion.

Twenty-eight family cemeteries were in the path the road was to take, and people weren't willing to move their beloveds' remains to make way for a highway. Also, concerns about the environmental impact on the pristine wilderness around it stopped construction.

You can drive down the road and when it comes to an end, explore the tunnel on foot. There are some great views of the Smoky Mountains from here. Both the road and the tunnel remain as mute witness to yet another example of a waste of taxpayers' money.

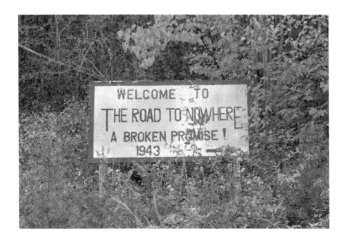

Q&A

Q. What type of architecture in farm buildings is seen almost exclusively in East Tennessee counties?
A. The cantilevered barn, with the second story larger than the first story, overhanging by about eight to ten feet.

Q. David Crockett was born in what town?
A. Limestone, west of Jonesborough. (Incidentally, there is no record of anyone calling him "Davy.")

Q. What county in the foothills of the Great Smoky Mountains received its name from the Cherokee word meaning "hazy" or "draped in fog"?
A. Unicoi.

Q. Since the 19902, what environmental role has Oak Ridge National Laboratory been playing?
A. Working with the Department of Energy to clean up and render harmless the toxic and radioactive wastes created in earlier years, not only in Oak Ridge, but in the United States and worldwide.

Q. Why was Tennessee chosen as the state in which to build components of the atomic bomb during World War II (in Oak Ridge) and later as the site for the Arnold Engineering Development Center (in Tullahoma)?
A. Relative security from German bombers and later from Cold War spies, in addition to adequate water and power supplies, access to rail lines and roads, and the availability of low-cost land.

Q. What designated National Wild and Scenic River that flows through the remote northern section of the Cumberland Plateau is one of the United States' last free flowing (undammed), unspoiled river systems?
A. The Obed.

Q. In 1949 what museum in an East Tennessee city had its opening coincide with the removal of the city's security gates?
A. American Museum of Science and Energy, in Oak Ridge, where top-secret work had been done to develop the atom bomb. (The museum was originally called the American Museum of Atomic Energy.)

CHAPTER SEVEN

Religion And Utopian Communities

Stories of Snake Handlers

Differences in interpretation of the Holy Scriptures often lead to the origin of new religions and cults. One of these, requiring serpent handling, derived from the Gospel of Mark (16:18): "they will take up serpents." Mark also referred to believers having the ability to speak in tongues and drink "any deadly thing" without injury. Many adherents who participated in the speaking in tongues and drinking of deadly substances (including strychnine and lye) were members of the Church of God.

George Went Hensley is generally credited with introducing the handling of serpents in Ooltewah, at Rainbow Rock on White Oak Mountain around 1905. An illiterate, Hensley had led a tumultuous life as an on-again-off-again minister in East Tennessee who, in his back-sliding days, had served time for selling moonshine. He was finally converted to the Church of God, which believed in the "following of signs," including handling serpents and drinking toxic substances, as part of its religious practices.

A worshipper handles rattlesnakes at a church service in Carson, Tennessee. Photo courtesy Mike DuBose.

At Rainbow Rock, Hensley prayed for a sign from God to tell him how to interpret Mark concerning snake handling. According to what he told his family, in midwinter, on snow-covered ground, a rattlesnake appeared and he picked it up without being bitten.

At a religious gathering in Owl Holler, Hensley began to preach and gained followers almost immediately. Some of his outlaw-type friends brought in a box of snakes, thinking this would discredit him. Instead, Hensley gathered up the rattlesnakes, water moccasins, and copperheads "like a boy gathering wood." The faithful saw this as a sign of God's approval, and other churches such as the Carson Springs Holiness Church of God in Jesus' Name, near Newport, took up the practice. Churches in West Virginia, North Carolina, and Kentucky followed suit, and Hensley became a kind of modern-day prophet.

The practice of snake handling was considered bizarre by the rest of society. In 1923 the Church of God split into two groups, forming the Church of God, which disassociated itself from the practice, and the Church of God of Prophecy, which continued it. In 1947 the first bill making snake handling illegal passed the Tennessee legislature.

In his years of snake handling, George Hensley was bitten at least four hundred times, but in 1955 at a religious meeting at an abandoned blacksmith shop in Calhoun County, Florida, he refused medical treatment for a bite and died. The practice persisted and in 1973 the Cocke County judge George Shepherd tried and convicted two deacons for snake handling.

Believers continue the religious practice to this day.

Strange But True!

Gideon's Bible... and Distillery

Gideon Blackburn was a Presbyterian minister who had more than one talent. Born in 1772, he settled on a farm in Fort Craig in East Tennessee, opened the New Providence Church, and later started two schools for the Cherokee people living nearby.

His industrious nature didn't stop there. He also owned a distillery, and in 1809 the Creek Indians accused him of using their land to illegally transport his whiskey to Mobile, Alabama. This caused nearly irreparable damage to the minister's reputation.

He did recover from the scandal, however, founded other churches, and even became the president of Centre College in Kentucky. History doesn't say if he ever built another still.

Members of a church in Carter County performed this baptism in a local creek. The photo is circa 1930. (Courtesy Tennessee State Library and Archives)

Did You Know?

Compared to other states, Tennessee has one of the highest percentages of Protestants, including over one million Baptists associated with the Southern Baptist Convention. The state is also home to many other varieties of the Baptist faith, some of which are found only in particular areas. The pull of evangelism is strong in Tennessee, and if you cross just about any river on a Sunday afternoon, you'll find some church members there, baptizing their own for God.

The Amish: Living Apart From The Modern World

The largest Tennessee community of the Amish is in Ethridge, in Lawrence County. The two-thousand-member group can be identified by their clothing. Boys and men wear brimmed hats and pants with suspenders; girls and women wear plain long dresses, aprons, and bonnets.

Mostly they are recognized by the way they live. These simple folk regard modern conveniences such as televisions, telephones, motor vehicles, electricity and running water as unnecessary and even burdensome. Their main focus is on the home and leading the simple life. An agricultural community, they are almost entirely self-sufficient. On the highways, their horse-drawn buggies serenely clop-clop along, as cars speed past them with their drivers intent on getting nowhere fast while fretting that their cellular phone batteries are running low.

This Protestant group broke away from the Mennonites in the 1690s and first came to America in 1728. The Lawrence County group came to Tennessee in the 1940s. Today the Amish live in twenty-three states and maintain their separation from the world. They do not go to war, swear oaths, or hold public office.

These simple, peace-loving people keep to themselves. Although their work on their farms is hard, by taking life more slowly, they seem immune to many of the ills and anxieties of modern society.

Today, you can learn more about the Amish and their way of life by visiting the Amish Heritage Farm Museum in Ethridge. This working farm is like a small village, complete with outbuildings, barns and an Amish schoolhouse. Not far from here, you will find the Amish Welcome Center, which offers horse-drawn carriage tours of the Museum. Also nearby is the Amish Country Market, where you can shop for and purchase wide-brimmed, hand-made hats, aprons and other items.

Did You Know?

The largest religious publishing house in the United States operated by African Americans is the National Baptist Publishing Board in Nashville.

Hey, Man, Look! It's The Farm!

In the 1960s and 1970s, young people and visionaries from all over the United States took off in search of America and themselves. Some of them formed a community that became world famous: The Farm in Summertown, Tennessee.

Stephen Gaskin

The Farm is called an "intentional community" because it was settled with a definite purpose in mind. In May 1971 Professor Stephen Gaskin left San Francisco with 350 students and friends. After a seven-month tour of the United States in brightly colored buses and vans, looking for a place to establish themselves, they decided to settle in Tennessee. By the end of

1980 The Farm had become, in its own terminology, "the largest hippie commune in North America," cresting at around 1,500 people

The philosophy of The Farm community is based on nonviolence and the belief that changing the world begins with the individual. In their tenuous first days, the newcomers were befriended by neighbors, who taught these "city folk" how to grow crops, use agricultural implements, and generally become self-sufficient.

Since that time, The Farm's culture has contributed to the acceptance of a variety of lifestyles in mainstream American culture, including vegetarian diets, environmental sensitivity, global responsibility, and the resurgence of midwifery. Today, The Farm is a thriving community and a proud contributor to the culture of Tennessee in general and Summertown in particular.

The people of The Farm have also reached out globally, trying to help others who are less fortunate. They now manufacture books, videos, electronics, and organic foods. It is headquarters for Plenty, International, a global outreach relief and development organization founded by the community in the mid-1970s. Their projects include soy nutrition in Central America, support for native peoples through fair trade, and a summer camp for children from homeless shelters.

The impact of The Farm has been felt worldwide. Its members have improved the lives of impoverished peoples to such an extent, Mother Teresa was once asked to meet with members of The Farm when they were working at a relief center in the Bronx. Speaking to Nancy Housel, one of the original members of The Farm, Mother Teresa reportedly had tears in her eyes when she said, "Oh, The Farm and Plenty! You are the heroes of the world!"

The Farm is available for tours, special events, retreats, and more. See "Virtual Tennessee" for websites.

Reverend Sam Jones and the Great Nashville Revival of 1885

In the spring and summer of 1885, Nashville was once again under siege, but this time it wasn't in the form of a threatening Union army. This threat came in the form of a spiritual challenge, made by a nondescript, slightly built man who filled the largest churches and biggest tents with penitential sinners seeking a messianic conversion for themselves and their world. The collective soul of Nashville was turned upside down by the Reverend Sam Jones.

No soft-spoken, kind-hearted shepherd type, this Georgia native looked the ministers who heard his righteous tirades right in the eye and challenged them as well. No wonder, he said, the churches were in such spiritual disarray, the people bewildered because they could not find their God. People were spending "all their time and all their money on the world," and "some people are actually ashamed to let the right hand know how stingy the left hand is."

He also turned his wrath on the churchgoers in the crowds. There was no room for the unrepentant sinners at barroom tables or card games because self-proclaimed Christians had gotten there first, he told the galvanized gatherings, assuring the sinners not to worry, because "the company in the Church ain't good enough for them yet."

These insults served to create controversy around the evangelist, which was the best kind of publicity. The Nashville Daily Union printed an editorial saying that the citizens of the city known as the Athens of the South "are past the age of being ridiculed or abused into religion."

Rather than turning away from Jones and his abusive, coarse, insulting verbiage, the throngs embraced him. Alternating his sermons with exhortations, jokes, and shows of temper at "Christians who attended dances Saturday night and

Ryman Auditorium

church Sunday morning," he kept his audiences enthralled, never knowing what to expect next. When he compared his attempts to convert the city to the Confederates' brave struggle in the Battle of Nashville, he won over hard-hearted men whose emotions were still in the 1860s. One night alone, five hundred stood up to dedicate their lives to the Lord.

One of these converts was "Steamboatin' Tom" Ryman. Ryman was a wealthy river man, with thirty-five steamboats plying the rivers. He was also said to be "a swinging soul who ran floating dens of iniquity." That part of his life ended when he heard Jones speak.

Ryman had come to protect his business interests, for Jones was speaking out against anyone who peddled or consumed the "devil's brew" and Ryman's boats often carried "old wine and young whiskey."

Thus, the crowds were astonished when Jones held out his hand, saying he knew Ryman and the others had come to protest his stance. He then asked them to take his hand. And Ryman, leaning on a cane, stumped up and did so, saying, "I came here for the purpose stated by Mr. Jones, and he has whipped me with the Gospel of Christ." Realizing that the new converts would need a more spacious place in which to worship, Ryman began building the Union Gospel Tabernacle in downtown Nashville, later known as the Ryman Auditorium and "the Mother Church of Country Music," one of the earlier homes of The Grand Ole Opry.

Today you can learn more about this time of religious fervor in Tennessee by visiting The Ryman. The Ryman offers guided tours and is open most days (musical performances are in the evenings). See "Virtual Tennessee" for website information.

You'll Love This Museum—It's the Gospel Truth!

For fans of traditional Southern Gospel, the Museum Center at 5ive Points in the town of Cleveland is a must-see. The Museum houses many artifacts related to the area's regional history, but on permanent exhibit is "The Red Back:

America's Best-Loved Hymnal." This exhibit has artifacts from more than six decades of Southern Gospel traditions.

It's appropriate that the exhibit on the old hymnal is in the town of Cleveland, for it was here that the hymnals were printed, using a typesetting machine known as a Linotype. Included in the exhibit is a working Linotype machine. The museum is on Inman Street East in Cleveland. See "Virtual Tennessee" for website information.

...And Two More Museums Paying Homage To Southern Gospel

I'm a huge fan of Dolly Parton, who's done so much for the people of her home state and has always been a great lover of Southern Gospel. In her hometown of Pigeon Forge, you can now visit the Southern Gospel Museum and Hall of Fame at Dollywood. It has many interactive exhibits and sound recordings which trace the history of Southern Gospel from its humble beginnings to today. Every fall, the National Quartet Convention is held here.

James Vaughan is known as the "Father of Southern Gospel Music." It was in Lawrenceburg in 1903 that Vaughan began publishing Southern Gospel hymnals and formed a quartet. The single quartet grew into more than a dozen, and their singing became so popular that they were traveling all over the country. Vaughan went on to establish a Southern Gospel radio station (also in Lawrenceburg). He is now memorialized with the James D. Vaughan Museum in Lawrenceburg, and every summer the town has a quartet festival which lasts four days. See "Virtual Tennessee" for website information.

The Bible Museum In Collierville

Approximately 30 miles outside Memphis you will find the quiet, charming village of Collierville. Collierville is the home to The Bible Museum on the Square. Located on the town square (as the name implies), the museum has welcomed people from all over the world since it first opened its doors in 1998. The museum is a kind of walk-through-Bible-history as you begin your tour; here, you will find everything from replicas of Bible-related artifacts to displays of truly ancient pieces. You will see exhibits containing items such as the Assryrian Flood Tablet to the Cyrus Cylinder and the Moabite Stone. The highlight of the tour for me was seeing the full-scale, operational model of the Gutenberg Press, as well as the many biblical manuscripts on display.

He Wore Out Some Horses!

Burton McMahan Martin, a McMinn County native, was a circuit-riding preacher with the Methodist Episcopal Church in 1898. He preached in churches located hundreds of miles from each other— Knoxville, Pikeville, Maryville, Athens, and Rockwood.

You can learn more about the early days of McMinn County at a lovely museum in Athens. Known as the McMinn County Living Heritage Museum, this establishment has more than 10,000 artifacts among its more than 30 permanent exhibits. See "Virtual Tennessee" for website information.

Wonder Why You Believe as You Do? The Wonders of Creation Center Will Help You Understand

There is a special and somewhat unusual kind of museum in Lewisburg, Tennessee. It is here that a minister by the name of David Rives established a museum he called Wonders of Creation Center, which celebrates God's creations. One docent, Halie Ayers, explained the purpose of this unique museum: "For those who want to have a deep faith in the Lord, oftentimes people want to witness but lack the tools and information to strengthen their faith using scientific discoveries that prove the

Bible to be true. The problem is that atheistic science claims to refute the Bible in support of evolution. If you don't have a Ph.D in science, you're often feeling helpless when trying to defend your faith. We understand how convincing the scientific arguments may sound, but you need the full story to support the truth. For that reason, we've become the most trusted name in Biblical science, interfacing with the top scientific organizations in existence to distill and give you the facts as they support your faith."

The Wonders of Creation Center offers guided tours through exhibits on Biblical astronomy, geology and flood evidences, human and animal biology, as well as dinosaurs and dragons. A Bible History and Accuracy exhibit spanning 6,000 years of history, with manuscripts and artifacts spanning 2,000 years, is part of this fascinating place. The gift shop contains nearly 800 books and DVDs, and a 200-seat event center offers a venue for presentations by guest speakers and classes on Creation Science.

The Story of Rugby

Thomas Hughes was an Englishman, former member of Parliament, social visionary, and author. His 1857 novel, Tom Brown's School Days, was popular both here and in England. It was based on Hughes's experiences while enrolled at Rugby, a prestigious British boys' boarding school. When Hughes visited America, he was enthralled by how relatively simple it was for a man of education to enter just about any field of endeavor he desired. He began to envision a place containing the best of both British and American worlds, one that offered the pleasant lifestyle he had always known yet did away with the social and economic barriers imposed by British elitist society.

Hughes became part of a venture company composed of capitalists from England and New England, who bought land in East Tennessee and called themselves the Board of Aid to Land Ownership. In the post–Civil War period, the plan for a utopian society in which southerners (especially Tennesseans) and Englishmen would work side by side was an appealing one.

When Rugby was officially named on October 5, 1880, it already had around 100 residents from both sides of the Atlantic. By midsummer 1881, the population had grown to about 300. Buildings such as the Tabard Inn and Christ Episcopal Church had been built, along with lovely homes and a library containing first-edition Victorian texts. For a while, it seemed that Hughes's vision had become a reality.

Then in the late summer of 1881, typhoid fever struck. Although only a handful of people died, many others left in panic and the utopian colony dwindled to about 60 souls.

Rugby's numbers grew again, with the population rising to around 450, but Hughes's grand dream never fully materialized. In the new millennium, however, there is promise for Rugby. A Rugby Restoration Association has been formed, and Historic Rugby is becoming a popular tourist stop.

Sue Bell, a docent at Historic Rugby, told me that the church, library, and Hughes' home have all been lovingly restored and guided tours are available. "My favorite place is the beautiful library," she said, "and children love the schoolhouse." Besides the day tours, Historic Rugby also has a Gift Shop and Commissary, and for those who would like to spend a night back in the late 1800's, lodging in Historic Rugby is available. See "Virtual Tennessee" for website information.

Q&A

Q. Established near Blountville in 1786, what was the first Methodist Church in Tennessee?
A. Acuff's Chapel. Now a Heritage Landmark of the United Methodist Church, the chapel and the cemetery (the latter of

which contains the remains of many early settlers and Revolutionary War heroes) are available for tours.

Q. What was one of the main causes of death for the early circuit-riding preachers?
A. Consumption (aka Tuberculosis).

Q. What Rutherford County native was a Methodist circuit rider between 1825 and 1827, served as a missionary to the Cherokee Indians, and during the Civil War was in charge of Methodist missionary work with the Army of Tennessee from 1861 to 1865?
A. John B. McFerrin, who also wrote The History of Methodism in Tennessee.

Q. Tennessee's oldest surviving African American church was built in what city?
A. Memphis (Beale Street Baptist Church, built in 1864). Lovingly restored in 2015, the church is open for tours outside of worship hours.

Q. What place of worship in Nutbush is the oldest of its kind in continuous use in the state?
A. Temple Adas Israel, established in 1882. Like Beale Street Baptist Church, this temple is also open for tours outside of worship hours. See "Virtual Tennessee" for websites.

Q. In 1796 Quakers from North Carolina established what town just west of Maryville?
A. Friendsville. The town is still known for its peaceful way of life and welcomes visitors.

Q. What was the first African American church to be established in Tennessee?

No

A. First Baptist Church, Colored, of Nashville, in 1848.

Q. What Presbyterian preacher came to the vicinity of Jonesborough in 1780 and organized not only a congregation but a school which later became Washington College?
A. Reverend Samuel Doak. His church is now the First Presbyterian Church in Greeneville.

Q. What was the first journal in the country solely devoted to the anti-slavery movement?
A. Manumission Intelligencer, published at Jonesborough by Quaker Elihu Embree, who had freed his own slaves in 1815.
Q. What Scottish lady and visionary heiress founded the short-lived utopian colony near Nashoba in 1827?
A. Frances Wright.

CHAPTER EIGHT

Sports, Recreation and Amusement Stories

It's Football Time in Tennessee!

All kinds of signs indicate when fall has come to the Volunteer State. Leaves change, the air gets chilly and crisp, and skies clear. For sports fans, though, the one thing that meant fall was the voice of John Ward saying, "It's football time in Tennessee!"

For more than thirty years the man known as "the Voice of the Vols" gave the details of University of Tennessee football games and got hearts racing with "Touchdown, Big Orange!" and "Give him six!"

There are many stories about John Ward, but Nashville Tennessean sports-writer Larry Woody recalled one that revealed a little-known side of the Voice of the Vols.

Dennis Fitzgerald, who had been deaf since an early childhood accident, worked in the newspaper's composing room. His favorite sports figures were NASCAR star Richard Petty and UT announcer John Ward. Fitzgerald had known Ward's family for many years: Ward's father had been principal at Tennessee School for the Deaf, and Ward's mother had been Fitzgerald's first-grade teacher. As a grown man with a family of his own, Fitzgerald would attend UT football games with his son, who used sign language to interpret what Ward was saying over the mike.

John Ward, the "Voice of the Vols" for more than thirty years, set fans' hearts racing with his "Touchdown, Big Orange!" (Courtesy University of Tennessee)

When Woody wrote an article about Fitzgerald, the deaf man mentioned his sports heroes and spoke of Ward in the most glowing of terms. Ward read the piece a few days later in The Tennessean, and the deaf man's words inspired Ward to find his address and write him a personal letter thanking him. Fitzgerald carried that letter with him until his death some years later.

On the eve of Ward's retirement, Woody recalled that single gesture, writing: "When I remember John Ward, I won't first think of football or basketball, of his descriptions of big games and thrilling victories. I'll think of a genuinely nice guy, a caring person. I'll think of class."

When Ward retired in 1998, his last post-regulation game was announcing UT's Fiesta Bowl that ended with UT earning a National Championship.

In 2012, Ward was inducted into the Tennessee Radio Hall of Fame; he was already in the Tennessee Sports Hall of Fame and the Knoxville Sports Hall of Fame, where there are now permanent exhibits about his life and accomplishments.

When in June 2018 Ward died, the entire football world grieved—even those who weren't Tennessee fans.

The Tennessee Titans: An Unprecedented Success

In the summer of 1995, meetings between then-mayor of Nashville Phil Bredesen and Texas businessman K. S. "Bud" Adams Jr. would forever change the sports landscape in the entire mid-south. The meetings resulted in the relocation to Nashville of the NFL's Houston Oilers, who became Tennessee's first major league sports franchise.

Tennesseans were treated to their first NFL game when the Tennessee Oilers defeated the Oakland Raiders at the Liberty Bowl in Memphis in August 1997, and the newly relocated team continued to play there before playing at Vanderbilt Stadium in Nashville the following season. The Oilers became the Tennessee Titans in the spring of 1999 when Adams changed the team name, colors, and uniforms to reflect the team's new surroundings; that same year, Nashville opened its new, 68,000-seat stadium, the Coliseum, for the Titans, and the love affair began between the team and its fans.

Since debuting in the Coliseum, the Titans have experienced a success unprecedented in the franchise's history. Every game since 1999 has been sold out, and the Titans have produced on the field as well, advancing to play in Super Bowl XXXIV (1999) and the AFC Championship Game (2002). The Coliseum itself is regarded as one of the toughest places to play in the NFL due to its football-savvy crowds and the skill of the Titans, who set a record for consecutive wins to . open a new stadium (twelve).

Some names shine through all this history, including Head Coach Jeff Fisher, Steve McNair (QB), Eddie George (RB), Frank Wycheck (TE), Jevon Kearse (DE), Bruce Matthews (OL), and Derrick Mason (WR). Seems like when anything moves to Tennessee, it only gets better.

One "Fang-Tastic" Story

You probably know that the Nashville Predators established themselves as a National Hockey League franchisee in what they termed "Smashville," on June 25, 1997, and since then the team has had phenomenal success. What you may not know is that the Predators' logo was inspired by the Ice Age: in August 1971 construction crews were digging in a cave below the city and discovered the bones of a

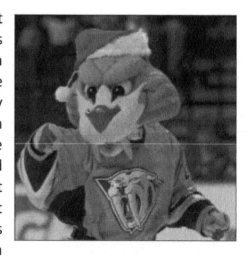

Gnash spreads holiday cheer as he cheers on the Predators

saber-toothed tiger, which had been the dominant "predator" on Earth for several millennia. This finding gave rise to the team's name, its logo of a saber-toothed tiger, and its mascot, appropriately dubbed "Gnash."

The "Preds," as locals call the team, make their home in downtown Nashville's Bridgestone Arena. You can see more about both the Titans and The Preds at the Tennessee Sports Hall of Fame in Nashville. See "Virtual Tennessee" for website information.

Rocky Top: Now You Can Sing Along

Okay, admit it: you've always wanted to sing along at football games.

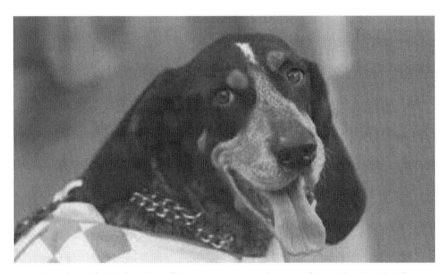

Smokey, the University of Tennessee mascot, pays close attention to the game. (Courtesy University of Tennessee Sports Information)

Now, you can. After all, it's one of the official state songs.

> Wish that I was on ol' Rocky Top
> Down in the Tennessee hills
> Ain't no smoggy smoke on Rocky Top
> Ain't no telephone bills

Once I had a girl on Rocky Top
Half bear, the other half cat
Wild as a mink, but sweet as soda pop I still dream about
that.

(Chorus)
Rocky Top, you'll always be
Home sweet home to me
Good ol' Rocky Top
Rocky Top Tennessee, Rocky Top Tennessee

Once two strangers climbed ol' Rocky Top
Lookin' for a moonshine still
Strangers ain't come down from Rocky Top
Reckon they never will

Corn won't grow at all on Rocky Top
Dirt's too rocky by far
That's why all the folks on Rocky Top
Get their corn from a jar

(Repeat chorus)

I've had years of cramped-up city life
Trapped like a duck in a pen
All I know is it's a pity life
Can't be simple again.

(Repeat chorus)

"La Gazella Nera" From Tennessee

Born in Clarksville in 1940, Wilma Rudolph was sickly and underweight, the twentieth child out of twenty-two in her family. As a child she suffered from a variety of illnesses, including pneumonia and polio. As a result, she didn't walk until age eight, and then only with a leg brace.

Wilma began playing basketball with her older brothers and sisters when she was around eleven. She had been told to wear corrective shoes but preferred to play barefoot. She ended up being a high school track and basketball star, qualified for the U.S. Olympic team in 1956, and won the bronze in the relay competition.

At Tennessee State College she played with the Tigerbelles, but various physical ailments sidelined her in 1958 and 1959. However,

Wilma Rudolf runs for the gold in the 1960 Olympics (Courtesy of the Leaf Chronicle)

she once again excelled in the Olympics in 1960, setting new world records and winning the gold in both the 100-meter and 200-meter dashes. On a post-Olympic European tour, Rudolph was popular with the Italians, who called her "La Gazella Nera" ("the Black Gazelle"), and with the French, who affectionately dubbed her "la Perle Noir" ("the Black Pearl"). She was named the Associated Press Female Athlete of the Year in both 1960 and 1961 and was only the third woman to win the prestigious Sullivan Outstanding Athlete of the Year award, in 1961.

Rudolph retired from athletics in 1962 and turned her energies to helping underprivileged children through her Wilma Rudolph Foundation, which also sponsors youth athletic competitions. She died in 1994.

The girl who physicians said would never be able to walk, ran to beat her obstacles, and became not only the fastest woman runner in the world but was ranked the number forty-one athlete among the top fifty North American athletes of the twentieth century by an ESPN panel. There are exhibits about her achievements at The Tennessee Sports Hall of Fame, and Rudolph penned her autobiography entitled *Wilma* some years before her death. There is also a statue of her in Clarksville, Tennessee, at the intersection of College Street and Riverside Drive. "Wilma Rudolph Day," on June 23, is an official day honoring this amazing woman.

Get Away from It All! Float the Best Streams in Tennessee

Here is a list, developed in consultation with the Tennessee Scenic River Association, of Tennessee's best recreational streams for paddling, canoeing, floating, and white-water rafting. The TSRA's website is www. paddletsra.org, for those who want to "paddle online." I've been on most, if not all, of these, and every single stream offers different challenges, with fantastic views you can only get from the bottom of a riverbed.

White Water Streams: Nolichucky, Ocoee, Hiwassee, Conasauga, Tellico, Big South Fork of the Cumberland, Obed-Emory System (National Wild & Scenic River System), Piney River, Whites Creek (in Rhea County), Crab Orchard Creek.

*D. L. Hayes displays his record-breaking smallmouth bass, caught in
Dale Hollow on July 9, 1955. (Photo © Mike DuBose)*

Pastoral Streams: Duck, Buffalo, Harpeth, Sequatchee,
"Ghost River" section of Wolf River (a black water stream called
"the Everglades of Tennessee").

Did You Know?

These coaches wore more than one hat! Robert Reese
Neyland became a brigadier general in the U.S. Army in 1944,
after serving as head coach at the University of Tennessee from
1926 to 1931. Jesse Neely coached football at Rhodes College
(then called Stewart College)

Breaking the Color Barrier: Ted Rhodes

When Tiger Woods donned his Master's blazer in 1997, he thanked someone very special to him. Woods had never known the man, but Ted Rhodes had done a great service for him and other African American golfers. He broke down the color barrier to the "game of kings."

A premier African American golfer at a time when such players were a rarity, Ted Rhodes was posthumously inducted into the Tennessee Golf Hall of Fame in Franklin in 1998 (he died in 1969). Rhodes won more than one hundred tournaments in his career, and CBS produced a

In 1948 Ted Rhodes successfully challenged the PGA's Caucasians only rule

documentary of his life. Tiger Woods's commercials for Nike include Ted Rhodes's image.

Ted grew up in Nashville, where in 1929, at the age of sixteen, he was a caddie at the Belle Meade Country Club, which banned African Americans from membership. The race issue in golf was first broached seriously in 1948 when Rhodes and another African American golf whiz, Bill Spiller, were among the top winners in the Los Angeles Open and went on to play in the Oakland Open.

The rules were different in the Oakland Open, though. After a couple of practice rounds, they were taken aside and told by George Schneiter, the head of the Tournament Players Bureau, "This tournament is only open to regular members of the PGA of America." Rhodes and Spiller were, of course, not members because of the PGA's Caucasians-only rule. They were humiliated, but they weren't going to take their clubs and go home.

Rhodes, Spiller, and another African American player, Madison Gunter, joined forces. First they held a news conference in Oakland, then contacted a sports producer with ABC, who aired their story across the nation. Finally, they filed a $250,000 lawsuit against the Professional Golf Association of America. The PGA offered a deal: if the players dropped their suit, the PGA would stop discriminating against players of color. Rhodes and his two fellow golfers accepted, and in 1961 competition in PGA tournaments became open to all players, regardless of skin color.

For Adrenaline Seekers: Go for a Walk in the Clouds

For those who seek beauty while getting a bit more than a thrill, the Gatlinburg SkyBridge is for you. The longest pedestrian suspension bridge in North America, the 680-foot bridge traverses a deep ravine which offers incredible views below. The Gatlinburg SkyBridge is accessible via a ride on the SkyLift at the SkyDeck, and it's the only way to get to the SkyBridge.

Part of the SkyBridge—near the middle, I'd say—consists of three panels of clear, thick glass, which is unnerving to some SkyBridge walkers (such as myself). From here, you can see straight down and view what's approximately 150 feet below where your feet are.

Some people will only go to the glass part of the SkyBridge and then walk back—after all, walking back is the only way down—but then, they can still say they braved walking the SkyBridge.

Their website proclaims a walk on the SKyBridge as "the most spectacular experience in the Smokies." I'm inclined to agree.

Did You Know?

In March of 2019, the city of Knoxville hosted the Geico Bassmaster Classic. It was a first for the city to host what has been referred to as the "Super Bowl of Bass Fishing." More than 50 bass enthusiasts competed for one million dollars in prizes. The response was so incredible, that by December 2019, registration was already open for the GBC of 2020. See "Virtual Tennessee" for website information.

Water, Water, Everywhere, and the Possibilities are Endless

For those who love water sports (kayaking, canoeing, paddle boarding, fishing, boating, swimming, etc.), then the Volunteer State has something for you. The Tennessee Department of Tourism folks have told me that the state encompasses more than 50,000 miles of rivers, streams and lakes.

For Those Who Like to "Hit the Links"

The "Golf Capital of Tennessee" is the lovely town of Crossville. Here you will find Fairfield Glade, which as of press time had 90 holes to play; also in Crossville is the Bear Trace

Cumberland Mountain State Park. The park is home to a challenging and scenic Jack Nicklaus-designed golf course.

Did You Know?

Johnson City hosts a motorcycle rally every September. Known as the "Hills & Hollers H.O.G. Rally," the event draws more than 2,000 biker enthusiasts and includes tours, entertainment and all kinds of food.

NASCAR and Bristol: The World's Fastest Half-Mile

In Bristol twice a year, the largest crowds of any sporting event in Tennessee gather to witness race cars going around the "World's Fastest Half Mile." What some of them might not know is that it's not really a half mile. In 1961 Bristol

Bristol Motor Speedway

businessman Larry Carrier constructed the track, an oval-shaped, perfect half-mile track. When it was first built, it could accommodate more than 20,000 fans, twice as many as most tracks.

It was originally banked at 22 degrees, but in 1969 the track was changed. Its new length measured .5333 miles, a little over a half mile, but it was now banked at 30 degrees. The track change was good for the fans because they could see all the competitors on the track all the time, and the increased banking, the steepest in Winston Cup racing, made the track faster.

Seating capacity now is even bigger since Bruton Smith's Speedway Motorsports, Inc., bought it from Carrier in 1996. You might not want to ask any of the 147,000 fans that can fit in the Bristol Motor Speedway as they watch Mark Martin, Darrell Waltrip, and others "swap paint" on the track if they realize it's not really the "World's Fastest Half Mile," because you might find yourself challenged to an old-fashioned settling of differences, Tennessee style.

You Might be a Nascar Fan IF...

The following items are all taken from real-life events.

You put off by-pass surgery because it's Race Day.

You help your mom get a job in a pawn shop so you can buy more NASCAR collectibles cheaply.

You have them bring a TV into the labor room so you and your newborn can watch the race as soon as he or she's born.

Your toddler knows all the cars and drivers but can't yet spell his or her own name.

You name your dog Dale, your kid Kyle, and your boat Darrell.

Pat Head Summitt: Netting History

Pat Head Summitt was born in the Clarksville area in 1953 and spent her childhood helping her family on the farm, milking

cows, cutting tobacco, and lending a hand in the family's grocery store. But her early life wasn't all work. She and her three brothers played basketball in the late afternoons after chores, in an old tobacco barn in which they'd built a basketball court.

The family moved from Clarksville to the tiny town of Henrietta when the budding basketball star was of high-school age. At Cheatham County High School Pat became a basketball all-star in 1966. While she was still in college at the University of Tennessee in Martin, she got a call from the University of Tennessee in Knoxville,

Pat Head Summitt

asking if she would take the job as head coach of the new women's basketball program.

During her first season the twenty-two-year-old novice worked on getting her master's degree while coaching her team to 18 wins. Twenty-four seasons later, her Lady Vols had won 664 games and lost a mere 143 and earned the title of National Champions in 1996, 1997, and 1998. In the 1997–98 season the Lady Vols went undefeated, something unheard of. Summitt herself has been driven to excel. She played in the 1973 World University Games, where her team won a silver medal, and in the 1975 Pan American Games, where her team took gold. She also co-captained the U.S. Olympic Team in 1976, where her team earned the silver.

Summitt coached UT to a total of 14 regular Southeastern Conference titles and 13 SEC Tournament titles. She established herself as the winningest coach in NCAA history when, in 2009, she completed that season with 1005 total wins.

Acclaimed as the greatest women's basketball coach in history, Pat Summitt was elected to the Basketball Hall of Fame in 2000. She commented then that coaching "is about opportunities and taking advantage of [them] and not being afraid." Although she died in June of 2016, this woman who made coaching history continues to inspire others through her legacy.

Today you can see more about Pat Summitt's achievements in more than one place in Tennessee. The Tennessee Sports Hall of Fame in Nashville has permanent exhibits about the life of this famous coach. In Clarksville, Liberty Park has open-air displays of Summitt's life and achievements, and there is a bronze statue of her there (as is one of Wilma Rudolph—see a previous story about her). The sculpture was created by Tennessee artist Brett Grill.

Q&A

Q. What competition has its national tournament in Standing Stone every year?
A. National Rolley Hole Marbles Championship, where more than thirty teams compete.

Q. What model company town was established in 1900 for the production of cotton bagging and jute bags and even constructed a golf course and YMCA for its resident employees?
A. Bemis, which was annexed into Jackson in 1975.

Q. What Grand Ole Opry star once signed a contract with the St. Louis Cardinals baseball team and died in a plane crash in Davidson County on July 31, 1964?
A. James Travel "Jim" Reeves. (He was unable to play with the Cardinals due to a leg injury.)

Q. On November 8, 1958, when rioting took place for nearly two hours after the game, who had played the Tennessee Volunteers?
A. Chattanooga Moccasins, who won 14-6. (The Knoxville News-Sentinel reported that one thousand people rioted after Moccasins fans uprooted the goalpost at the north end of Shields-Watkins Field, resulting in police using water hoses and tear gas, with nine injuries and ten arrests.)

Q. Who was known as "the Mother of the Tigerbelles"?
A. Mae Faggs; she and Barbara Jones were the first Olympic gold medalists on the Tennessee State University track team in 1952, paving the way for Wilma Rudolph.

Q. What Vols player from 1928 through 1931 was said to be the greatest player Coach Bob Neyland had ever coached?
A. Gene McEver.

Q. What was the real name of the Chattanooga native who earned the nickname of "the Mad Bomber" as an All-American basketball player?
A. Richard Fuqua.

Q. Who won the Winston Cup for two consecutive years, 1981 and 1982?
A. Darrell Waltrip.

Q. In what year did the University of Tennessee Volunteers first wear their orange jerseys?
A. 1922.

Q. In 1931 what Tennessee professional baseball player, playing for the Boston Red Sox, broke the major league record for the most doubles in one season?
A. Earl W. Webb, with sixty-seven doubles. As of press time (2020), that record still stands today.

Q. Where is the Southeastern 500 race held?
A. Bristol.

Q. Born in 1880 in Murfreesboro, what writer was acknowledged to be the dean of American sportswriters?
A. Grantland Rice.

Q, What is Tennessee's most heavily fished trout stream?
A. South Holston.

Q. In 1877 what city was the first to have a professional baseball team?
A. Memphis, with the Red Stockings, which lasted only one season.

Q. The Memphis Red Sox player Ted Radcliffe was given the nickname "Double-Duty" because he held what two positions?
A. Catcher and team manager.

Q. With what league were the Memphis Red Sox and the Nashville Elite Giants affiliated?
A. Negro Southern League (NSL).

Q. During the 1926–27 season, Satchel Paige played with what Chattanooga team?
A. Black Lookouts (NSL).

Q. For the 1945–46 season, what sixteen-year-old Chattanooga Choo-Choos outfielder played without a contract?
A. Willie Mays. (His mother wanted him to finish high school.)

Q. In 1881 what was the first American-bred horse to win the English Derby?
A. Iroquois, owned by William Hicks Jackson of Belle Meade Plantation, Nashville.

Q. On what river were kayaking and other white-water competitions of the 1996 Summer Olympics held?
A. Ocoee.

Q. The stickball game that was a favorite with the Choctaw people ultimately became what modern-day competition?
A.Lacrosse.

Q. What sports hall of fame devoted entirely to women opened in Knoxville in 1999?
A. Women's Basketball Hall of Fame.

Q. What NBA team from Vancouver, Canada, settled in Tennessee in 2001?
A. Now known as the Memphis Grizzlies, the team was one of the first of two non-U.S. teams to join the NBA in 1995 (the other team was the Toronto Raptors)

CHAPTER NINE

The Civil War in Tennessee

Frankly, My Dear, Maybe This is Why Tennesseans Still Give a Damn

The War between the States. The Battle over States' Rights. The War of Northern Aggression and Southern Rebellion. By whatever names you've heard it called, the Civil War remains a source of endless fascination, even for people who are not history buffs. For Tennesseans especially, the Civil War is often still discussed as if it happened yesterday and not more than a 150 years ago. Perhaps one reason is that, with the exception of the state of Virginia, Tennessee had more battles fought within its borders than any other state.

Did You Know?

In 1824, William Driver, a New England sea captain, named his U.S. flag "Old Glory." He later moved to Nashville, where, during the Civil War, he kept the original Old Glory hidden in a quilt at his home. After the war, when Driver died in Nashville, the U.S. Congress made his grave in the City Cemetery one of the few places where a flag may be flown twenty-four hours a day. His family gave Old Glory to the Smithsonian Institution in 1922.

Still a Mystery: The Battle of Spring Hill

In 1864 the Confederate army under General John Bell Hood returned to Middle Tennessee, hoping to rekindle the South's dying flame and recapture Nashville. Fighting began at Spring Hill on November 29, and as darkness fell, both sides stopped for the night.

The Confederates thought they had the 17,000 Union troops trapped, but inexplicably left the road from Columbia to Franklin open. Under cover of darkness, Union troops marched past Confederate campfires 150 yards from the road and by morning were safely ensconced behind earthworks in Franklin.

General Hood, whose left arm had been shattered at Gettysburg and whose right leg was lost at Chickamauga, ordered his senior officers to meet him at Rippavilla Plantation in Spring Hill, where he gave them a verbal thrashing for allowing the Union

General John B. Hood couldn't understand how his men allowed seventeen thousand Union troops to slip through their fingers at the Battle of Spring Hill.

troops to escape. Among them was General Nathan Bedford Forrest, who blamed Hood, saying, "If you were a whole man, I'd whip you within an inch of your life."

Nevertheless, the Confederates followed the Federal troops and the disastrous Battle of Franklin ensued.

To this day, it's still a mystery as to how 17,000 Union soldiers slipped out of the grasp of what should have been a tremendous Confederate victory. There are still heated debates about who allowed it to happen.

Strange... but True!

The young man was struggling with math. He already had a problem with too many demerits, and if he didn't pass math, he couldn't graduate. This filled him with despair.

Another student, seeing him struggle, offered to help him. The offer was gratefully accepted, and that was how the future General Schofield tutored the future General Hood so he could graduate from West Point in 1853.

In 1864, tutor and pupil fought each other, Schofield leading his Union army and Hood his Confederates at the Battle of Spring Hill (Tennessee).

Did You Know?

The Chickamauga and Chattanooga Military Park was the first national military park in the United States. Established in 1890 and containing 8,200 acres, it is the nation's oldest military park. The re-enactment of The Battles for Chattanooga is held in the park every November. The park's headquarters is officially in Fort Oglethorpe, Georgia. See "Virtual Tennessee" for website information.

Fighting in the Buff

On more than one occasion, soldiers on both sides were obliged to go au naturel, such as when fording a deep creek. They'd roll their clothes around their guns and carry them over their heads when crossing rivers. Other times they'd be in this vulnerable circumstance when bathing in the rivers, just trying to wash a few lice off their bodies. Sometimes they would use this tactic as an element in surprising the enemy.

U.S. Colonel James P. Brownlow of the First Tennessee Cavalry once led an "in the buff" attack. In July 1864 he had his men disrobe, cross a river, and sneak up on unsuspecting Confederate soldiers. Union General E. M. McCook wrote in his journal of that day: "They drove the enemy out of their rifle-pits, captured an . . . officer and 3 men... They would have got more, but the rebels had the advantage in running through the bushes with clothes on. It was certainly one of the funniest sights of the war, and a very successful raid for naked men to make."

Want to Really Immerse Yourself in Civil War Sites? Here's a Partial List!!

For true, die-hard Civil War buffs, here is a (mostly complete) list of places in the Volunteer state where you can learn more about the War Between the States:

Tennessee State Museum: located in Nashville and opened in 2018, this fascinating museum is not to be missed. There are exhibits spanning the entire history of the Volunteer State, including the Civil War.

Carnton Plantation: see the story about the family and the war in this chapter. Carnton Plantation is located in Franklin, Tennessee.

Carter House: also in Franklin, the historic Carter House is a wonderful, sometimes sobering, memorial to this tragic war. In late 2019, Carter House unveiled its new, $3 million visitor center and museum. Touring Carter House could take most of a day, and you'll be happy you came.

Chickamauga National Military Park. See the Did You Know? Story near the beginning of this chapter.

Stones River National Battlefield: Located a few miles northwest of Murfreesboro in Rutherford County, this 570-acre park memorialized the Battle of Stones River, one of the bloodiest conflicts of the Civil War. Inside the Visitor Center you can see interactive exhibits of true, firsthand accounts of the battle, along with a short film documentary and a bookstore. The cemetery here is the final resting place to more than 6,000 who died in this battle.

Lotz House Museum: located in Franklin, the museum also offers walking tours of the former battlefield.

Shiloh National Military Park: located outside the town of Shiloh, near the border of Tennessee and Mississippi, lies Shiloh National Military Park. This park is both a salute to the heroes of the war, and a memorial to the fallen—Shiloh National Cemetery is the final resting place of more than 23,000 casualties of the largest engagement in the Mississippi Valley campaign. The park also contains some prehistoric Indian mounds that are well preserved.

Travellers Rest: a historic plantation house in Nashville, it was the former home of Judge John Overton, and during the Civil War served as headquarters of Confederate General John Bell Hood. The home and grounds are supported by the Battle of Nashville Preservation Society. Inside you can see what is said to be the largest collection of Civil War artifacts of any place in Tennessee.

Belle Meade Plantation: located in the town by the same name, this Greek Revival plantation was founded in 1805. Tours include viewing of the plantation house itself, slave quarters, and outbuildings such as a dairy and carriage house.

Monthaven Arts and Cultural Center: Located in Hendersonville, this antebellum home was once used as a Civil War hospital and is now a combination museum and art gallery.

Belmont Mansion: located in Nashville, this was the former home of the wily Southern belle, Adelecia Acklen. See her story in this chapter.

Fort Negley Park: a Civil War fortification that Union soldiers built after the capture of Nashville, it is the largest inland stone fort built by either side during the conflict.

East Tennessee Historical Society and Museum: located in Knoxville, this museum houses an amazing array of all things related to the history of East Tennessee, including the Civil War.

Fort Pillow State Historic Park: located in western Tennessee, this 1,642-acre park in Lauderdale County (Henning) tells the story of the Battle of Fort Pillow. This fort was built in 1861 along the steep Mississippi River bluffs.

Johnsonville State Historic Park: a state park in New Johnsonville (Humphreys County), it is named after former U.S. President Andrew Johnson (who was the first president ever to be impeached). The Battle of Johnsonville occurred here in November 1864, and every November Civil War re-enactors hold an encampment in the park.

Abraham Lincoln Library and Museum: this museum often surprises people that "Honest Abe" has a museum about him in the Volunteer State. Located in the town of Harrogate on the campus of Lincoln Memorial University, the museum houses a collection of more than 30,000 books. Artifacts include the walking cane Lincoln carried the night of his assassination.

The Mabry-Hazen House: this lovely home built in 1858 houses many artifacts related to the Civil War, especially events that occurred in Knoxville. It served as headquarters for both the Confederate and Union armies.

Dickson-Williams Mansion: TripAdvisor hailed this mansion as "one of the crown jewels of the South." Located in Greeneville, Tennessee, it was originally the home of Catherine Dickson and her new husband, Dr. Alexander Williams. This Federal-style mansion was used by both Union and Confederate soldiers, at various times during the Civil War. Touring this home, you will learn of how this family was truly divided, with some sympathizing with the Confederacy, and other family members, with the Union cause. The family was so divided, that there was even a murder on the grounds as a result!

Farragut Folklife Museum: this museum in the town of Farragut (near Knoxville) is named after Admiral David Farragut, famous for his part in the Battle of Mobile (Alabama) Bay and his defiant shout, "Damn the torpedoes! Full speed ahead!" Outside the museum (which opened in 2010), the Memorial Plaza and Civil War trail markers, along with a statue of Farragut in his Union garb, add to your visit.

Slave Haven Underground Railroad Museum: This, to me, is a must-see. Located in Memphis, this 19th century home (originally known as the Burkle Estate) features all sorts of secret places, such as trap doors and tunnels, where abolitionists hid runaway slaves to help them get to freedom.

Sam Davis Museum and Hanging Site: located in Pulaski, this museum exhibits mementoes of the "Boy Hero of the Confederacy." One sobering exhibit contains his execution shackles; the ground on which he was hanged is marked with a large rock.

Emerald Hill: also known as Eagle's Nest, this lovely antebellum home in Clarksville was once the home of Confederate Senator Gustavus Adolphus Henry, Sr. It is now home to the local state university alumni association, Austin Peay. After renovations in 2019, the mansion is open to special events.

It's worth mentioning here that many of these places have special events, such as battle re-enactments, during the year; some other places, such as mansions, offer their venue as a backdrop for events such as weddings. See "Virtual Tennessee" for websites.

The Mystery of the Headless Corpse

Colonel William Mabry Shy of the Twentieth Confederate Infantry was fighting with his men under the command of General Thomas B. Smith. It was December 16, 1864, during the Battle of Nashville, and Shy and his infantry were defending the area outside Nashville then known as Compton's Hill. They

Colonel William Mabry Shy

were part of a Confederate line of defense that stretched for five miles.

The battle went awry for Shy and his men, and the Union soldiers succeeded in breaking the Confederate lines. The Southerners retreated to the Overton Hills with General Nathan Bedford Forrest's cavalry giving them cover.

General Smith was captured by the Union army, but Colonel Shy was killed in the battle. A friend of the family found him bayoneted to a tree, shot through the head, and completely naked. His body was taken to his home in Franklin, where he was buried. But that's not the end of the story.

In December 1977 some grave robbers opened Shy's grave. His casket was made of cast iron, but that didn't stop them. The graverobbers broke the front of the casket open using a heavy metal object, probably a post-hole digger.

Accounts don't say what (if anything) was taken from Shy's body or casket, but the morning after the grave was robbed, police found a headless corpse with the torso sticking out of the coffin. They saw that the body was extremely well preserved, and they thought it might be the victim of some recent murder.

The body was given a cursory examination by Dr. William Bass, forensic anthropologist and head of the Department of Anthropology at the University of Tennessee, Knoxville, who searched for and found the missing head. For a short time he thought that they were conducting a homicide investigation because of the well-preserved state of the body. Finally, he determined for certain that the body was that of the long-deceased Colonel William Shy. "I was right about the age of the victim and the cause of death," he told me in an interview in 1999. "I was only off on the time of death—off by about 113 years."

In January 1978 Shy was reburied with full military honors. His old casket is now on view at the Carter House Museum in Franklin. Incidentally, the hill he defended, Compton's Hill, has been renamed Shy's Hill in his honor. Carter House is open for tours, and recently opened a $3 million Visitor Center. See "Virtual Tennessee" for websites.

"Waterloo Teeth" and Civil War Dentistry

Before the advent of modern dentistry, teeth were more often pulled than saved, and many different types of materials were used in the making of dentures. Bone, ivory, and wood were some of the most common materials carved to make replacement teeth.

Sometimes, too, human teeth were used, called "Waterloo Teeth" because they were often gathered from dead soldiers as they lay on the battlefield. During the Civil War, barrelsful of teeth were taken from dead soldiers, and shipped to England for use in dentures. There is a fine display about "Waterloo Teeth" at a museum in downtown Clarksville, known as the Customs House Museum and Cultural Center. See "Virtual Tennessee" for websites.

The Headquarters for Both Armies in the Same Day!

The first person to build a permanent home on Lookout Mountain was Robert Cravens in 1856. It was a simple L-shaped, single-storied home with six rooms. For some years, peace reigned at Cravens House. Then the Civil War came to Lookout Mountain.

In September 1863 Confederate troops occupied the mountain and for a time held the Union army in Chattanooga. Then on November 24 General Joseph Hooker's Union troops attacked Lookout Mountain. That same day the Confederate army made the Cravens House their headquarters as they tried to fend off the Union soldiers. When the Confederates retreated in mid-afternoon, Cravens House became Union army headquarters under command of General W. C. Whitaker.

Cravens House is now maintained by the National Park Service as a part of the Lookout Mountain Battlefield and is open for tours. See "Virtual Tennessee" for website information.

Button, Button, Who's Got the Button?

After Abraham Lincoln was assassinated by John Wilkes Booth, Lincoln's vice president took over to face the task of reuniting the country in the aftermath of the war. Himself a Tennessean, President Andrew Johnson did everything in his power to protect his beloved state and the rest of the South from the full vengeance of the victorious North. Everything he did, however, came under scrutiny and suspicion, since he was a southerner. Johnson later missed being impeached and removed from office by only one vote. He was the first U.S. President to have impeachment proceedings against him.

Tennessee was under the strict governance of William Gannaway Brownlow, a Virginia-born Methodist minister and journalist. At one time, he and Johnson had taken the same side in the fight against secession. On every other issue, however, they were at opposite ends of the political spectrum. Brownlow succeeded Johnson as governor of Tennessee when Johnson ran on the ballot with Lincoln.

As much as Johnson was compassionate toward the Southern states, Brownlow was vengeful against those who had voted to secede from the Union. Although he backed government bonds to rebuild railroads and other infrastructure in Tennessee, his vengeance against Tennesseans who had remained true to the Confederacy was unflagging. For example, after Lee surrendered at Appomattox, in many states there was a military prohibition against, of all things, Confederate soldiers' buttons.

William Gannaway Brownlow

No Confederate soldier—whether he was just straggling home from the battlefield, the hospital, or a POW camp—was to wear his uniform's buttons. The buttons must be covered or replaced (and the rule did not consider that these men were destitute and without "button resources"). What a final humiliation it must have been for one returning, beaten and dispirited, to come upon a Union soldier who would cut off the buttons with a saber, leaving the poor Confederate in a state of near undress.

Brownlow and his Tennessee legislature tried to have a "Button Bill" passed as law, which would impose a fine of anywhere from five to fifty dollars on soldiers who wore their buttons on their tattered uniforms. Fortunately, it did not pass, but "the Button Trouble" was one more festering wound Tennessee endured after the Civil War.

Did You Know?

In Tullahoma one of the largest U.S. Army training bases during World War II was named after Nathan Bedford Forrest. Camp Forrest also served to house eight hundred alien civilians in the early days of that war. Later, it was used as a prisoner of war camp, and at one time it was home to more than 24,000 members of the German Wehrmacht. Camp Forrest itself no longer exists; the site today is occupied by Arnold Engineering Development Center (under the auspices of the U.S. Air Force). Today, you can see more about Tullahoma's history at the Mitchell Museum, and you can tour Tullahoma's Confederate Cemetery. See "Virtual Tennessee" for website information

The County That Left Tennessee to go with the North

Just before the outbreak of the Civil War, to say "times were tense" was an understatement. Everyone from politicians to yeoman farmers talked of secession. Some felt it was akin to treason for Tennessee to leave the Union; others answered they were following in the footsteps of their Revolutionary War ancestors who wouldn't abide tyranny. For many regions the issue was clear-cut—but not for East Tennessee. This was a geographically and strategically desirable region with natural deposits of saltpeter and niter. East Tennessee also had its railroads branching from Knoxville into Georgia, Kentucky, and

Virginia. The Confederacy needed East Tennessee as much as the Union wanted to set it free from the Confederate grip. One Richmond journalist called East Tennessee "the Keystone of the Southern arch."

There were many East Tennesseans whose sympathies were with the Union; this caused hard feelings among neighbors and kinsmen. The war became a very personal thing.

When Tennessee voted to secede from the Union, the members of the Scott County Court convened a special session. To a man, the members voted to secede from Tennessee, and even renamed their county the "Free and Independent State of Scott." Ellis O. Butler wrote of the bizarre incident this way: "The brave squires dispatched a messenger to Nashville to inform the governor and the state legislature that the former Scott County was now independent and no longer a part of Tennessee but, unlike the rest of Tennessee, still a loyal part of the United States of America."

Confederate soldiers quickly took arms against the insurgents of Scott County, but the men responsible for the county's divorce from the state hid and evaded the attacks of their neighbors.

The matter was not solved with the end of the Civil War, either. In 1866, Tennessee rejoined the Union, but Scott County waited longer to adopt a resolution to dissolve the "Free and Independent State of Scott" and "petition the governor and legislature of Tennessee for readmission into the state of Tennessee as Scott County."

Maybe it procrastinated a little or maybe it wanted to prove a point, but Scott County didn't make a move to formally rejoin the state of Tennessee until 1986, 125 years after it had seceded from the state.

You can learn more about this interesting era of Tennessee history by visiting the Scott County Museum in Huntsville, Tennessee. See "Virtual Tennessee" for website information.

Whistle-Stops Along the Underground Railroad

Benjamin "Pap" Singleton, who called himself "the father of the Black Exodus," made his way to freedom along the Underground Railroad, from Nashville to Canada. A Memphis mansion now called the Slave-haven/Burkle Estate served as a stopping place for slaves trying to gain their freedom via the Underground Railroad. Because of its labyrinth of trap doors and tunnels, the Bell-Herrin House in Jonesborough is also thought to have been a haven for fleeing slaves. Both places are open for tours.

"Secret Soldiers" of the Civil War

During the Civil War, many civilians changed their identities so they could take part in defending their respective countries. One of these was a Pulaski native by the name of Sullivan.

In 1861 Sullivan joined up with a close relative in Company K of the First Tennessee Infantry Regiment. With the rest of the infantry, Sullivan marched long miles, carrying knapsack and weapons, set up camp, and endured sleepless nights on the cold, hard ground. Sullivan fought in West Virginia and then in northern Virginia, serving under Stonewall Jackson.

Sullivan's close relative was wounded on the battlefield in Perryville, Kentucky. When he was made a prisoner of war, Sullivan accompanied him to prison. From there this "secret soldier's" records are lost in the mists of time.

Sullivan was Betsy Sullivan. Her relative? Her husband, John. Like every other woman living in the South then, her life was affected by the Civil War. Some women responded by caring for the wounded after battles. Other women hid Confederate soldiers in their attics or spring houses or defended their homes from marauding bands of Union soldiers in the aftermath of battles. Others packed their families and what belongings they had left and moved on.

But women like Sullivan, whether they wanted to join their husbands or sweethearts in battle, serve as spies, or seek adventures home and hearth didn't provide, responded to the war by cutting their hair, donning men's uniforms, and keeping their true gender a secret.

In *Patriots in Disguise: Women Warriors of the Civil War* (New York: Paragon House, 1993), Richard Hall wrote, "A surprising number of women served in combat on both sides during the American Civil War." The unfortunate thing is that, like Betsy Sullivan, these "secret soldiers" have been all but forgotten in the annals of mainstream American history.

The Soldier Who Fought for Love

Colonel Harry T. Buford of Memphis had several goals during the war, one being to become known for his courage. Buford raised a cavalry troop and came to be recognized as a courageous fighter, especially in the Battles of Bull Run and Shiloh. Colonel Buford also served as a spy and special agent for the Confederacy. It was after the war, when Buford wrote a book on these experiences, that the public came to know the soldier's true identity.

For Colonel Harry Buford was not Harry Buford, but Loreta Velazquez, who had disguised herself to be near her fiancé. In 1876 she published a memoir to support herself and her son.

You can learn more about people like these by visiting the Pink Palace Museum in Memphis. See "Virtual Tennessee" for website information

From Private to General: Nathan Bedford Forrest

Indisputably one of the greatest leaders and military tacticians of the Civil War, Nathan Bedford Forrest, who was born in Chapel Hill in 1821, never had formal military training or experience prior to the war. He was the only man on either side to enter the war as a private and leave a general.

Possessed of an incredible fearlessness and determination, Forrest joined the Southern army as a lowly private. His Civil War deeds are many: he killed more than thirty men in personal combat, had 29 horses shot out from under him, and planned and led the first major raids, in several Kentucky towns, on November 14, 1861.

One of his greatest and most remarkable military achievements was on November 4, 1864. Forrest led his men to Johnsonville,

Nathan Bedford Forrest

Tennessee, where they attacked and destroyed the Federal supply and munitions depot located along the river known as Trace Creek. This resulted in the fall of the Union-controlled town and was the first defeat in military history of a naval force by a cavalry force. Since then, the state has created in the vicinity of the raid a park named after this military genius. Nathan Bedford Forrest State Park in Eva, Tennessee, now is a peaceful place, with camping, cabins, hiking, and other outdoor activities. This scenic park overlooks beautiful Kentucky Lake. See "Virtual Tennessee" for website information.

The Battle of Fort Sanders

It was a gray and cruelly cold day on November 29, 1863, in Knoxville. Union Major General Ambrose Burnside was defending Fort Sanders against the onslaught of Confederate Lt. General James Longstreet, and Knoxville itself was under siege. The city of Knoxville had been under Union occupation for two months, and its citizens were feeling the effects of the privations of war.

The Battle of Fort Sanders was thus a crucial engagement of the Civil War. Longstreet's forces seized Cherokee Heights, a bluff just south of the Holston River (now known as the Tennessee River), which was about 2,400 yards from Fort Sanders. His plan was at first to use artillery to hammer down on Fort Sanders and the Union troops, but at the last minute he decided on a surprise infantry attack early next morning. He squandered his intent of surprise by sending skirmishers ahead just hours before the planned "surprise" attack.

By letting the Union become aware of his plans, Longstreet and his men were doomed. In their attack, they were thwarted by both the Union soldiers' use of tripwire and icy, rough terrain. Longstreet and his men withdrew, failing to take Fort Sanders and Knoxville.

Today you can see more about the Battle of Fort Sanders and the Knoxville campaign. Bethel Cemetery is a lovely place to stroll the grounds and view the places where more than 1,600 Confederate soldiers are interred (there are 50 Union soldiers buried here also, as well as Civil War veterans). A monument, placed in the cemetery in 1892 by the Ladies Memorial Association, is the centerpiece of the cemetery. On the grounds you can tour the caretaker's cottage (Winstead Cottage), which has recently been restored and is now a museum with exhibits pertaining to this battle. See "Virtual Tennessee" for website information.

Q&A

Q. What Knoxville-born admiral in the U.S. Navy uttered the words, "Damn the torpedoes; full speed ahead!" during the battle of Mobile Bay?
A. David Glasgow Farragut (1801–1870).

Q. The Confederacy's principal army on the western front had what official name?
A. The Army of Tennessee.

Q. What was Nathan Bedford Forrest's occupation prior to the war?
A. Slave trader.

Q. What Nashville woman served time in the Tennessee State Penitentiary for being a Confederate spy, and after the war established Nashville's first day-care center, which is still in existence?
A. Fannie Battle.

Q. What was the name of the temporary "housing" that General Ulysses S. Grant ordered Chaplain John Eaton to establish for the destitute and starving slaves fleeing their masters' homes in anticipation of the arrival of Union soldiers?
A. Contraband camps, nicknamed "New Africa." Eaton established the first such camp at Grand Junction.

Q. What Civil War dentist from Washington County is credited with inventing a splint for treating facial gunshot wounds and pioneered the use of aluminum for dental plates?
A. Dr. James Baxter Bean (Bean's Splint).

Q. Shelbyville was given what nickname because of its pro-Union stance?
A. "Little Boston."

Q. What county provided both sides of the war with a nearly equal number of soldiers?
A. Bedford.

Q. Of what general was General William T. Sherman speaking when he said, "I think [he] was the most remarkable man our Civil War produced on either side"?
A. Nathan Bedford Forrest. (Sherman also once called him "that devil Forrest.")

Q. The Battle of Lookout Mountain was given what descriptive name?
A. "Battle above the Clouds."

Q. What Union general was nicknamed the "Rock of Chickamauga"?
A. General George H. Thomas.

Q. During the war, Tennessee civilians made do with dried sassafras leaves and okra seeds as a substitute for what?
A. Coffee.

Q. Confederate soldiers ground corn with their rifle butts, mixed it with bacon drippings, molded it around their bayonets to bake in the campfire, and gave what name to this concoction?
A. Swoosh or sloosh.

Q. Of the approximately 180,000 African Americans who fought for the Union army during the Civil War, how many came from Tennessee?
A. Around 20,000.

Q. What profession were New Yorkers Albert Richardson and Junius Browne following when they were captured and subsequently put in a Confederate prison for almost two years, until some East Tennesseans helped them escape?
A. Journalism, working for the New York Tribune.

Q. When did the Tennessee legislature ratify the Thirteenth Amendment, abolishing slavery, which was introduced in the U.S. Congress in January 1865 and became the law of the land in December 1865 when two-thirds of the states had ratified it?
A. March 1865.

Q. What was the first Union vessel to succumb to the Confederate Merrimack's attack?
A. The USS Cumberland, which was named after the river in Tennessee.

Q. When John P. Buchanan was the twenty-eighth governor (1891–93), what law was enacted to help Confederate veterans in the state?
A. Granting of pensions for war service.

Q. Known as the "Boy Hero of the Confederacy," what member of the Coleman Scouts, serving in the Army of Tennessee, was captured and executed as a spy in Pulaski in 1863?
A. Sam Davis.

Q. What Confederate general, the last one to surrender, later became president of the University of Nashville and then a math professor at the University of the South at Sewanee?
A. Edmund Kirby Smith.

Q. According to census records, when the Civil War began, slaves comprised what percentage of the population of Tennessee?
A. Around 25 percent (283,019 people).

Q. When Franklin County considered seceding from the state of Tennessee, what state did these "Franklinites" consider joining?
A. Alabama.

Q. Concerning leaving and rejoining the Union, how is Tennessee unique?
A. Tennessee was the last to secede and the first to rejoin the Union.

Q. What was the difference in monthly pay between a Confederate brigadier general and a Union one?
A. $14 ($301 for the Confederate and $315 for the Yankee).

Q. For what is Virginia "Ginnie" Bethel Moon, who lived in Memphis in 1862, noted?
A. She was a Confederate spy.

Q. The fall of Forts Henry and Donelson on the Tennessee and Cumberland Rivers in 1862 brought nationwide fame and a nickname to what general?
A. General Ulysses. S. "Unconditional Surrender" Grant.

Q. What was the first Confederate state capital to fall?

A. Nashville, on February 23, 1862.

Q. What Confederate general was killed at Shiloh?
A. Albert Sidney Johnston.

Q. What was the first great bloody battle of the war?
A. Shiloh, with casualties totaling 23,500.

Q. What Irish-born Confederate general who died in the battle of Franklin was known as the "Stonewall Jackson of the West" because of his brave stance at Missionary Ridge?
A. Patrick Cleburne (1828-1864)

CHAPTER TEN

From Civil Wrongs to Civil Rights

THE CIVIL RIGHTS TRAIL IN THE VOLUNTEER STATE

The Tennessee Civil Rights Trail was established in 2018, and this was long-overdue, in my opinion. If you'd like to learn more about Tennessee's role in the struggle for Civil Rights, there's plenty to see. Here is a brief overview of most of them:

THE NATIONAL CIVIL RIGHTS MUSEUM, MEMPHIS

The first place that comes to mind is the Lorraine Motel in Memphis. The site of where famed Civil Rights leader and visionary Martin Luther King, Jr., was assassinated, the Lorraine was made into the National Civil Rights Museum in 1994 (it closed as a motel in 1988). You can read the story about King's assassination in Chapter 1 of this book.

Even before the Civil Rights movement was in full swing, the Lorraine Motel was listed in "The Negro Motorist Green Book," a guide to hotels, restaurants, beauty and barber shops, gas stations and other businesses friendly to traveling African

Americans. Since the Lorraine was close to Beale Street and Stax Records, many musicians would stay at the Lorraine while recording or performing in Memphis. While a hotel in its heyday, The Lorraine housed many famous guests, including members of the Harlem Globetrotters basketball team, the Negro League Baseball League, and famous singers and entertainers such as Nat King Cole, Aretha Franklin, Ray Charles, Otis Redding, Louis Armstrong, Isaac Hayes and Sarah Vaughan.

As a museum, The Lorraine houses 260 artifacts, interactive media and more than 40 films. The exhibits and recordings lead the visitor through the dark days of slavery, through the Civil War and the Reconstruction era, and the events of the 1960s, 70s and 80s up to today, that continue to inspire people from all walks of life to take a stand for equality between people.

Lorraine Motel. The wreath marks the spot where MLK stood when assassinated

Part of the Civil Rights Museum Complex is The Legacy Building. It is thought that the assassin's bullet was fired from this building. This building houses artifacts and exhibits surrounding the 1968 assassination of King, including conspiracy theories. The exhibits include a timeline of the struggle for human rights and equality that goes back more than 400 years.

CLARK MEMORIAL UNITED METHODIST CHURCH, NASHVILLE

This brick church in Nashville, the oldest African American church in Music City, is said to be "the cradle of the Civil Rights movement in Nashville." It was a meeting place for civil rights leaders and those who wanted to learn more about how they could play a part in the movement. In the late 1950, it was here that James Lawson offered workshops on nonviolent protests; in 1961, Dr. Martin Luther King, Jr., hosted the annual meeting of the Southern Christian Leadership Conference at the church. Still an actively functioning church, Clark Memorial UMC welcomes visitors.

MASON TEMPLE CHURCH OF GOD IN CHRIST

"I've been to the mountaintop," Rev. Martin Luther King, Jr., said to the thousands who filled this temple on April 3, 1968. It was the night before King's assassination, and some say that the minister's words that night were eerily prophetic when he also said, "I've seen the Promised Land...and I might not get there with you." He was killed by an assassin's bullet the following night as he stood on the balcony of The Lorraine Motel.

Also located in Memphis, Mason Temple is a Christian international sanctuary. It is also central headquarters of the

Church of God in Christ (COGIC), which is the largest African American Pentecostal group in the entire world.

Incidentally, the church has nothing to do with the brotherhood known as the Masons. It was named for the founder of the Church of God in Christ, Bishop Charles Harrison Mason. He lies buried in a marble crypt inside the church. The church welcomes visitors.

GREEN MCADOO CULTURAL CENTER

Melba Patillo Beals wrote of her experience as a young teenage student integrating Little Rock, Arkansas, in her book, *Warriors Don't Cry*. But integration with its surrounding turmoil was happening all over the country, and Tennessee was no exception. The Green McAdoo Cultural Center tells the

courageous story of the twelve African American teenagers who, in August of 1956, entered the doors of formerly all-white Clinton High School, which made this school the first public high school in the South to be integrated. Today, the Center tells the dramatic story of the "Clinton 12." Located where the former high school used to be, the Center has recreations inside of 1950s-era classrooms and exhibits taking visitors back to this tumultuous time and tells of the bravery of the 12 young people. In the front of the Center, life-size bronze statues of the Clinton 12 show them as they might have appeared, entering the doors of Clinton High School.

According to docents at the Center, Tennessee supported the law (Brown vs. Board of Education) and many whites offered aid and solace to the brave 12 teens (especially Rev. Paul Turner). But there were others who were against integration and committed acts of violence to try and stop the movement. For example, in 1958, white supremacists bombed the school; undeterred, citizens from the towns of Oak Ridge and Clinton came together, refurbished an unused elementary school in Oak Ridge, and the school was up and running in one week.

The Green McAdoo Cultural Center was listed on the National Register of Historic Places in October of 2005. In 2018, the Center became an official part of the Tennessee State Museum system. It is a new gem in the crown of Tennessee's museums.

CHEROKEE REMOVAL MEMORIAL PARK

Located at the confluence of the Hiwassee and Tennessee Rivers, this park commemorates those who were forcibly removed from Tennessee in the terrible march known as the "Trail of Tears." The park includes a Visitor Center, which houses a library where people can research their ancestral native roots. Outside you can find a History Wall, which describes how local native people moved from being hunter-gatherers to a highly civilized and literate culture (see my story on Sequoyah in chapter 5). The deplorable and cruel conditions

Cherokee Removal Memorial Park, Meigs County, TN

of the forced march west, which resulted in many thousands of native people dying along the way, is also described. The Memorial Wall has the names of more than 2,500 heads of Cherokee households. According to the park's website, "this is the closest thing to a headstone they will have."

The area also is home to the Hiwassee Wildlife Refuge, which has a small population of American Bald Eagles. In the late fall and early winter months, visitors such as myself were thrilled to see migrating flocks of Sandhill and Whooping Cranes in the refuge. The park is free to visit.

CLAYBORN TEMPLE

Located in Memphis, this iconic Romanesque Revival church is just south of Beale Street. In the late 1890s it was known as the Second Presbyterian Church with an all-white congregation. During the sanitation workers' strike in 1968, both labor reform activists and civil rights workers gathered here to plan and organize protests in Memphis. Listed with the National Trust for Historic Preservation, the temple is currently under restoration. A new 3-D free-standing sculpture, "I Am A Man," is outside the temple, reminding visitors of the signs that African American males carried during the height of the Civil Rights movement.

Clayborn Temple is currently available for special events such as concerts.

FISK UNIVERSITY AND THE JUBILEE SINGERS

Fisk University's Jubilee Singers attained international fame for their singing talents, and Fisk University students worked with African American students from Meharry Medical Center and Tennessee State University to non-violently promote civil rights and equality for all. It was their employment of non-violent protests that led to Nashville becoming the first integrated city in the entire South.

AMERICAN BAPTIST COLLEGE

"If not us, then who?" the voice of John Lewis, one of the famous and skilled orators of the Civil Rights movement, boomed throughout Griggs Hall, the first building on the campus. "If not now, then when?" His words are now famous, and so is the American Baptist College, for it was here that Nashville's lunch counter sit-ins and other non-violent protests were planned (see more on that story, below). John Lewis would go on to become a Congressman, and Nashville, to fame for its role in the fight for Civil Rights.

Griggs Hall offers tours to the public Monday through Thursday.

COUNTER-CULTURE

"Whites only," the sign at the Woolworth lunch counter read. But that was before the 1960s. Finally, visionary whites and determined African Americans decided to challenge this ridiculous rule. Sit-ins at lunch counters of Woolworth stores took place in not only Greensboro, N.C., but at the location of the downtown Woolworth on 5th Street in Nashville. The protestors were inspired by the words of Martin Luther King,

Jr., and the aforementioned John Lewis (whose first arrest happened here).

Now a place where all people can freely intermingle, Woolworth on 5th is a restored restaurant, which honors the efforts of those peaceful protestors of the Civil Rights movement. The restaurant also offers live musical entertainment and is a wonderful venue for special events such as wedding receptions and corporate gatherings.

Four Nashville students eat at lunch counter

And this iconic place, which has as its saying, "the soul of downtown Nashville," is open to everyone!

NASHVILLE'S CIVIL RIGHTS ROOM

Located in the downtown public library, you can pore over amazing historic photographs, documents, and other memorabilia related to Nashville's Civil Rights movement. It's a great way to spend some time, educating yourself and your children about the difficult and challenging path to equality for everyone.

See the section, "Virtual Tennessee," for websites of these places of interest along the Civil Rights Trail in Tennessee.

Q&A

Q. In what establishments in Nashville did the first black protesters stage lunch-counter "sit-ins" in February 1960?
A. Woolworth, Kress, and McClellan department stores.

Q. What former slave published the Chattanooga Blade, which in 1905 challenged Jim Crow laws and addressed other social injustices based on race?
A. Randolph Miller.

CHAPTER ELEVEN

Wheelers and Dealers (Business and Entrepreneurs)

The Chattanooga Choo Choo: An Old Train Saved from the Wrecking Ball

The first Chattanooga Choo Choo was a passenger train that began running to Cincinnati, Ohio, in 1880. Chattanooga's present Terminal Station was completed in 1909, designed by an American artist in Paris's Beaux Arts Institute. Its entrance inspired awe, with the Grand Dome resting on four steel supports 75 feet apart. It was an architectural wonder, spanning the entire 68-by-82 foot waiting room.

The last train rolled into the station in 1970, and for a time it seemed the grand old place would be sacrificed to the wrecking ball. Some visionaries in Chattanooga, however, decided to renovate the station instead, and make it a landmark for the city.

In 1973 Terminal Station reopened its doors as a hotel— the Chattanooga Choo Choo. It has since become part of the Holiday Inn family, but don't think that it hasn't kept its originality. Just walking around the romantic gardens and fountains, peeking into the train cars that are now used as guest quarters, and strolling the lobby lets you step back in time. There's even an old trolley to take you around the grounds, and many of the antique train cars in the yard have been refurbished and are now unique dining establishments.

Their following signature recipe helped make the hotel restaurants famous. Did I hear someone say, "All Aboard"?

Chattanooga Choo Choo Peanut Butter Pie

1 9-inch graham cracker pie crust
1⁄2 cup peanut butter, heaping
1 (4-ounce) package cream cheese, softened
1 1⁄4 cups powdered sugar
2 1⁄2 cups heavy cream
1⁄2 cup toasted almonds

Cream peanut butter with cream cheese until blended. Add powdered sugar and mix well. Whip cream until light and stiff, being careful not to whip into butter. Reserve some of the cream for garnish. Blend remaining cream into peanut butter mixture, with about two-thirds of the almonds. Spread filling in crust, pipe or spoon remaining cream on top, and sprinkle with remaining almonds.

Chill before serving. Serves 8.

The Song Behind the Train

Americans older than baby boomers connect the Chattanooga Choo Choo with Glenn Miller's big band hit of the 1940s. Mack Gordon wrote the lyrics to "Chattanooga Choo Choo," and Harry Warren wrote the catchy music. The Glenn Miller Orchestra first performed the song in 1941; it later appeared in the movie "Sunset Serenade" and was sung by Tex Beneke and the Modernaires. During World War II, the song was popular in Europe as well as the United States.

Lyrics to "Chattanooga Choo-Choo"

Pardon me, boy, is that the Chattanooga Choo Choo?

Track twenty-nine . . .

Boy, you can give me a shine.

I can afford to board a Chattanooga Choo Choo;

I've got my fare and just a trifle to spare.

You leave the Pennsylvania Station 'bout a quarter to four,

Read a magazine and you're in Baltimore.

Dinner in the Diner . . . Nothing could be finer

Than to have your ham 'n eggs in Carolina.

When you hear the whistle blowing eight to the bar,

Then you know that Tennessee is not very far.

Shovel all the coal in . . . gotta keep it rollin'.

Woo Woo, Chattanooga, there you are!

There's gonna be a certain party at the station,

Satin and lace . . . I used to call funny face.

She's gonna cry until I tell her that I'll never roam,

So, Chattanooga Choo Choo, won't you choo-choo me home?

Chattanooga Choo Choo, won't you choo-choo me home?

[Words by Mack Gordon. Music by Harry Warren. © 1941 (renewed 1969) Twentieth Century Music Corporation. All rights controlled by Leo Feist, Inc. All rights of Leo Feist, Inc., assigned to EMI Catalogue Partnership. All rights administered by EMI Feist Catalog, Inc. All rights reserved. Used by Permission.]

Did you Know?

Born in1887, a Knoxville businessman and one-time mayor helped construct the Panama Canal and had been a hobo before he founded a construction company that built infrastructures of all sorts—railroads, highways, and dams—throughout the south-eastern United States. However, he's probably most well known for inventing the Dumpster.

His name? George Roby Dempster. In 1964 he was awarded the U.S.Navy Public Service Award for the merits of the Dumpster.

Adolph Ochs: One Stubborn Tennessean

There's a bit of a stubborn streak in just about any Tennessean worth his or her salt. Adolph Ochs had that, plus what Northerners call "chutzpa." Born in Cincinnati in 1858, little Adolph was raised in Knoxville, the son of German-Jewish immigrant parents, and fell in love with the newspaper business. Even as a young boy, he had a dream to one day own a big, successful newspaper.

At age eleven, he became a newsboy and then a floor sweeper at the Knoxville Chronicle, and five years later, "Ochsie" had become a full-fledged printer. For a short while he worked with the Louisville Courier-Journal as assistant foreman of the composing room; he then took a job with the Knoxville Tribune where Colonel John MacGowan, an editorial writer, took an interest in him. MacGowan and another party invested their funds so Ochs could buy Chattanooga's newspaper, The Dispatch. Tough post–Civil War economics, however, caused Ochs's fledgling journal to go bankrupt. Ochs was back to square one.

Adolph Ochs, publisher of the Chattanooga Times and the New York Times, came up with the slogan, "All the News That's Fit to Print," which is still on the front page of the New York Times today. (Photo courtesy the Chattanooga Times)

Borrowing printing presses and in need of cash, Ochs put together a Chattanooga city directory through which he came into contact with many influential people in the area. He discovered the Chattanooga Times was for sale and boldly approached a bank for a loan. His determined demeanor resulted in a loan of three hundred dollars, and once again he and MacGowan worked together. When times were tight, Ochs used a kind of "company store" tactic, getting credit slips in lieu of payment from his advertising clients, and giving the slips to his employees.

The newspaper was doing well until a land deal in which Ochs had invested turned sour. Instead of declaring bankruptcy, he decided that if one newspaper could make a little money, two could make more. He checked around and discovered the New York Times was soon to be on the auction block.

Ochs was without resources but not without what Tennesseans call "grit." Riding in a parade in Chattanooga, he met President Grover Cleveland and used the opportunity to tell the president of his plan to buy the Times. Before the Times was sold at auction, Ochs had put together a financial plan to please his stockholders (which eventually gave him controlling interest). At auction time in 1896, Ochs was the sole bidder.

Ochs put all his energies into producing the best newspaper anyone had ever seen. He stayed away from the "yellow journalism" style popular at that time, and came up with the slogan, "All the News That's Fit to Print," which is still on the front page of the New York Times today. You can learn more about the newspaper business in the Volunteer State at the Tennessee Newspaper and Printing Museum in the town of Rogersville.

Opryland Hotel: Tennessee's "City Under Glass"

This is a true city under glass, with its own power and water supplies, too many restaurants to count, more than 2,800 guest rooms, dozens of retail shops, with a staff of several thousand people. The Opryland Hotel was built in 1977 with six hundred rooms, twelve miles from downtown Nashville. It's now grown to nearly three thousand rooms with 600,00 square feet of meeting and convention space. The exhibition hall, called the Ryman, is 288,000 square feet and is the largest single-level exhibition facility in a hotel in the United States. It contains five ballrooms, the largest being the Delta, which covers more than 55,000 square feet and can accommodate nearly 6,000 diners or up to 12,000 people for a concert. Its golf course, the Springhouse Golf Club, is home to the Bell South Classic, which is part of the PGA Senior Tour.

There are nine acres of gardens under glass. In 1983 the Conservatory opened with over ten thousand tropical plants. In 1988 the Cascades area was completed, with three waterfalls from 25 to 35 feet tall coming out of a 45-foot-tall mountain into a 12,500-square-foot lake.

Visitors can ride a flatboat in the Delta at the Opryland Hotel. (Courtesy Opryland)

The third "interior-scape," the Delta area, added one thousand rooms to the hotel. It contains four and one-half acres. A quarter mile long river runs through it, with flatboats available for rides. The Delta is also home to the largest restaurant in the state, Old Hickory Steakhouse; the first and only Coca-Cola General Store in the country; and the only Ben & Jerry's ice cream shop in the state.

With so much to offer, especially with its fabulous decorations and seasonal entertainment at Christmas, the Opryland Hotel attracts enough visitors to maintain an 80 percent occupancy rate year-round, an unusually high figure for hotels. It's a premier meeting and entertainment destination — the world's largest under one roof.

Here is a favorite recipe from the Cascades Restaurant:

Grilled Asian Mahi-mahi with Thai Curry Sauce

>   5 garlic cloves, chopped
>   2 tablespoons fresh ginger, chopped
>   2 tablespoons cilantro, chopped
>   juice of 2 whole lemons
>   1/2 cup rice wine
>   1/2 cup olive oil
>   1/4 cup sesame oil
>   5 6-ounce mahi-mahi fillets

Place all ingredients in a bowl and marinate the fish fillets for one hour.

Sauce
>   2 tablespoons curry paste
>   1/2 cup diced fresh pineapple
>   1/2 cup diced Granny Smith apples
>   2 tablespoons chopped fresh ginger
>   1/4 cup chopped onions
>   1/2 teaspoon chopped garlic
>   1/2 cup rice wine

1/2 cup apple juice
1/2 cup pineapple juice
1 cup chicken broth
4 tablespoons sesame oil

Sauté the fish fillets in oil 3 minutes on each side until done. Set aside and keep warm. In the same pan that fish was sautéed in, sauté together the curry paste, pineapple, apples, ginger, onions, and garlic. Remove from pan. Deglaze the pan with rice wine, apple juice, pineapple juice, and chicken broth. Simmer for 20 minutes. Add sautéed ingredients. Strain and pour over the fish.

The Wheeling and Dealing Belle of Belmont

Tennessee women have a way of retaining their femininity while getting exactly what they want; Adelicia Hayes Acklen was a perfect example of this Tennessee trait.

Born in 1817, Adelicia Hayes was the daughter of a prominent Nashville lawyer. At age twenty-two, she married Isaac Franklin, twenty-eight years her senior. They had four children, but none survived childhood, and after seven years of marriage Franklin left Adelicia a very wealthy widow. Her estate included four cotton plantations in Louisiana, 750 slaves, and a large farm in Middle Tennessee.

When she was thirty-two Adelicia married an Alabama lawyer, Colonel Joseph Acklen, who agreed to sign a prenuptial agreement allowing Adelicia to keep all her properties and other assets. This was unusual in those days. Together, they built the twenty-thousand-square-foot Belmont Mansion in Nashville (now part of Belmont University) and had six children, four of whom lived past childhood. Joseph Acklen increased

Adelicia's fortune three times over before his death during the Civil War.

Alone again, Adelicia Acklen found herself facing financial ruin; the Confederate army, fearing her 2,800 bales of market-ready cotton would fall into Union hands, threatened to burn them. Adelicia secretly traveled to Louisiana, where she negotiated cotton sales with each side, unbeknownst to the

LEFT: Adelicia and Joseph Acklen built the twenty-thousand-square-foot Belmont Mansion in Nashville. RIGHT: During the Civil War, plantation-owner Adelicia Acklen avoided financial ruin by negotiating with both sides. (Courtesy Belmont Mansion Association)

other. The Confederates promised not to burn her cotton; the Union, to help her move the cotton to New Orleans.

She then slipped her cotton through the Union blockade and sold it to the Rothschilds of London, who paid her in gold. She made $960,000 on the deal. Three weeks after Lee's surrender at Appomattox, Adelicia traveled to England to retrieve her fortune.

The Greek Revival-style Belmont Mansion is listed on the National Register of Historic Landmarks and is open for tours, weddings and special events during holidays. See "Virtual Tennessee" for website information.

The Mecca for Shoppers: Opry Mills

When attendance at Nashville's Opryland USA theme park began to decline, the management razed it and built in its place an incredibly huge shopping-and-entertainment Mecca. Opry Mills opened in May 2000 and features an IMAX theater, interesting shops such as the Gibson Bluegrass Showcase (where visitors can see the company's musical instruments being created), and exotic restaurants such as the Rainforest Cafe.

When You Could See the World in Tennessee: The 1982 World's Fair

When it was announced that Knoxville would host the 1982 World's Fair, there was more than a little skepticism by politicians and professional event planners. Many said that, although Nashville had hosted the Tennessee Centennial Exposition in 1897, that Knoxville was a "scruffy little city" that was nowhere near up to the Herculean task of hosting such an event.

But Knoxville proved skeptics wrong: It was an incredible year, with twenty-two nations, seven states, and eighty-nine international corporations participating in the World's Fair held in Knoxville. Some of the events at the fair included its opening by President Ronald Reagan and an appearance by comedian Bob Hope, who celebrated his seventy-ninth birthday at the fair.

By July 15, attendance had reached 5,249,131. By the time the World's Fair closed its gates that year, Knoxville had welcomed more than 11 million visitors.

The European Community (EC) had its first pavilion at a world exposition at this fair, and the first touch-screen computers were there.

For a season, Tennessee was host to the world; they built it, and the world came. Today, you can tour parts of the World's

The Sunsphere
1982 Worlds Fair

Fair that remain open to visitors. One prime example is the Sunsphere, a 266-foot high hexagonal structure with an observation deck on the fourth floor. The Sunsphere was closed for restoration and repair but reopened to the public in 2014. It's worth going inside just to see the city, especially at sunset.

See "Virtual Tennessee" for website information.

Food and Drink from Tennessee

Here are the stories behind some favorite foods and drinks that began in Tennessee.

- **Christie Cookies:** In 1985 former Vanderbilt football player Christie Hauck decided to perfect a cookie he remembered a neighbor used to make when he was just a kid. It took Hauck two years, but he finally came up with the Christie Cookie. He opened his first retail store on Church Street in Nashville; now there are more than five retail stores and the cookies are distributed wholesale to universities and other institutions. Hauck also has an online ordering service, so almost anyone in the world can have a taste of the now-famous Christie Cookie. For those who want to visit the company, in the community of Germantown of Nashville, Christie Cookies welcomes visitors—just "follow your nose."

- **Moon Pie:** The Chattanooga Bakery, founded in 1902, was having trouble breaking into the Appalachian market. One frustrated salesman returned from the area and reported: "They don't want anything we make. They want something round, with marshmallow inside, and as big as the moon!"

  From this, the now-famous Moon Pie was created. It became an everyday thing for the average working man to go into a grocery store, buy an RC Cola and a Moon Pie, and have lunch for less than fifteen cents

- **Goo-Goo Clusters:** The Goo-Goo Cluster, the first combination candy-bar ever created, is made primarily of peanuts, milk chocolate, caramel, and marshmallow. When Howell Campbell Sr. created it in 1912 at the Standard Candy Company in Nashville, no one knew what to call the round candy bars. Campbell rode the trolleys, asking people to make suggestions. One woman he spoke to, a "lady school-teacher," suggested Goo-Goo, the name you see today emblazoned on the silver foil wrappers in red letters.

Although the factory itself is currently not open for tours, you can take a "Make Your Own Goo-Goo" at the store in downtown Nashville.

- **Coca-Cola in bottles:** As late as 1899, Atlanta-based Coca-Cola was still sold only as a fountain drink. Then Benjamin Thomas and Joseph Whitehead of Chattanooga got together with Coca-Cola's owner, Asa Candler, and asked him for the bottling rights to the beverage. As a formality, they agreed to pay him one dollar, which he never collected. With another Chattanooga businessman, John Lupton, they began bottling and distributing Coca-Cola, the container of which was made to resemble a dress shape popular in that time, the hobble skirt. Coca-Cola is still bottled in and distributed from Chattanooga, at the rate of more than 30,000 cases a day.

- **Maxwell House Coffee:** In 1872 Kentucky-born Joel Owsley Cheek made his own green-bean coffee blend and began selling it to hotels and other establishments in Tennessee and Kentucky. Finally, in 1892 the elegant Maxwell House hotel in Nashville agreed to serve his coffee in its restaurant.

Cheek must have known his success was assured when in 1907, President Theodore Roosevelt was a guest at the Maxwell House. Upon tasting the coffee, he remarked it was, "Good to the last drop." That slogan is still the Maxwell House Coffee slogan today. Although the company was eventually bought out by Kraft Heinz, Maxwell House Coffee is still "Good to the last drop."

Other Tennessee Goodies

- **Mrs. Grissom's Salads:** Grace Grissom's chicken salad, potato salad, and coleslaw are still packed and marketed out of Nashville.

- **Brock Candy:** Chattanooga businessman William E. Brock started the Brock Candy Company, which may be best known today for concocting the nation's first gelatin-based "gummy" candies.

- **Little Debbie Snack Cakes:** Created in Chattanooga in 1933 by O. D. and Ruth King McKee, and named after their granddaughter, Little Debbie is now the nation's leading snack cake.

- **Colt's Bolts:** Started by Mackenzie Colt of Hee-Haw fame, this candy is sold internationally.

- **Double Cola**: Charles Little of Chattanooga invented it in 1933.

Strange... But True!

Here's a Really Weird Story about TVA.

Little did President Franklin D. Roosevelt know when he presented his bold plan for the new economy in 1933 that some of his "dam plans" would go awry, but not for lack of a girdle.

As part of Roosevelt's First One Hundred Days of the New Deal, the Tennessee Valley Authority proposed to do away with flooding by building a series of dams. The dams would also help the economy of the poverty-ridden region by improving living conditions.

By the end of World War II, TVA had built sixteen dams along the Tennessee River and its tributaries and had purchased five others from the U.S. Corps of Engineers. From this, TVA had created fourteen million acres of flood storage and by 1946 was providing electricity to nearly 700,000 households, where previously there had been no power supply.

In preventing flooding in the Tennessee Basin, malaria and other diseases were brought to a halt. Economically, many of the people were better off, although there were some who spoke bitterly of losing their lands to the government agency.

Unfortunately, there was a problem with one of the older dams bought from a local power company. Hales Bar Dam leaked because of problems with the limestone foundation. There was so much flooding, some people said there was more water leaking out from under the dam than there was flowing over it. A construction firm was called in and decided to try something innovative to stop the leak. It dumped truckloads of women's corsets into the water above the dam, hoping the suction would pull the corsets against the face of the dam and stop the leaks.

It didn't work. Eventually, TVA dynamited the dam in 1968 and replaced it with Nickajack Dam, a few miles downstream. In 2017, part of Nickajack Dam opened for tours.

And in Case You Like Something Brewed--

You'll visit the right place for prize-winning beer when you go to Big River Grille and Brewing Works in downtown Chattanooga. In 1998 its Iron Horse stout won the top medal in the World Beer Cup Competition in Rio de Janeiro, Brazil. Its Sweet Magnolia brown ale took the gold medal at the 1998 Great American Beer Festival. This brewery has expanded so much and has garnered international attention to the extent that it also has establishments at the Disney Parks.

They Got Their Start in Tennessee

Piggly Wiggly: This self-service grocery, the prototype of American supermarkets, was started in Memphis by Clarence Saunders in 1916. (Saunders's 36,500-square-foot home built of pink marble is now the Memphis Pink Palace Museum, open to the public).

Shoney's: Yeah, it was the Big Boy himself. Nashvillian Ray Danner bought franchise rights for Big Boy from West Virginia entrepreneur Alex Shoenbaum. Danner opened Shoney's Big Boy restaurant in Madison in 1959.

Cracker Barrel: Dan Evins opened the first restaurant in 1969 in Lebanon, Tennessee. Now there are thousands of restaurants, and millions of folks make this their stop as they're travelling. It's good food they can consistently count on—and the gift shops are worth a look as well.

Krystal: Founded in 1932 by Chattanooga businessmen J. Glenn Sherrill and Rudolph B. Davenport, the Krystal Company sold its square-shaped hamburgers for a nickel, along with "a good cup of coffee." Although the headquarters moved from Chattanooga to Atlanta some years ago, you can still dine at the oldest Krystal Hamburger restaurant, located at 307 Cherokee Boulevard.

The Largest Collection of Aluminum Cans in the World

The name of the town Alcoa is an acronym for the Aluminum Corporation of America, which began buying property along the Little Tennessee River in 1910. The company built a series of dams to make its own inexpensive electricity, which is one of the biggest costs in making aluminum. The factory itself was built outside Maryville in 1913, after which the town of Alcoa was incorporated.

It must have been like something from a science fiction novel: everything was provided for the workers, from schools to housing to grocery stores to playgrounds and parks, and everyone who lived there worked for the company.

Although the Great Depression brought trouble, World War II brought an economic boom to Alcoa. By 1941 the factory had grown so much it was one of the largest plants in the world. In later years, the Tennessee Valley Authority entered the picture and challenged the city's hydroelectric business, and Alcoa was no longer at the proverbial top of the heap in the aluminum market.

Now it's no longer a town with a "Big Brother" attitude. Alcoa has opened its doors to competition and regular folks who just want to live there, and the company no longer requires its workers to live in its housing. Alcoa has a working force of more than two thousand people, making aluminum for beverage cans. The city of Alcoa now offers bus tours and more. See "Virtual Tennessee" for website information.

The Slave Who Created His Own Fate

Born a slave, Shelbyville resident Wade Gosling vowed he would make something of himself one day. In 1878 he borrowed twenty-nine dollars from a man named Albert Frierson and opened his first business, called the Great Variety Store. Then Gosling, a voracious reader, began to teach himself law and finally, as he put it, "stood a verbal examination and was admitted to the Bar." He became the first black lawyer in the state and one of Shelbyville's most successful entrepreneurs, holding more land than most whites. You can learn more about Gosling and his courageous and inspiring life by visiting the Tennessee State Museum in downtown Nashville. See "Virtual Tennessee" for website information.

Entrepreneurial "Spirits": Jack Daniel and George Dickel

The areas around Lynchburg and Tullahoma are lovely, with rolling hills, natural limestone springs, iron-free water, and fertile soil. Agricultural folks might look at this and think "corn" or "cattle." Jasper Newton ("Jack") Daniel and George Dickel thought "whiskey."

Daniel got into the distillery business in 1860 at the young age of 12, when he worked with Dan Call near Lynchburg. By 1863, Daniel was Call's partner; three years later, he bought out Call's interest. The teenaged Daniel was a distillery owner, but by today's laws was still too young to drink what he produced.

Also in the late 1860s, Tullahoma resident George A. Dickel became a partner in the whiskey-making business with two Nashville families, the Schwabs and Davises. They got their whiskey from several regional sources; the most favored was out of Cascade Creek in Coffee County. Eventually Dickel created his own blend made especially for the tastes of his fans in Nashville. When he died in 1894, his wife Augusta managed the business with his partners.

In 1910, when Prohibition became the law in Tennessee, both distilleries moved—Jack Daniel's to St. Louis (after Daniel's death when his nephew Lem Motlow had taken over the business), and George Dickel's to Louisville. When in 1933 the national Prohibition Amendment was repealed, the distillers both moved back to their original counties.

Although their home counties were still both "dry," the counties' politicians finally relented and voted (by narrow margins) to allow the distilleries to once again make whiskey.

Today, both distilleries are in full production. Dickel's distillery produces roughly 900 barrels of whiskey a week, while Jack Daniels' churns out 30,000 a day. For those of you who want to learn more about the two distilleries, both offer tours and tastings. See "Virtual Tennessee" for website information on both.

Want to Be a "Whiskey Tourist"? Take the Tennessee Whiskey Trail Tour!

Distilling of spirits has grown in popularity since the early days of Jack Daniel and George Dickel. By the year 2017, there were so many micro-distilleries and other, larger distilleries, that they all joined forces. The Tennessee Distillers Guild created the Tennessee Whiskey Trail (TWT) that takes the adventurous "spirit" through 26 distilleries across the Volunteer State. Their website states that an efficient Whiskey Trail tourist could see all 26 distilleries in as little as 10 days. Costs for tours, as well as length of tours and availability of tastings, vary by each distilling company.

The TWT is so high-tech, they even have an app for your phone. Users of the app can collect virtual stamps for each tour they take, earning a t-shirt when they've toured all 26 distilleries.

As of press time, the most-popular tour is the Mint Julep tour, which runs 5 days a week, departing the Omni Hotel in Nashville. The TWT folks say that many tours have additional offerings, such as food, and many are kid friendly. One enterprising company known as Whiskey Trail Tours offers, according to their website, "customized tours in private vehicles for groups of all sizes," whereby all you have to do is enjoy the tours, worry-free. See "Virtual Tennessee" for websites.

A Pyramid In Memphis

This thirty-two-story structure is used for sports, entertainment and exhibitions.

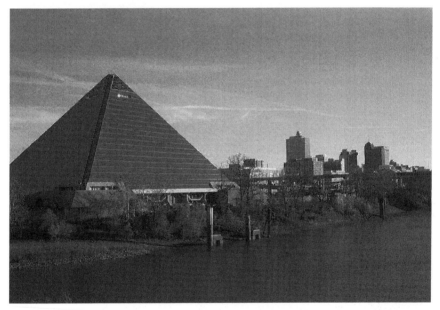

A view from Downtown Memphis.

Hatch Showprints

One of the oldest poster-making companies in the country still operates in Nashville at 316 Broadway. The company was founded by C. R. and H. H. Hatch in 1879. In the 1920s Will T. Hatch hand-carved the woodblocks used in the letter-press process. Many a country music fan and memorabilia collector has at least one Hatch Showprint, whose clients include the Grand Ole Opry and many of its artists. The Hatch brothers were fond of saying, "Advertising without posters is like fishing without worms."

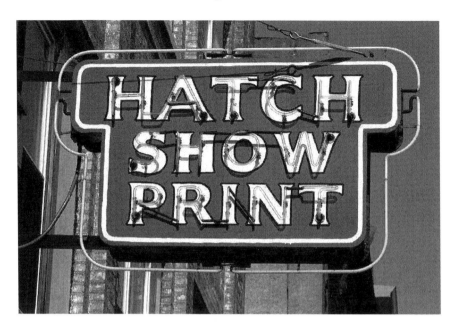

Today, you can take a tour of Hatch Showprints, see it in action and even make a poster of your own as a memento. See "Virtual Tennessee" for website information.

McKissack and McKissack Architectural Firm: Story of Another Moses

In a story sounding like a page right out of Alex Haley's novel Roots, a young man of the West African Ashanti tribe was taken from his homeland and sold into slavery. "Moses," as he was called, was purchased by William McKissack of North Carolina.

As was the tradition then, the young slave took his master's last name. Moses McKissack was interested in building and became a master builder. After he married and had children, he taught his sons the building trade. His sons taught their own sons. Moses McKissack III took the skills he'd inherited from his grandfather a step further and in 1905 moved to Nashville, where he opened his own construction business. Word of his skill spread, as he constructed buildings for Vanderbilt University and the Carnegie Library at Fisk University. Through advertising and word-of-mouth, the grandson of a slave was designing buildings for clients throughout the state.

When his brother Calvin joined him, they formed McKissack & McKissack, Tennessee's first and the nation's oldest professional African American architectural firm.

After Moses III died, the reins were taken by his wife, Leatrice Buchanan McKissack, and daughters, who opened satellite offices in Memphis, Washington, D.C., and New York City. The current CEO is Deryl McKissack Greene, so the family tradition continues.

You can learn more about the McKissack family and their contributions to Tennessee architecture at the recently opened Tennessee State Museum in downtown Nashville.

The Story of the "Black Patch War"

In Middle Tennessee, tobacco has been a major source of income for farmers and those who deal in the buying and selling of the dark leaf. In the first decade of the 1900s, the tobacco industry was stained with acts of violence and oppression known as the "Black Patch War" (black patch refers to the region of the state that grows dark-fired tobacco).

Falling tobacco prices starting back in the 1890s caused some tobacco farmers to form an alliance to market tobacco more effectively, called the Dark Tobacco District Planters' Protective Association of Kentucky and Tennessee (PPA). Some growers refused to join the PPA; the PPA gave those non-joiners the derogatory name "hillbillies." The buyers' monopoly, headed by the American Tobacco Company, was termed "the Trust" by the PPA. The stage was set for violence, and some growers took to vigilante-type acts to attempt to coerce non-PPA growers to join the ranks.

In Robertson County, PPA members adopted the "Resolution of the committee of the Possum Hunters Organization," which aired their grievances against "the Trust" and "the hillbillies" and outlined their plan to "visit" both in the area. They planned on visiting in bands, to "convince" both groups to join them.

Their "convincing" methods became violent, and over the next several years, vigilantism by groups called "the Silent Brigade" and the "Inner Circle" used dynamite, fire, and other forms of assault on people, their crops and their farm animals. In Kentucky, several towns were taken over by these violent PPA members, and nonaffiliated tobacco growers in Montgomery and Robertson Counties, Tennessee slept little at night.

The violence did result in the price of tobacco being raised, but much of the trouble was effectively ended by the presence of troops in trouble spots and by the lawsuits against the individuals involved. The final blow to the PPA'S existence was the outbreak of World War I, which caused the European markets for dark-fired tobacco to close.

You can learn more about the history and culture of tobacco farming in Tennessee at the Museum of Tobacco Art and History. Located in Nashville, the museum memorializes the contributions of tobacco farmers of The Volunteer State.

Did You Know?

There was a time when iron-deficiency anemia was practically nonexistent, and a doctor-friend of mine (Dr. Bill Grabenstein of Clarksville) tells me that that was because, in the old days, everyone cooked their meals with and even baked in cast iron. Cast iron cookware, he explained, naturally leaches iron out with every dish you cook in it (especially acidic things such as tomato-based spaghetti sauce). If you want to enjoy cooking healthier meals for your family using heirloom-quality cast iron cookware, then Lodge cast iron is your "go-to" cookware of choice.

Founded in 1896 by a man named Joseph Lodge, Lodge Manufacturing is one of the oldest cookware companies in continuous operation in the entire United States. The two forges in South Pittsburgh (Tennessee) are only available for tours during the National Cornbread Festival, held every year the last weekend in April; at other times, you can visit their factory store nearby. There are currently two other locations of Lodge stores: one in Pigeon Forge, Tennessee, and another in Charlotte, North Carolina.

I use my Lodge deep skillet to make everything from quiches to birthday cakes, and, of course, cornbread.

Running a Sweet Business in Manchester

It was in 2006 that George "The Honey Man" Martin left his home in North Carolina and put down roots in Manchester. He brought with him his honey-making expertise and eventually had more than a hundred hives across three counties in

Tennessee. Today, his "Honey House" produces raw, unfiltered local honey, along with other products such as lip balms, lotions, and infused honey. You can visit his "Honey House" and chat with him when he's not working at a farmer's market. His place is the bee's knees!

Tennessee's Businesses Enjoying the Sweet Taste of Success for the Longest Time

There are more than 100 businesses in the Volunteer State who have been doing business for more than 100 years.

For example, the Chattanooga Times Free Press was first established as the Chattanooga Times in 1869 but merged in 1999 with the Chattanooga Free Press. It remains the only daily newspaper for Chattanooga.

Q&A

Q. Starting in 1884, why did the Tennessee Coal and Iron Company begin making annual lease payments of $101,000 to the state?
A. For the use of convicts as "free labor" instead of having to pay union miners. (The convict lease system as a government business subsidy was dropped after the union workers employed violence to halt it, in the insurrections of 1893–96.)

Q. What is the nation's oldest, continuously operated African American bank?
A. Nashville's Citizens Bank, established in 1904 by members of the National Negro Business League.

Q. In 1953 what Madison company, a maker of pedal steel guitars, became part of the large instrument-manufacturing corporation Baldwin, Inc.?

A. Sho-Bud, founded by Harold B. "Shot" Jackson and Buddy Emmons.

Q. Nashville has been home to what well-known vacuum-bottle and lunch-box company since 1949?
A. Aladdin Industries.

Q. What is Tennessee's most valuable (profitable) agricultural crop?
A. Soybeans, celebrated in Martin, Tennessee, at the annual Soybean Festival in September.

Q. What major international shipping company was established in Memphis in 1973?
A. Federal Express. The shipping company was a "star" in the 2000 movie Castaway, starring Holly Hunter and Tom Hanks.

CHAPTER TWELVE

Film, Music and Drama

Les Paul and Gibson Guitar: Two American Icons

Already a popular guitar player in the early 1950s, Les Paul was also a leading innovator in electric guitar design. Thinking that a solid-bodied guitar should have a solid sound to match, he attached guitar strings to a miniature railroad tie (a four-inch-by-four-inch piece of pine) and made the first solid-body electric guitar. He named this first model "the Log" and Nashville-based Gibson Guitar produced it. Today Les Paul is an active spokesman for Gibson, and the Les Paul signature model guitar is one of the greatest musical instruments of the 20th century.

There are two Gibson Guitar factories in Tennessee: one in Nashville and the other in Memphis. Both offer repairs, music schools, and tours. I toured the one in Music City USA and, although I knew little about guitars, was totally impressed. See "Virtual Tennessee" for website information.

A Lemons-into-Lemonade Story About Gibson

In the spring of 1998, tornadoes ripped through parts of Nashville, destroying churches, damaging historic buildings, and uprooting trees. Some of the trees were on the grounds of Andrew and Rachel Jackson's home, the Hermitage.

While some people bemoaned the loss of the great old trees, Gibson Guitar Company went into action. Henry Juszkiewicz, its CEO, took the usable parts of trees and created guitars, thus commemorating the Hermitage in a unique way and making music from disaster.

Vice President Al Gore, who attended the unveiling ceremonies of The Hermitage Guitars, said that Gibson turned "the debris of disaster into beautiful instruments."

The Birthplace of Rock 'N Roll

Just thinking about the famous voices who have sung and recorded within the walls of Sun Studio in Memphis and the music that was played there is enough to give a visitor goosebumps. The walls are lined with memorabilia of artists who recorded there, including Elvis Presley, U2, Carl Perkins, Johnny Cash, Def Leppard, Tom Petty, Jerry Lee Lewis, Roy Orbison, B. B. King, Howlin' Wolf, Ike Turner and Paul Simon. Ringo Starr once said, "If it hadn't been for what happened at Sun Studio, there wouldn't have been a Beatles."

Sun Studio gives tours seven days a week, all day long. You can also make your own musical and voice recordings with the aid of computers and CD-music backup. See "Virtual Tennessee" for website information.

Sun Studio in Memphis is said to be the birthplace of rock 'n' roll.
Artists such as Elvis Presley, Jerry Lee Lewis, and Roy Orbison
recorded here. (Courtesy Clay Tomas & Hansom Graphics)

Strange But True!

W.C. Handy's first musical instrument of choice was not the piano, the violin or the horn, although he became proficient at all three. When he was eight years old, he bought his first musical instrument, a Manson guitar. His father, a preacher who disapproved of musicians, made Handy take the guitar back to the store and exchange it for a dictionary.

Did You Know?

A music store owner tricked W. C. Handy out of the rights to his song "Memphis Blues." He told Handy the song wasn't selling well and bought it from the future "Father of the Blues" for one hundred dollars. Handy got his rights back later when he discovered the ruse. You can see more about Handy at the

W. C. Handy Boyhood Home in Memphis. See "Virtual Tennessee" for website information.

Hollywood in Tennessee

Los Angeles and New York City have realized for some time that the Volunteer State, long hailed as music's "Third Coast," is also a great place in which to make movies. In 1997 music, film, commercial, TV, and music video production resulted in more than $4 billion for the state's economy. David Glasgow of the Tennessee Film, Entertainment, and Music Commission once told me, "Memphis can look like one of a dozen big cities. It's very adaptable. A lot of places in Tennessee can look like a lot of other places in the world." Regal Cinema, the world's largest chain of movie theaters, is also based in Tennessee.

So what's been filmed here? Here's a partial list:

Raintree County (1956): Starring Elizabeth Taylor and Montgomery Clift. This movie was filmed in Reelfoot Lake State Park.

The River (1984): Starring Sissy Spacek. TVA flooded part of Hawkins County to make this movie.

Starman (1984): Starring Jeff Bridges. Much of this movie had footage shot in Chattanooga and Nashville.

Mystery Train (1990): Starring Masatoshi Nagase and Elizabeth Bracco.

This film, directed by Jim Jarmusch, takes a look at some of the more colorful characters of Memphis. It was one of the first widely distributed independent films shot there.

Days of Thunder (1991): Starring Tom Cruise. This movie was filmed at the Bristol Motor Speedway.

The Firm (1993): Starring Tom Cruise, Hal Holbrooke, Gene Hackman, and Holly Hunter.

The Client (1994): Starring Susan Sarandon and Tommy Lee Jones. Both based on John Grisham novels, these films were shot in Memphis.

Love Potion No. Nine (1993): Starring Sandra Bullock. Chattanooga provided the set for this film.

Against the Wall (1994): Starring Kyle MacLachlan. Clarksville simulated the town of Attica, New York, in this made-for-HBO movie.

Rudyard Kipling's The Jungle Book (1994): Starring John Cleese. About 80 percent of the location shooting for this live-action Disney film, set in India, was done in Fall Creek Falls State Park in Middle Tennessee.

The Specialist (1995): Starring Sylvester Stallone and Sharon Stone. The first twenty minutes of the movie (when the dam is blown up) were shot at Fall Creek Falls State Park, simulating Colombia in South America.

The People vs. Larry Flynt (1997): Starring Woody Harrelson, Edward Norton, and Courtney Love. This film was shot in the same lake and swamp area of Reelfoot Lake State Park as Raintree Country.

U.S. Marshalls (1998): Starring Tommy Lee Jones and Wesley Snipes. The chase scene through the swamp in this film was also shot in Reelfoot Lake State Park.

The Green Mile (1999), starring Tom Hanks, was filmed at the old Tennessee State Penitentiary in Nashville.

In Dreams (1999): Starring Annette Bening. The critical scene at the dam in this movie was filmed in Blount County.

October Sky (1999), starring Laura Dern, was shot in six counties around Knoxville.

Since this book first came out in 2000, many additional blockbuster movies and documentaries have been filmed in whole or in part in the Volunteer State. Those include such notables as:

Hannah Montana The Movie—filmed in Columbia, the town was made to look like a California beach village, complete with palm trees. Released in 2009.

Walk the Line—filmed entirely in Memphis and released in 2004, this blockbuster about Johnny Cash and the love of his life, June Carter (later Cash) featured Joaquin Phoenix as Johnny Cash and Reese Witherspoon (the latter a Tennessee native) as June.

An American Haunting—released in 2002, this film, loosely based on the Bell Witch of Adams, Tennessee (see Chapter 15, Unusual Grave, Ghost and Burial-Site Stories), featured Donald Sutherland as the accursed John Bell, haunted by the Bell Witch. It was filmed in

Sevierville. You can read the complete story of the Bell Witch in Chapter 15 of this book.

A Painted House—filmed in Memphis and released in 2002, the novel is based on the novel by the same name by author John Grisham. Starring in this movie were then-unknowns, Scott Glenn and Logan Lerman.

Cast Away—filmed partially in Memphis and released in 2000, this movie starred Tom Hanks and Helen Hunt.

Strange… but True

The Boy Who Didn't Get His Wish

In a small town in northern Mississippi in 1946, an eleven-year-old boy begged his parents, once again, for a bicycle. It cost too much, his parents told him, way too much; but he was their only child, and his mother wanted to give him something special. She thought and thought about what else he might like that she and his daddy could afford.

Finally, she found something at the Tupelo Hardware Company. It cost $12.95.

Elvis Presley, shown here at age ten, had to settle for a guitar as a birthday gift because his parents couldn't afford a bicycle. Courtesy Memphis Department of Tourism.

The boy accepted the gift, a guitar, and he learned how to play it. He played and sang so well that when they moved to Memphis in 1948, he began spending a lot of time on Beale Street, learning the blues and picking gospel tunes. In 1953, wanting to hear what his recorded voice sounded like, he dropped into Sun Records' Memphis Recording Service and made a demo for his mother, singing "My Happiness" and "That's When Your Heartaches Begin."

You know the rest of this boy's story. Now you know that if his parents had been able to afford a bicycle instead of a guitar, we might never have heard of Elvis Presley.

Incidentally, Graceland is THE most visited private home in the entire U.S. A relatively recent addition to Graceland is The Guest House at Graceland, a small yet elegant hotel that puts visitors in walking distance to "The King's" original domicile. See "Virtual Tennessee" for website information.

Guess Who?

He grew up in Union County outside Maynardville and his dream was to play professional baseball. Earning twelve letters in high school, he had good prospects to realize his dream. Then he was invited to try out for the New York Yankees, but the young man first went to Florida, where he acquired a terrible sunburn. It was so severe that he required hospitalization and a year of bed rest. Recuperating from his burns, his pro-ball dreams shattered, the young man began to listen to the Grand Ole Opry, and he decided to try to play the kind of music he heard. His first appearance on the Opry was in 1938.

Roy Acuff

Who is he? Roy Acuff, now known as one of the kings of country music. He was the first living member inducted into the Country Music Hall of Fame, and his name is synonymous with the Grand Ole Opry.

In Maynardville, you can visit the Roy Acuff Union Museum and Library, and in Nashville, the "King of Country Music" has an exhibit in the Country Music Hall of Fame. One of the rare fiddles Acuff played is on display at the Mountain Music Museum in Kingsport, Tennessee.

An Impromptu Concert Series

In the summer of 1962 a young man first came into Collins Music Store in Clarksville. He introduced himself to the owner, Sam Collins, saying he was stationed nearby at Fort Campbell and would like to drop in from time to time. Collins got to know the young man and remembered him later as someone who talked fast yet not discourteously. "He'd come in here and pick up any guitar and just start playing it," he once recalled to me. "He liked to play rock and roll . . . and I knew he had a sound I didn't hear every day. And he had a set of lungs that could really belt out the songs."

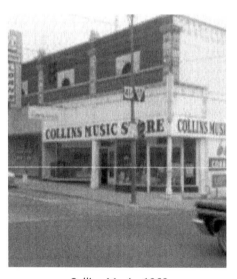

Collins Music, 1962

239

Collins and others who were in the music store when the young man came by now consider themselves lucky to have heard those impromptu concerts. The young man was none other than the legendary Jimi Hendrix.

When Barbara Mandrell Entertained the Troops

When Opry star Barbara Mandrell was a teenager, she and her family left their home in California to entertain the soldiers at military bases. When she and her mother, Mary, had to take makeshift baths in crude shelters outdoors, they took it in stride, until they realized they were being spied upon by soldiers! Undaunted, Barbara's mother said matter-of-factly, "Well, we came over here to entertain the boys, and I guess that's what we've done!"

W. C. Handy and Beale Street

A native of Florence, Alabama, William Christopher Handy was living in a small shotgun house at 325 Beale Street in Memphis and working as a band leader and cornet player when in 1909 he wrote the campaign song for E. H. Crump, who was running for mayor of Memphis. It was later entitled "Memphis Blues" and in 1912 was the first blues composition ever published. Two years later he wrote "St. Louis Blues," possibly the most popular blues song of all time.

Derived from field songs (called "hollers") sung by slaves, blues became a popular musical form and aspiring musicians came in droves to Beale Street to learn to play the blues and perhaps make names for themselves. Then the Great Depression brought hard times; nightspots closed, the musicians went north, and Beale Street sank into a seedy travesty of its former self.

A local blues musician performs outside a Beale Street café. (Courtesy Memphis Convention & Visitors Bureau)

In the 1970s some savvy Memphians recognized what a tourist draw Beale Street could be and launched a redevelopment campaign. Among the many attractions on Beale Street are the W. C. Handy Home; the Orpheum Theater for the performing arts; the New Daisy Theater, which hosts everything from musicians to boxing matches; and the famous dry-goods store A. Schwab. The old honky-tonk bars and pawn shops are being revitalized into new restaurants, shops, and nightspots.

Composer George Gershwin, who wrote "Rhapsody in Blue," once told Handy, "Your work is the grandfather of mine." Now a statue of the "Father of the Blues" smiles over everyone in W. C. Handy Park, and a "whole lotta shaking" is still going on.

Fans meet Country Music Hall of Fame member Eddy Arnold at the museum.
(Courtesy Country Music Hall of Fame, Nashville, Tenn.)

The Grand Ole Opry

It all began in 1925 as a local radio program called Barn Dance, and every Saturday night, more and more area listeners gathered around their crystal (radio) sets to hear country music played from the WSM studio in Nashville. To miss that show was like having fried eggs without grits for breakfast.

WSM attained network status in 1939, and the show, now known as the Grand Ole Opry, could be heard all over the U.S. As more people came to see the live performances, the Opry outgrew WSM studios. In 1941 it moved to the Ryman Auditorium. In 1943 the Acuff-Rose Publishing Company was founded by Roy Acuff and Fred Rose, and in 1945 Decca began recording country music at Studio B, WSM Radio. Country music had made its mark, so much so that on Okinawa it is said that one Japanese banzai battle cry was, "To hell with

242

Roosevelt; to hell with Babe Ruth; to hell with Roy Acuff." The Opry has been successful because of the music that comes from the heart and the musicians that have played from theirs. They've written and sung about love, lost and found; about dying parents, sweethearts, or children; about driving trucks or trains; about being lonesome, hungry, heartbroken, imprisoned, and otherwise wretched. Deep in "Bible Belt Country," they've also sung about their love of Jesus and waiting to see loved ones gone on to the Other Side. Songs going out into radio land (and later TV land) from the Grand Ole Opry touched hearts and brought tears to eyes because so many people could relate to the words being sung.

Ryman Auditorium

Lots of Opry fans came to be onstage themselves. Loretta Lynn, who first listened to the radio as a poor coal miner's daughter from Van Leer, is one. Dolly Parton, Floyd Tillman, Hank Snow, Tammy Wynette, Charlie Walker, Barbara Mandrell, Roy Acuff, Kitty Wells, Hank Williams, Patsy Cline, and more all made their mark on Opry history. Sara Ophelia

Cannon—you know her as Minnie Pearl—was a regular comedienne at the Opry.

In 1974 the Opry moved to the auditorium built especially for it at Opryland USA. Since Decca began recording in Nashville, many other studios and related recording businesses have followed. What turned Nashville into Music City, USA, began with a small Saturday-night broadcast and is approaching its 100th birthday in 2025.

There are several tours offered if you want to see the Grand Ole Opry in person, but If you really want to get a feel for the true excitement of the place, the Backstage Tour is THE tour. This tour includes a visit to stars' dressing rooms (including the "King of Country Music," Roy Acuff, and a view of where the fans send mail (each Opry star has their own, brass-plated name on their personal mailbox). Finally, near the end of the roughly hour-long tour, you can stand in "The Circle," which is a round piece of wooden flooring cut from the center of the Ryman Auditorium's stage. See "Virtual Tennessee" for website information.

So...You Want to be in the Opry?

An official at the Grand Ole Opry had this to say regarding membership requirements: "A member of the Opry is inducted by showing interest that being a part of the Opry is important to him or her, both musically and to their career. They don't really have to audition because by the time they're inducted, they have already played the Opry several times. They must have a desire to be a member and a commitment to make appearances, but there is really no set number of performances required by the Opry." Hey, does that sound democratic or what?

It Started with a KISS

This country music singer, who moved to Nashville in 1984, recalled the time he thought he was getting his first big break: "One night around six o'clock," he related to interviewer Ralph Emery, "we got a call from a promoter asking us if we could put a band together and get down to the [Norman, Oklahoma] civic center by eight o'clock." When he saw the marquee announcing the rock band KISS was playing that night, the would-be star was incredulous and thought surely, he couldn't be opening for that particular group.

But they played their best as the warm-up band. The audience was—to put it nicely—unappreciative, yelling and booing the band. The band finally quit the stage, after shouts and taunts from the crowd became too loud to bear.

This tough beginning was just one of the early experiences of the country star you now know as Vince Gill. Once, when I was talking with Vince Gill in the alley behind Tootsie's Orchid, I asked him about his memory of this experience.

Gill just smiled.

Roll Call: Grand Ole Opry Members

Here's a current list of members of the Grand Ole Opry, with the years they were inducted.

1948 Little Jimmy Dickens
1953 Billy Carlisle
1953 Teddy Wilburn
1955 Charlie Louvin
1955 Jean Shepard

1956 Jimmy Newman
1957 Wilma Lee Cooper
1958 Porter Wagonner
1958 Roy Drusky
1958 Don Gibson
1959 Skeeter Davis
1959 Billy Grammer
1960 George Hamilton IV
1960 Hank Locklin
1960 Billy Walker
1961 Bill Anderson
1962 Loretta Lynn
1963 Jim Ed Brown
1964 Ernie Ashworth
1964 Jim & Jesse
1964 The Osborne Brothers
1966 Ray Pillow
1966 Del Reeves
1967 Jack Greene
1967 Stu Phillips
1967 Jeannie Seely
1967 Charlie Walker
1969 Stonewall Jackson
1969 George Jones
1969 Dolly Parton
1971 Jan Howard
1971 Connie Smith
1972 Barbara Mandrell
1973 Jeanne Pruett
1976 The Gatlins
1976 Ronnie Milsap
1980 Tom T. Hall
1980 The Melvin Sloan Dancers
1981 John Conlee

1982 Riders in the Sky
1982 Ricky Skaggs
1984 Lorrie Morgan
1984 The Whites
1985 Johnny Russell
1986 Mel McDaniel
1986 Reba McEntire
1986 Randy Travis
1987 Roy Clark
1988 Patty Loveless
1988 Ricky Van Shelton
1989 Holly Dunn
1990 Garth Brooks
1990 Mike Snider
1991 Clint Black
1991 Vince Gill
1991 Alan Jackson
1992 Emmylou Harris
1992 Marty Stuart
1992 Travis Tritt
1993 Joe Diffie
1995 Bashful Brother Oswald
1995 Martina McBride
1996 Steve Wariner
1997 Johnny Paycheck
1998 Diamond Rio
1999 Trisha Yearwood
2000 Ralph Stanley
2000 Pam Tillis
2001 Brad Paisley
2003 Del McCoury
2003 Trace Adkins
2004 Terri Clark
2005 Dierks Bentley

2007 Mel Tillis
2007 Josh Turner
2008 Charlie Daniels
2008 Carrie Underwood
2008 Craig Morgan
2009 Montgomery Gentry
2010 Blake Shelton
2011 The Oak Ridge Boys
2011 Rascal Flatts
2012 Keith Urban
2012 Darius Rucker
2013 Old Crow Medicine Show
2014 Little Big Town
2017 Crystal Gayle
2017 Dailey & Vincent
2017 Chris Young
2018 Chris Janson
2018 Dustin Lynch
2019 Mark Wills
2019 Kelsea Ballerini
2019 Luke Combs

Did You Know??

As a young man, Mel Tillis couldn't keep a job because of his terrible stutter. He'd been a fireman, a strawberry picker, and a house painter. When he applied to be a driver of a candy-company truck, the employer wouldn't hire him but gave him a copy of the Serenity Prayer, which asks for wisdom to "accept the things I cannot change." The young man began to write songs, which he could sing without stuttering. He started out as a backup musician and songwriter, and he's now a famous country music singer.

What started out as the Grand Alt(nerative) Opry

The house band is named Vacation Bible School and is billed as "the most righteous band in the land." Now known as Billy Block's Western Beat, Block started the show in an effort to bring back a love of country and alternative music to Nashville. The Cinderella-type story began in 1995, when Billy Block came to Tennessee from California, where he had been the house drummer at the famous Hollywood honky-tonk, the Palomino Club. He started his show, first billed as the "Grand Alt Opry," on a shoestring and a prayer. Within months his Tuesday-night live concert series and radio show at a small south Nashville bar outgrew its setting and moved twice to accommodate larger audiences. It's now located at a club called the Exit/In.

Billy Block

Block's Western Beat idea, with its frequent switching of musicians who perform with the Vacation Bible School, was an instant hit. Since its inception, Western Beat has showcased more than six hundred artists, including Steve Earle, Lucinda Williams, Emmy Lou Harris, Leroy Parnell, the Derailers, Marty Stuart, and Trisha Yearwood, with some of them appearing on a Country Music Television (CMT) weekly series that debuted Block's show in July 2000.

Billy Block died in 2015 after a long fight with cancer, but the man Nashville now calls the "godfather of Americana" continues to have his legacy cherished by Music City and its musicians and fans. Hatch Show Prints made a collector's edition poster of one of his shows from 2004, and Exit/In shows are still a part of the Nashville scene, thanks to Block's vision.

Embracing the newest technology, the show Western Beat is aired every Tuesday night via the Internet (Live on the Net at www.westernbeat. com), which reaches a potential audience of at least seventy million listeners and viewers. This way, if you can't walk in, log on.

Twice in a Lifetime: The Comeback Queen of Blues and Jazz

When the eighty-two-year-old African American singer arrived on stage in 1979 at The Cookery, a New York City nightclub, the sensation of appearing before an audience was something she hadn't felt in more than twenty years. The songs she sang that night, from "My Castle's Rockin'" to "Down-Hearted Blues," echoed her life from her early days in Memphis where she grew up to where she now stood, at the beginning of her come-back. This woman was Alberta Hunter, one of America's legendary singers of blues and jazz.

Her life was successful against improbable odds. Her mother worked in a Memphis brothel as a maid, and Hunter began singing there, performing tunes she'd heard on Beale Street.

Alberta Hunter

Hunter's throaty voice made her a star from the 1920s through the mid-1950s; she had toured with the first all-black USO troupe to entertain troops at the front in World War II and the Korean War.

Abruptly quitting showbiz and becoming a nurse when her mother died, she worked at a Manhattan hospital until she was eighty-two.

That's when her career took off. Again.

Barney Josephson, the owner of the Cookery, heard that Hunter was living as a retired nurse in New York. He called and told her, "Get on down here. You're going to be a singer again." Someone who heard her remembers: "She had an incredible presence. She had our attention . . . and even at eighty-two, she was sexy!"

Alberta Hunter performed at the Cookery until her death in 1984, a star twice in her lifetime. Hunter is featured prominently in the Memphis Music Hall of Fame. See "Virtual Tennessee" for website information

GUESS WHO?

This man was born in Covington in 1942, the son of a sharecropper. He was raised by his grandparents in Memphis, where he learned to play the saxophone and piano. In 1962 his first band, Sir Isaac and the DooDads, did gigs at local clubs. By 1964 he was playing backup on the keyboard for Otis Redding, Carla Thomas, and others at Stax Recording Studio. His shaved head in the time when afros were popular made him stand out. He was, and is, a symbol of black pride and success, the first African American composer to win an Academy Award. The voice of Chef on the animated TV show "South Park" belongs to this man.

Who is he? Isaac Hayes, whose "Theme for Shaft" won him that Academy Award. Like Alberta Hunter, his life and accomplishments are featured in the Memphis Music Hall of Fame.

A Job from Chet Atkins

The following story was told by Muriel Anderson, internationally renowned guitar player, who was lucky enough to have Chet Atkins as a mentor.

Chet Atkins gives Muriel Anderson a guitar lesson. He also gave her a job helping out in his chicken coop. (Courtesy Muriel Anderson)

"Like many young guitarists, I often stopped by Chet Atkins's office in Nashville with the hopes he might be practicing a tune, and I could learn some music by watching his fingers. Chet was always very generous with his music, and sometimes he would slow it down so that I could catch the notes as they went by. I learned a lot of music this way.

"One day as I was talking to his secretary, Mr. Atkins came down the stairs and said, 'Muriel, I have a job for you!' The greatest guitarist in the world giving me a job? What could it be, the Grand Ole Opry? Carnegie Hall?

"'You see," he continued, "my pet rooster, Hot Shot, has come down with a case of feather mites, and my wife and I are getting too old to crawl into the chicken coop, and we're just too big, and . . . you see, you're about the smallest person I know.' He went on to tell me that he was going to ask [Grand Ole Opry star] Little Jimmy Dickens, but I just happened into the office that day.

"That afternoon I went to the Atkins' home. They put a plastic bag with head- and armholes over me to protect my clothes, and with a great deal of coaching, I caught the rooster by both legs at once (so the spurs didn't get me) and with the other hand grabbed its neck. Then Chet's wife, Leona, spread bacon grease around its neck for the mite dust to adhere to. Then I caught the hen (also named Leona) and we covered her with mite dust as well, while the rooster complained loudly.

"With that, I was invited to stay for lunch. Chicken stew, I believe it was."

Did You Know?

Besides being a judge on "The Voice" (since 2011), country music megastar Blake Shelton has launched entertainment venues in Tennessee. Ole Red Nashville opened in spring of 2018; Old Red Gatlinburg, in spring of 2019. See "Virtual Tennessee" for website information.

Johnny and June Cash Retreat

Once he achieved international-celebrity status, country music icon Johnny Cash needed some kind of retreat where he and June Carter Cash could escape the paparazzi and enjoy life as regular folks. Cash's accountant found and purchased an 1800s-era general store and farm in the tiny town of Bon Aqua, and this became the retreat for the Cash family and their guests.

They restored the old general store and built a stage inside. As time went on, local musicians began coming over to play on the weekends. These "jam sessions" became known as Saturday Night in Hickman County. The Cash family lived in the old farmhouse off and on for the next 30 years.

In 2015, two brothers bought the farm and general store and converted the old store into a Johnny Cash Museum. It is now known as the Storytellers Museum and Hideaway Farm. The museum contains tons of Cash-related memorabilia, including the "One Piece at a Time" car. The brothers also re-started the show, "Saturday Night in Hickman County." You can find the Storytellers Museum on Old Highway 46 in Bon Aqua. See "Virtual Tennessee" for website information.

Did You Know?

I've always been a big fan of Hatch Show Prints, a company that has been printing playbills, music posters and the like for more than 140 years. Since they moved from their old spot on Broadway in downtown Nashville to where they make their home today (in the lobby of the Country Music Hall of Fame), visitors can see letterpress printing in action. Kids of all ages love to visit Hatch and take part in making their own letterpress art! See "Virtual Tennessee" for website information.

Take a Road Trip Down Rockabilly Highway

U.S. Highway 45 South goes from Jackson to Selmer, Tennessee, and is known by the nickname, "Rockabilly Highway." Travelers who take this route might want to stop and have a "selfie" made in front of the two murals that highlight this road, paying homage to the "King of Rockabilly," Carl Perkins.

Tennessee's Got Drama!

If you think great plays, ballets and concerts can only be had in New York City's Broadway, think again: The Volunteer State is awash with beautiful and historic theaters, all of which offer a variety of entertainment. Many of the smaller towns, such as Franklin, have charming theaters to claim as their own (Franklin Theater). Other, larger cities boast theaters that have been a part of the entertainment scene for nearly a millennium, and their historic architecture adds to the experience of theater going (such as The Roxy in Clarksville). But two theaters are the gems in the crown that Tennessee wears.

Tivoli Theater – The Jewel of the South

One, Tivoli Theater in Chattanooga, is known as "The Jewel of the South." It first opened in 1921 and has been on the National Register of Historic Places since 1973. After major renovations in 1989, it continues to offer all sorts of musical and entertainment and is home to the Chattanooga Symphony and Opera.

The top of the list for theaters in the state, however, would have to be the Tennessee Theatre in Knoxville. Open since 1928, it closed for a time for renovations and re-opened in 2005. Seeing the beautiful architecture (such as the domed ceiling) and overall opulence of the theater is an experience in itself. "The Tennessee," as locals call it, is the official State Theater and is a world-class theater.

For those who feel a kinship with The Bard (as I do), Nashville's Shakespeare Festival is a must. The year this edition went to press, they offered performances of what I will call here "The Scottish Play." There is also a summer camp for aspiring thespians ages 7-18.

Many of these theaters, such as The Tennessee, offer tours, and also are available for hosting special events, such as weddings, corporate conventions, and more. See "Virtual Tennessee" for website information.

HOME TO HARD ROCK CAFÉ AND HOUSE OF BLUES: CARNEGIE MUSEUM IN JACKSON

The town of Jackson in west Tennessee offers a surprising number of amazing things to see and do within its borders. One of my favorite places to visit in Jackson was the Carnegie Museum, which originally was a Carnegie Library. The town of Jackson has as one of its claims to fame as the place where Rock and Roll, and Rockabilly, originated, and this is celebrated at Carnegie.

Y ou'll enjoy seeing the vast array of classic guitars, clothing worn by celebrities and all sorts of memorabilia. There is also an audio-tour, so you can better understand what you're seeing in the exhibits. The museum celebrates Jackson's two "home-boys," Carl Perkins and Isaac Tigrett (the latter of whom founded both the House of Blues and Hard Rock Café). The museum, docents told me, houses the largest Carl Perkins exhibit in the entire world, but there are also exhibits about other Tennessee musical celebrities such as Eddy Arnold and Tina Turner.

Carnegie Museum, Jackson, Tennessee

The docents are very friendly and knowledgeable, and for those who want to have a memento of their experience, items such as t-shirts are available in the gift shop. You can find the Carnegie Museum on East College Street in Jackson. You'll have a severe case of "the blues" if you don't visit this gem of a museum!

The Story of Sleepy John Estes

Born in Brownsville, guitar player John Estes earned his nickname, "Sleepy," because he could drop off for a nap at a moment's notice. After recording in Chicago for a few years with both the Bluebird and Decca record labels, he returned to West Tennessee. Estes was recording at Sun Studio in Memphis in the early 1950s when tragedy struck. Sleepy John's vision started to fail (his sight was already impaired from a childhood eye trauma). As his vision diminished, his despair intensified, and the notes issued less frequently from his guitar. Once he was completely blind, he dropped out of the music scene and returned to Brownsville to live out his life in obscurity.

But the blues were rediscovered in the 1960s, and along with them, Sleepy John Estes. He was brought from his shack in Brownsville back into the music scene. He picked up where he left off and from then on recorded and toured

John Estes

internationally until his death in 1977. Now the town that calls itself the "heart of the Tennessee Delta" has created a museum in honor of its own "Delta blues man," Sleepy John Estes.

You can learn more about Estes, his life and contributions to music in the town of Brownsville. The John Estes House is restored and available for tours; also in Brownsville, the West Tennessee Delta Heritage Center and Tina Turner Museum has exhibits about the life and times of Estes. See "Virtual Tennessee" for website information.

Cinderella Story: One Coal Miner's Daughter

Born in 1935 in Kentucky coal mining country, Loretta Lynn sang about as soon as she spoke her first words, and when the Grand Ole Opry came on the radio each Saturday night, she'd be found glued to the speaker, absorbing every note. Married at the age of thirteen, she went from coal miner's daughter to coal miner's wife.

Loretta Lynn

After seeing so many of his friends and family die young, their lungs choked by coal dust, her husband, "Mooney," left coal mining soon after their marriage and they moved to Washington State. Music was still in Loretta's veins, though, so Mooney encouraged her to try singing professionally. By 1950 she had started performing at area honky-tonks, and by the 1960s she'd performed on Buck Owens's radio show out of Tacoma and had released her first single, which she wrote herself, "I'm a Honky Tonk Girl."

With her husband as manager, Loretta achieved success in her singing career, with appearances on Ernest Tubb's Midnight Jamboree on WSM Radio and an invitation to become a regular on the Grand Ole Opry. Her closest friend was Patsy Cline, who influenced her singing style. The coal miner's daughter became one of Tennessee's diamonds when she and her husband made their home in Nashville and then at Hurricane Mills in Humphreys County.

It is the story in her songs that makes people love Loretta Lynn. Her audiences share the experiences of the girl who grew up in oppressive poverty and a life of back-breaking work, but with dreams about which she sings. Her story has been such an inspiration that her book *Coal Miner's Daughter* (1976) was made into a blockbuster movie starring Sissy Spacek as Loretta Lynn and Tommy Lee Jones as Mooney.

You can learn more about Loretta Lynn's life and accomplishments by touring the Country Music Hall of Fame (Nashville), the Coal Miner's Daughter Museum (Hurricane Mills) and the Loretta Lynn Home and Museum (also in Hurricane Mills). See "Virtual Tennessee" for website information.

Two "Cash" Coincidences

In 1987 when Rosanne Cash recorded "Tennessee Flat-Top Box," she thought the song was in the public domain. Until it debuted on the Billboard charts and reached the number one spot, she was still unaware that her father, Johnny Cash, had written and recorded it in 1962.

In 1999 June Carter Cash recorded the famous song "Ring of Fire" on her CD Press On. Previously it had been one of her husband Johnny Cash's hit songs, but when she performed it during a TV interview, she revealed that she had written the song when she first realized she was in love with the famous Man in Black. She said that for years he hadn't known who had inspired her to write those lyrics (they had married in 1968).

A bittersweet postscript to this story is that in May 2003, June Carter Cash passed away. She was joined by the man who had written the first song and inspired the second when Johnny Cash died in September 2003.

Johnny and June Carter Cash are buried in Hendersonville

Johnny and June Cash

in Memory Park, near some of their other famous and not-so-famous family members. They both have exhibits about their lives in the Country Music Hall of Fame and Museum in Nashville.

The Country Music Hall of Fame and Museum

Located in Nashville, the Country Music Hall of Fame was originally founded in 1961 by the Country Music Association (CMA) but is now its own entity. The first inductees were Jimmie Rodgers, Fred Rose, and Hank Williams Sr., that same year. Inductees are chosen every year by an anonymous panel of two hundred people who have actively participated in the music business for fifteen years or more and who themselves have made a significant contribution to the music industry. As of press time, the most recent exhibit at the museum was in honor of Kenny Rogers; popularly known as "The Gambler" for that hit song, Rogers "cashed in his chips" in February of 2020.

The Country Music Hall of Fame and Museum has been visited by more than twenty million people, making it one of the most visited musical museums in the country. It includes more than four thousand items relating to the people and history of country music. The media center contains over two hundred thousand recorded discs, sixty thousand photographs, five thousand films and videotapes, posters, songbooks, and hundreds of audiotapes.

Important to country music and its history is what the museum does in the fields of restoration and education. It restores priceless historical commercial recordings and each year helps over twenty thousand students and teachers with lesson plans, classroom materials, and other musical educational aids. A mentoring program for promising young songwriters and a Girl Scout program called Camp

SummerSong engender a love of country music and music in general. All this has given country music a new, more sophisticated image.

Did You Know?

The only person with four relatives in the Country Music Hall of Fame is June Carter Cash. She has an aunt (Sara Carter), an uncle (A. P. Carter), her mother (Mother Maybelle Carter), and her husband (Johnny Cash) honored there.

Country Music: So They Say

"A song ain't nothin' in the world but a story just wrote with music to it."—Hank Williams Sr.

"Country music springs from the heart of America."—Tex Ritter

"A good country song taps into strong undercurrents of family, faith, and patriotism."—George Bush Sr.

"When you stop dreaming, you stop living."—Lorrie Morgan

Keep learning, keep doing, and get your ducks in a row. Then, when opportunity knocks, you're ready."—Buck Owens

"True country music is honesty, sincerity, and real life to the hilt."—Garth Brooks

"If you want the rainbow, you've got to put up with a little rain." —Dolly Parton

"As an artist, it tells me we are doing our job when we're touching people's hearts."—Ty Herndon

"God respects you when you work, but he loves you when you sing."—Cliffie Stone

"Applause surely must be the most powerful aphrodisiac known to mankind. The quest for it is a disease of the blood. Or, at best, a genetic disorder."— "Whisperin' Bill" Anderson

"I started in rock and worked my way up to country."— Conway Twitty

"Pretty Women Don't Need Money"

One day Roy Orbison's wife, Claudette, was about to go out shopping. He'd written a song for her and was discussing just what to name it with his friend Bill Dees. As Claudette was leaving, Roy asked her if she needed money.

Dees looked at Roy and quipped, "Don't you know that pretty women don't need money?" Orbison and Dees looked at each other and said in unison, "Pretty Woman!" It was the perfect title for Orbison's song, which has enjoyed enduring popularity and was used as the title song for the movie Pretty Woman, starring Julia Roberts and Richard Gere.

In addition to the Roy Orbison Museum in Wink, Texas, the famous crooner, and this iconic song, were honored with an exhibit in 2014 at the Musicians' Hall of Fame in Nashville.

Good thing Claudette decided to go shopping that day.

She's Got L'eggs

Born in the West Tennessee town of Nutbush of sharecropper parents, Anna Mae Bullock picked cotton and did all the other necessary back-breaking work in a hardscrabble farm family. As she grew, she began to listen to WDIA, the black radio station in Memphis, where she heard the music of blues greats such as Sleepy John Estes, Bootsie Whitelow, and B. B. King. Moving to St. Louis with her mother, she became lead singer of a band, the Kings of Rhythm. She and the bandleader married, and they became the most famous husband-and-wife act in Rhythm & Blues and, later, rock music; however, their

Tina Turner

marriage ended because it was said he was abusive.

Now she is perhaps one of the highest achievers in musical entertainment. She has written her autobiography, and although she was born in 1939, she still has such great legs that she's been the spokesperson for L'eggs pantyhose.

266

You know her as Tina Turner; her husband was Ike Turner. You can learn more about her at the West Tennessee Delta Heritage Center and Tina Turner Museum in Brownsville.

The Legendary Brenda Lee

Here are some tidbits from Ralph Emery, music celebrity interviewer, about rock and country legend Brenda Lee, who began singing in Nashville in 1956.

She's sold more double-sided hit singles than any other female in pop music's history.

She's charted in more categories more consistently than any other female in recording history.

During the 1960s Lee was the top female act and fourth overall (the top three being Elvis Presley, the Beatles, and Ray Charles).

She's ranked number nine for most consecutive top ten hits of all time.

Her first hit song in the United States was the 1960s release, "Sweet Nothings."

You can see more about her in exhibits at the Country Music Hall of Fame and Museum In Nashville.

Garth Brooks: A Prince, On and Off the Stage

We were in the labor and delivery unit of Nashville's Baptist Hospital in 1990, getting ready to have our first baby. But the nurses and staff seemed to have their minds elsewhere. Finally I asked, "What's going on?"

"Garth Brooks and his wife, Sandy, are down the hall," they said. "They're having their first baby."

That was the closest I've ever gotten to the star whose lyrics, showmanship, and singing style have endeared him to died-in-the-wool country music fans and who has made fans out of people who weren't country music fans. Some of Brooks' biographers say he's the biggest-selling solo artist in U.S. music history.

Garth Brooks

One reason he's done so well is that he's in it for the music. Instead of thinking of studio schedules and other time-restrictive considerations, Brooks plays the recordings until they sound right, experimenting with different approaches and various instruments until the sound in his imagination and the sound in his ears are the same.

Even despite the challenging times in his personal life, Brooks has taken the proverbial high road. When he and Sandy divorced in 2001, Brooks went into semi-retirement until sometime after his marriage to fellow country music star Trisha Yearwood in 2005, upon which time he began a "comeback tour," and his fans fell in love with him all over again.

Besides his many awards for his music, he's been inducted into the Songwriters Hall of Fame in 2011, the Country Music Hall of Fame in 2012 and the Musicians Hall of Fame in 2016.

His heart's as big as Tennessee is wide. In the spring of 1999 he lived a dream of his, training with the San Diego baseball team, the Padres, and donating all his earnings to his charity for children, Touch 'Em All. There have been many other times when Brooks has shown his love for others. When he was on tour in 2014, a daughter took her mother (who was undergoing chemo for Stage Three breast cancer) to a Brooks concert. They made a sign that read, "Chemo This Morning, Garth Concert Tonight." When Brooks was made aware of the two, he brought them to the front row, serenaded the mother, and gave her his guitar. Later, on a YouTube video, he said, "You know, we might complain about two shows on Friday and two on Saturday. This mom's gone through chemo this morning, and still came to the show."

The Birthplace of Country Music

The title "Birthplace of Country Music" is proudly claimed by Bristol. Ralph Peer came to the mountains in 1927 to record "hillbilly" music for the Victor Talking Machine Company. During his stay there, he recorded such notables as Earnest "Pop" Stoneman and his family, the Carter Family, and Jimmie Rodgers. The Smithsonian celebrated the so-called Bristol Sessions in 2003 with a Salute to Appalachia to honor Peer's achievement in Bristol.

Deana Carter: "Sing or Wash the Dishes"

"In our family you either had to sing harmony or wash dishes," Deana Carter quips. "So naturally I picked the harmony part."

Her father, Fred Carter Jr., played on virtually all the recording sessions in Nashville during the 1960s and 1970s, with such greats as Roy Orbison, Simon and Garfunkel, and Elvis Presley. Deana Carter's own first break came when Willie Nelson heard one of her demo tapes and asked her to perform in a Farm Aid concert.

She was the only female soloist in the show but made friends with the crowd and became an overnight sensation, recording such hits as "Did I Shave My Legs for This?" and "Strawberry Wine."

All the times she sang to get out of washing dishes finally paid off.

Bessie Smith: "Hold It!"

Chattanooga-born Bessie Smith (1894–1937) is said to be the "Empress of the Blues." The songs she made famous, such as "Jail-House Blues" and Alberta Hunter's "Down Hearted Blues" left music fans enthralled. She was raised by her sister in a one-room wooden shack in a poor neighborhood in Chattanooga called Blue Goose Hollow. She and her brother Clarence were street musicians by the time she was nine, with Bessie singing and Clarence accompanying her on his guitar.

The renowned blues singer Gertrude "Ma" Rainey took her on as a pupil, and Frank Walker, head of Columbia Records' Race Division, had her come for an audition on February 15, 1923.

Two weeks before the Columbia audition, Smith is said to have "blown it" at a New York audition. She had been invited to audition at Okeh Records in New York. She cut a test song, then interrupted the audition with, "Hold it! I gotta spit!" That was the end of that audition; the studio personnel said she was "too rough" for audiences.

Bessie Smith

When Smith auditioned for Columbia, apparently, she didn't spit, because they asked her back the following day. On that day she sang songs that would comprise her first release as a professional blues singer: "Gulf Coast Blues" and "Down Hearted Blues." Bessie Smith was on her way.

You can learn more about the life and contributions of the "Empress of the Blues" at the Bessie Smith Cultural Center in Chattanooga. The Center—what locals refer affectionately to as "The Bessie"--hosts musical performances and is available for special events such as conventions and wedding receptions. See "Virtual Tennessee" for website information.

Film, Music and Drama

According to the entertainment e-zine Insider.com, here is a short list of other country music stars, and cross-genre ones, that you might want to be keeping an eye on right now:

Kacey Musgraves, who in 2019 won not one but four Grammys, including Album of the Year ("Golden Hour").

Maren Morris, who's currently probably best known for her hit single "The Middle."

Kane Brown, whose energetic and smooth baritone voice may remind you of country music singing legends of the early days. In October 2017, Brown became the first country music artist to top all five Country Billboard charts at the same time.

Thomas Rhett, a cross-genre musician of country and pop music, sings a dearth of love songs, including "Marry Me" and "Die a Happy Man." He also writes for other musicians, such as the group Florida Georgia Line, so you've probably heard his lyrics if not his actual singing voice.

Jillian Jacqueline is fairly new to the music scene, but it seems right off the proverbial bat, she collaborated with Keith Urban on a pop-country song, "If I Were You," which became an instant hit. She's going to be one to watch!

Ryan Hurd, who's married to Maren Morris, is making a name for himself in the country music industry. He also writes for other artists, such as Blake Shelton ("Lonely Tonight") and Luke Bryan ("Sunrise, Sunburn, Sunset").

Kelsea Ballerini won a nomination for Best Country Album for "Unapologetically" in 2018.

Blanco Brown is, in the words of Insider.com, helping bring "the traditionally white [country music] genre into the 21st century." Brown has proven adept at blending country with hip-hop; one of his songs, "The Git Up," made the number 16 rank of the new Hot 100 hits of 2019. It also hit the number one spot on the Hot Country Songs Chart in July of that same year.

Brandi Carlile's music has been across genres, from Americana to country and folk. Her performance of her song, "The Joke" at the 2019 Grammys won her a dearth of new fans.

Lil Nas X is a cross-genre singer, who does rap as well as country. When his rap song, "Old Town Road," was removed from Billboard as "not country enough," instead of being discouraged, he recruited Billy Ray Cyrus to help him re-record it, with Cyrus also singing vocals, and did another remix of the song featuring yodeler Mason Ramsey. The song became what Insider.com referred to as a "smash single."

These rising stars are just a few to watch, as they challenge the old norms and expectations of country music and raise the proverbial bar.

Toby Keith: Saluting Those on the Front Lines

I've always admired Toby Keith and other country music artists who appreciate and salute those in uniform, risking their lives abroad so we can live free. One night, for example, singer Toby Keith had the wife of a soldier deployed to Afghanistan come on stage while he sang "American Solider." After the song, he had her husband, newly returned from Afghanistan, surprise her onstage with his unexpected homecoming.

This kind of musician is my kind of hero!

Trace Adkins, Nashville Icon

Mention the name Trace Adkins and anybody who's into modern-day country music knows who you're talking about. Adkins has made the Nashville country music scene going on roughly three decades now and has sold more than 11 million albums and received awards from Country Music Television (CMT) among others. He's been a long-time member of the Grand Ole Opry, but loves most to create music, collaborating with fellow musicians, and take his music on the road. He's also made a name for himself as an actor: as of press time, he has starred or appeared in thirty films.

He has another passion, though, that's impressed me about as much as anything else: that is, he is an avid supporter of the Wounded Warrior Project and has been since 2010. Furthermore, he brings veterans' needs to the forefront during his concerts and interviews. To me, this man's blood runs red, white and blue.

Did You Know?

There is a relatively new musical performance venue that is also as old as the hills, literally. Set in a cave in Pelham near the base of Monteagle Mountain, The Caverns is the setting for the PBS series, "Bluegrass Underground." Seating is limited (currently, 750), but you'll never have to worry about the weather (constant cave temperature is around 60 degrees year 'round).

She Couldn't Act, But...

Twenty-eight-year-old Sarah Ophelia Cannon just couldn't make it in acting and had gone back home to Centerville, frustrated, to get a job as a recreation-room director. One night the children in her program entertained a group of banker conventioneers. While waiting for the main speaker to arrive, Ophelia filled in with her monologue about a fictitious girl from the fictitious mountain village called Grinder's Switch.

That did it. She went on to become a star of the Grand Ole Opry— named Minnie Pearl. Today, you can see quite a bit of

Minnie Pearl

memorabilia related to the life of Minnie Pearl at the Country Music Hall of Fame and Museum in downtown Nashville, and there is a Minnie Pearl Museum In the town of Centerville (and in front of City Hall, you can find a bust of her likeness, complete with hat price-tag). A lovely bronze sculpture of Minnie Pearl, sitting on a park bench in an amicable chat with Roy Acuff, can be found in the Ryman Auditorium.

Unusual Country Music Titles

"There's a Tear in My Beer"—Hank Williams Jr. and Hank Williams Sr.

"I Ain't No Communist"—Grandpa Jones

"Truck-Crashin' Cousin"—Curtis Danny Glen H

"Achy-Breaky Heart"—Billy Ray Cyrus

"White Trash Shine My Shoes"—Mark Gilman and Jay Smith H

"A Truck Called Sunday School"—Don Schauda

"Truck Accordion"—Jonathan DeWitt Sampson

"Did I Shave My Legs for This?"—Deana Carter

"Did I Shave My Back for This?"—Cletus Judd (in response to Carter's song)

"She Ran Out of Give Before I Ran Out of Take"—Phil Lee

"Cheatin' Ain't Cheatin' When Nobody Knows"—Thomas Allen and Larry Lee

"Barroom Bathroom Stall"—Steven Tracy

"Scarlet O'Hara Is Alive and Well"—Mike Rayburn

Records Setting Records

Here are some record-breaking entries from the 1999 Guinness Book of World Records:

Garth Brooks became the most successful country music recording artist, selling more than $80 million worth of albums between 1989 and 1998.

The late Tammy Wynette, who was often called the "First Lady of Country Music," was the first female country music singer to sell a million records in 1969.

The late Conway Twitty had the most songs make the number-one spot on the country charts, with forty tunes on the Billboard hit list.

How Tootsie Kept Order in Her Lounge

In March 1960, Hattie Louise "Tootsie" Bess bought a lounge in Nashville near the Ryman Auditorium, then the home of the Grand Ole Opry. Tootsie's Orchid Lounge was

Hattie Louise "Tootsie" Bess

essentially a place for Opry performers and down-on-their-luck musicians to come, take their breaks, and have some of Tootsie's fried chicken and beer. Some of her regulars included Patsy Cline, Roger Miller, Willie Nelson, Kris Kristofferson, Tom T. Hall, and Loretta Lynn ("she usually came in to get Mooney," one long-time patron said).

How did Tootsie keep her patrons from getting too rambunctious? She didn't use a pistol to keep the peace, or even a burly bouncer. She used the time-honored lady's tool: a bejeweled lady's hat pin, that legend says crooner Charlie Pride gave Tootsie as a gift. Whoever acted up got stuck!

Although it's now under new ownership, it is rumored that proprietor Steve Smith still uses the hatpin, and I have never seen anyone act up at Tootsies.

Q&A

Q. What classical music label made Franklin its world headquarters in 1999?
A. NAXOS.

Q. What name was given to the Grand Ole Opry's show that performed for American soldiers at home and overseas during World War II?
A. Camel Caravan.

Q. In 1871 spirituals were introduced to other parts of the country by what group of black singers?
A. The Jubilee Singers, of Fisk University, Nashville.

Q. A 1963 plane crash near Camden killed what four musicians?
A. Patsy Cline, Cowboy Copas, Randy Hughes, and Hawkshaw Hawkins. An engraved boulder now marks the spot, which also has an interactive kiosk and gazebo.

Q. With what well-known Memphis personality did Isaac Hayes open a branch of the L. Ron Hubbard's School of Scientology in Memphis in 1997?
A. Lisa Marie Presley, daughter of the late Elvis Presley.

Q. The Country Music Awards were first broadcast on network TV in what year?
A. 1968.

Q. Who first coined the term "country music"?
A. Connie B. Gay.

Q. What country music celebrity interviewer wrote three books of memoirs entitled Memories, More Memories, and The View from Nashville?
A. Ralph Emery.

Q. After leaving the Opry, what singer/songwriter moved to Missouri, where he was host of one of the first successful country television programs, Ozark Jubilee?
A. Clyde Julian "Red" Foley (1910–1968).

Q. What man, known as the world's lowest bass singer, performed with the Blackwood Brothers and the Sunshine Boys, and toured with Elvis Presley?
A. J. D. Sumner.

Q. What popular Memphis entertainer, who (before his death in 2005) blended his music with Cajun, bluegrass, and jazz, was known as "Gatemouth"?
A. Clarence Brown.

Q. What grandfatherly type on the syndicated country TV show Hee Haw loved to belt out the song "Old Rattler"?
A. Grandpa Jones.

Q. On what nationally televised show did Elvis Presley first appear?
A. The Ed Sullivan Show, in 1956.

Q. What 1962 hit song by Lester Flatt of Flatt and Scruggs became the song for a popular TV show about some mountain people who discovered oil and suddenly became rich?
A. "The Ballad of Jed Clampett."

Q. "You Light Up My Life" was the hit song for what daughter of Pat Boone?
A. Debby Boone.

Q. What U.S. president said he favored country music above all other kinds of music?
A. George Bush Sr. (His favorite artist was Roy Acuff.)

Q. What group did Hendersonville resident Roy Orbison open for in England in 1963?
A. The Beatles. (They later wrote "Please Please Me" for him.)

Q. After he filled in for Hank Williams in 1952, what singer was immediately offered a contract with the show Louisiana Hayride?
A. Jim Reeves, who joined the Grand Ole Opry in 1955.

Q. Known as the "singing cowboy," what Grand Ole Opry star was also a stock-car racer?
A. Marty Robbins.

Q. What musician, with his "galloping guitar" method of picking, was the youngest member of the Country Music Hall of Fame when he was inducted in 1973?
A. Chet Atkins.

Q. What banjo-playing star of Hee-Haw and the Grand Ole Opry was tragically murdered in his home in Goodlettsville in the 1960s?
A. David Akeman, nicknamed "Stringbean."

Q. What do the call letters WSM stand for in the radio station that has always broadcast the Opry from Nashville?

A. "We Shield Millions," the motto of National Life and Accident Insurance Company, which originally owned the station.

Q. What was the "chitlin circuit," and how did it relate to the blues?
A. Blues nightclubs would serve chitlins as a side dish to their dinners.

Q. What Bristol-born entertainer, known for the song "Sixteen Tons," closed his TV shows with the signature line, "Bless your little pea-picking hearts"?
A. Tennessee Ernie Ford.

Q. What Jackson native wrote the hit song "Blue Suede Shoes"?
A. Carl Perkins.

Q. In 1967, the Country Music Association's first Entertainer of the Year award went to what country music singer?
A. Eddy Arnold.

Q. With their headquarters in Hendersonville, what group of contemporary country-pop groups released such well-known songs as "Sail Away" and "Elvira"?
A. The Oak Ridge Boys.

Q. When President Richard M. Nixon visited the Grand Ole Opry in 1974, what Opry star gave him yo-yo lessons?
A. Roy Acuff.

Q. James D. Vaughn transformed what city into the "capital of gospel music in America"?
A. Lawrenceburg.

Q. In the 1980 TV special Hank Williams: The Man and His Music, actor Henry Arnold played the part of what Nashville-based music publisher?
A. Fred Rose.

Q. What country music star was a heavyweight boxer in the Washington, D.C., area before making it in country music?
A. Roy Clark.

Q. In what Tennessee town did Elvis play his last concert--as a warm-up act?
A. Kingsport in 1955. (He preceded the Louvin Brothers and Cowboy Copas, for which he was paid around thirty-seven dollars.)

Q. What country music star, who made her acting debut in the science-fiction movie "Tremors," also starred as fictional race-car star A. J. Ferguson in the 1994 version of the movie, "The Little Rascals"?
A. Reba McEntire.

Q. The spiritual "They That Sow in Tears Shall Reap in Joy," which premiered in 1955 at Overton Park in Memphis, was written by what composer who died in 1958?
A. W. C. Handy.

Q. From 1954 to 1956, who was Hank Snow's manager?
A. Colonel Tom Parker

Q. When he appeared on the show "The Louisiana Hayride" in the 1950s, who called himself "the Singing Fisherman"?
A. Johnny Horton.

Q. What famous RCA studio in Nashville was built in 1957, at the insistence of Chet Atkins?
A. Studio B.

Q. What tune was played when Governor Frank Clement went to the podium to make the keynote address at the 1956 Democratic National Convention?
A. "The Tennessee Waltz."

Q. What was the first publication for country music and musicians to be published in the United States?
A. Country Music Roundup.

Q. Where is Elvis Presley's 1960 "Solid Gold Cadillac"?
A. Country Music Hall of Fame and Museum.

Q. What is the name of one of the world's largest music festivals, held every year in Manchester?
A. Bonnaroo.

Q. What small musical venue in Nashville is so intent on hearing the performers, that if you're talking you might get shushed?
A. The Bluebird Café. Many earnest, budding musicians come here, and you'll never know who you'll see or hear.

Q. Who was the first woman to be named Entertainer of the Year by the Country Music Association?
A. Loretta Lynn, in 1972.

Q. What name was given to musicians Willie Nelson, Waylon Jennings, Jessie Colter, and Tompall Glaser (and band), who found fame in Nashville?
A. The Outlaws.

CHAPTER THIRTEEN

Flora, Fauna, and Natural Phenomena

Reelfoot Lake: Earthquake City, Land of Eagles

In northwestern Tennessee, where Missouri, Kentucky, and Tennessee borders meet, there is a place unlike any other. Visiting Reelfoot Lake is like being on another planet or going back in time, when Earth was ruled more by animals than by humankind. Its topography gives it a sense of the surreal.

Reelfoot Lake is situated on the New Madrid fault, and back in the winter of 1811–12 huge earthquakes occurred there. Violence was such that a fissure opened between the Mississippi River and the Cypress Bottoms of the lake area. Archeologists have said that for three days the Mississippi River flowed backward, filling the bottoms and creating Reelfoot, the only large natural lake in Tennessee.

The cypress trees still stand, their wide wooden "knees" just above water level. Reelfoot has a lot of the fauna you might see in the rest of this part of the country: egrets, loons, ospreys, cormorants, and blue herons. You'll see evidence of quail, deer, doves, and turkeys—and if you're quiet enough, you might even spot them. The forests around the lake abound with raccoons, rabbits, and squirrels, and there have been more than fifty-six different species of fish caught in the lake.

Bald Eagles nest in the cypress swamps of Reelfoot Lake

From October through the end of March, Reelfoot is the busiest.

Ducks, not by the thousands, but by the hundreds of thousands, come to Reelfoot to winter. The mallard population alone has surpassed four hundred thousand, with nearly one hundred thousand Canada geese.

When you think of Tennessee, do you think of bald eagles? Probably not, but Reelfoot Lake is one of their winter homes and nesting areas, and you can take guided tours to see their aeries—incredible nests of twigs and sticks that average six feet across.

There are quite a few ways to experience Reelfoot Lake, even if you don't have a boat. The park offers "eagle tours" in winter months, when the eagles are there and active. Guides also offer "Deep Swamp Canoe Trips," and if you've ever been lost in a swamp, you'll want to avoid that, and take advantage of a guide. The park also offers pontoon boat cruises. There are also angling tournaments throughout the year for those who would like to see what they can catch in the lake.

When you see it for yourself, you'll understand why this area was the favorite hunting ground of David Crockett and Jim Bowie. See "Virtual Tennessee" for website information.

Did You Know?

Shelby County has more horses per capita than any other county in the United States.

What in the Sandhill?

Every February the people of the Birchwood community (about thirty miles northeast of Chattanooga) hold the Sandhill Crane Festival to celebrate the more than thirty-five thousand sandhill cranes that use the nearby Hiwassee Wildlife Refuge to rest from their migrations. The cranes arrive from southern Canada and the Great Lakes region every October to winter in northern Florida or southern Georgia, but more and more of them have been choosing to remain in Tennessee. In the middle of one recent winter, for example, there were more than five thousand sandhill cranes staying in the Hiwassee Wildlife Refuge. The last ones leave by the latter part of March each year.

Hohenwald's Elephants

In the tiny hamlet of Hohenwald, people who live a few miles outside the town are awakened every morning, not to birdsong, nor to rooster crow, but to elephant trumpeting. Hohenwald is the host to the Elephant Sanctuary, the "first natural environment for elephants in the United States," according to its codirectors, Carol Buckley and Scott Blais.

Residents of the Elephant Sanctuary in Hohenwald enjoy a light snack of watermelons. (Courtesy of the Elephant Sanctuary in Hohenwald)

When circuses, zoos, and other entertainment-oriented businesses had no further use for their old elephants, there was no place for the pachyderms to go. And when elephants are no longer capable of performing, their upkeep becomes too expensive. Elephants eat around 150 pounds of hay and grain daily, at an annual cost of around twelve thousand dollars.

Thus, many elephants, especially Asian ones, were neglected—even starving.

Enter Buckley and Blais. Recognizing that Hohenwald's environment is similar to Asia's, they decided to settle their sanctuary in that part of Tennessee. Their first elephant arrived in 1995. True to the meaning of the term sanctuary, no tourists are allowed, although you can see the elephants via teleconferencing or accessing the Elephant Sanctuary's website.

Here the pachyderms are free to graze, wander the 112-acre sanctuary—and paint. "With more than one hundred thousand muscles in their trunks," Buckley explained, "they're very adept at picking up small things or wielding a paintbrush." Their best artist is Tarra; when I wrote the first edition for this book, I got to watch her paint, and I still have her "signed" original. As of press time (2020), Tarra was still going strong. Now, besides viewing the pachyderms on cameras, people can get involved in other ways, and donate by adopting elephants, purchasing needed supplies, and buying clothing and other goods that support the Elephant Sanctuary's mission. See "Virtual Tennessee" for website information.

Did You Know?

The town of Sweetwater is home to the Lost Sea, the largest underground lake in the country. Here, under the guidance of the tour staff, you can ride a glass-bottomed boat and see some of the largest rainbow trout on this continent, breathtaking cave formations, and rare cave flowers called "anthodites," found in only a few caves throughout the world. See "Virtual Tennessee" for website information.

A "Gem" of a Tale, or the Story of "Many Pearls"

Tipper Gore and first lady Hillary Clinton wore Tennessee pearls at President Bill Clinton's inauguration. Elizabeth Taylor visited Tennessee and bought an exquisite strand. Others, unaware that the Tennessee state gem is the freshwater pearl, have virtually stumbled upon where the pearls are cultured. They come from the Birdsong pearl farm in tiny Camden, the only commercial pearl farm in the nation. Since the pearl farm's first days in the early 1960s, Tennessee's pearl industry has grown to a multimillion-dollar-a-year business.

It all started when South Dakota–born John Latendresse and his wife, Chessy, became interested in starting a commercial pearl farm. He had picked up a knowledge of the "musseling business" when he served in the marines in World War II and then began pearl trading along the Mississippi and Tennessee Rivers. After he and his wife studied the pearl-buying business in New York City, they decided to locate their pearl-making operation on the banks of the Tennessee River.

They chose Tennessee as the site for their pearl farm because of its moderate water temperature—fifty to seventy degrees—and for its lime content, two conditions that help set the stage for pearl production. The Latendresses spent thirty years adapting culturing techniques used on Japan's saltwater akoya oysters to Tennessee's freshwater mussels, and their efforts have paid off. Their operation has been written about in National Geographic, Southern Living, and other highly regarded national and international publications.

When I first visited and interviewed Birdsong's owners and asked about details, neither they nor their operation's tour manager, Bob Keast, would tell exactly how they do it. What do you know? They "clammed up."

A Duck's Tale

A ritual involving ducks has been happening twice a day at the Peabody Hotel in Memphis for nearly 100 years. It is here that ducks parade, marching to the large marble fountain in the lobby, waddling their way from the elevator over red carpet for a swim.

This "ducky" tradition was started in 1932, when hotel manager Frank Schutt returned from a hunting trip and thought the addition of his live decoys to the lobby fountain would be an interesting touch. Making their feathery march at 11:00 a.m. and 5:00 p.m., the ducks take twice-a-day constitutionals, which have made them, and the Peabody Hotel, world-famous.

Tennessee Walking Horses

Tennesseans, with their neighbors from all over the world, get together for ten days every summer in Shelbyville, for what is now called simply "the Celebration," a festival and competition featuring the famed Tennessee Walking Horse.

Originally bred for long rides around the plantation, these horses were called a lot of different names, including "all-purpose horse" and "southern plantation saddle horse." As breeders in Middle Tennessee came to have a reputation for raising horses with a smooth, even gait, buyers came from outside the area wanting to buy "those walking horses," and that was the name that stuck. If it's a good walker, the horse has a disposition that is as easy as its ride.

The Tennessee walking horse became a recognized breed in 1935, when the Tennessee Walking Horse Breeders' Association was organized in Lewisburg. From that time on, this special breed of horse has enjoyed an incredible popularity, as has the Celebration. The original Tennessee Walking Horse was F Allen One. Another famous stud, Strolling Jim, was trained by his owner, Floyd Carothers, on the grounds of the hotel now called the Walking Horse Hotel in Wartrace.

In the 1939 competition, Strolling Jim was named the first Tennessee Walking Horse World Grand Champion. Wartrace then became known as "the Cradle of the Tennessee Walking Horse." Strolling Jim is buried behind the old hotel, but folks around there say they sometimes see his ghost strolling the grounds as he did in the old days.

Mule Day in Columbia

Since the 1930s, if you were in the market to buy a mule, you'd come to the town of Columbia to look for one. What started with some mules and their traders gathering to meet with prospective buyers has become known as Mule Day, now the world's largest mule market.

Mule Day is a regular event held every April, complete with music, dancing, and a big parade. (Mule Day 2000 was celebrated as "the Mule-Lennium.") But who really buys mules nowadays? Well, the Amish for one. And ever ride a mule down into the Grand Canyon? Those mules are bred in Tennessee. Good mules don't come cheap. A proper pair of mules might lighten your wallet by around six or seven thousand dollars.

Puts mules in a whole other light, doesn't it? Maybe next time you pass a mule, you'll tip your hat.

Kind of Like a Beauty Contest: The Rules for Mules

Curious as to exactly how mules are judged, I located a man by the name of Jerry Erwin, who used to be co-chairman of the Mule Day event. Here's what he said:

"It's kinda like a beauty contest. I mean, if you're judging a mule, you want the best-looking one. They must have long ears erected on the corners of the head. The face must have little fat under the jawbone. They must have a thin neck, wide chest, and a straight back. Their body must have graceful lines, and the back legs must be only slightly bowed.

"Their hooves should be medium-sized, not too big or small. No pigeon-toes. No knock-knees. They should be a big-boned animal with good muscle tone and development. They should have a nice walk and carry themselves well."

He almost made me break out in song—something like, "There she is..."

Tiger, Tiger...

On forty-seven acres outside Kingsport in East Tennessee, the residents do the kinds of things you might expect on a farm, like go out and feed the livestock. But in this case the "stock" isn't cows, pigs, and chickens. Here the stock is fed twelve hundred pounds of red meat. This is a sanctuary known as Tiger Haven, a safe place for unwanted tigers, leopards, lions, and other big animals in the feline family, one of only about five in

the United States.

Tiger Haven was established in 1991 for big cats who had been abused and mistreated, and it has grown to include more than sixty-three such animals. Despite anxiety from nervous neighbors, there have never been any escapes from Tiger Haven.

Where do these unwanted cats come from? A problem occurs when regular folks buy the cats, thinking they would make a "different" or exotic kind of pet. Well, they are different, but they are not meant to be pets. When I first interviewed owner Joe Parker back in 2000, he said, "When people see big cats perform on TV and in circuses, it creates a desire to possess such beauty and power while leading us to believe we can contain and control the power and emotions of a great cat. With most states having no laws regulating the commerce and keeping of cats, the regular folks wanting to raise a giant, lovable "Tigger" for their kids suddenly found themselves broke from feeding the cat--and fearing for their lives. Even if a big cat means no harm, playing with a heavy animal with sharp claws and teeth can end in disaster."

Zoos don't take these unwanted animals because of their licensing requirements—no stray cats allowed. So what happens to a big cat when it's no longer wanted or needed by its original owner? It may be euthanized or even sent to a "game ranch" to be hunted.

At Tiger Haven, the big cats roam, play, and live out their days in one of the few places in the nation designed solely for their safety and sanctuary. There are many ways to support Tiger Haven, including adopting a cat and purchasing t-shirts and other products to support the cause. See "Virtual Tennessee" for website information.

Gotta Have a Dog Story!

In 1927 a blind man in Nashville named Morris Frank heard about a program in Switzerland that trained dogs to be used by the police and the military, and as guide dogs for the Red Cross. If dogs could do that, he thought, why couldn't they be used to assist sightless people? Franks contacted Dorothy Harrison Eustis, the woman who trained dogs in the Swiss Alps. She wasn't certain if dogs could be trained to assist blind persons, but she found a dog and trainer.

When Franks returned to Nashville with his new best friend, Buddy Fortunate Fields, called simply "Buddy," he commenced to challenge the "no dogs" rule prevalent in business establishments in the city. Stemming from this

success, Franks established the Seeing Eye, the oldest guide dog school in America, now with its headquarters in New Jersey.

The Seeing Eye, the world-famous dog guide training school, was first incorporated in the city of Nashville in 1929. Its headquarters was at the First National Bank Building. Franks and his guide dog, Buddy, played a critical role in the founding of the school and its success. The Seeing Eye was moved to New Jersey in 1931. There is a historical marker near where the first dog guide training school was held, in downtown Nashville.

Since This Chapter Includes Flora...

Tennessee is home to an incredible abundance of plant life, a lot of it noteworthy. The variety and abundance of trees alone is enough to give Tennesseans bragging rights. In the Great Smoky Mountains National Park, there are more species of trees than in all of Europe. In the spring, throngs of people come to Tennessee just to see the wildflowers. In the fields and forests of Tennessee you'll find virtually every wildflower there is, from arbutus and bloodroot, to trillium and yarrow (no, I couldn't find one that started with z).

Folks at the Chattanooga Department of Tourism told me that, that in their area, more than three hundred kinds of trees and nine hundred varieties of wildflowers grow—and this is more than any other place on earth with the exception of Central China.

Like its neighboring states, Tennessee is partly covered with a vine that most consider a nuisance: kudzu. It drapes across old barns, nearly covering the words "See Rock City" painted on roofs and adorns interstate signs. Brought to the Southern U.S. from Asia as part of an anti-erosion campaign, it has become like the proverbial four-day guest: no longer welcome. It grows at the prodigious rate of nearly a foot a day in good conditions, so you can't just cut it back and think you're done for the season. A hard frost stops it, but it never really goes away. It's so prevalent that not only have Tennesseans just about given up fighting it, they've embraced it as part of their culture. There's even a cartoon strip named Kudzu.

The interest in alternative medicine has brought with it research into what herbs and wildflowers (and even kudzu) can do for people. Guess what? Kudzu has been found by some medical researchers to be an effective aid in the fight against alcoholism. Maybe it'll become another of Tennessee's cash crops.

In the old days, when a Tennessean needed medicine, he or she just went out into the back yard or the nearby woods to locate the plant that would do the trick. Now it seems all of America has discovered this, but it's not "alternative medicine" to a lot of old-timers; it's just the way they've always done it.

And While We're on the Subject of Alternative Medicine...

The village of Red Boiling Springs is aptly named, because of the red-tinted water that was discovered there in 1830, bubbling up from the ground. Early settlers claimed this water had healing properties, and Red Boiling Springs boomed as a mineral springs resort until the Great Depression of the 1930s. Three hotels from that time have survived, and tourists still come to "take the waters." Every May, Red Boiling Springs hosts a three-day-long Folk Medicine Festival. People who visit Red Boiling Springs swear it's a cure-all—and at the very least, it's fun.

Unique Features of Great Smoky Mountains National Park

When in 2000 I was writing the first edition for this book, I interviewed Nancy Gray, park spokesperson. She related these intriguing facts to me: "The diversity of plants, animals, and trees is unique because of the elevation and orientation of the park (the way the mountains are positioned, going from north to south).

"At least sixteen native mammals live there, including the black bear (the park is the largest black bear reserve in the East).

"There are about two hundred species of birds, including the scissor-tailed flycatcher, the western kingbird, the cliff swallow, tanagers, and finches.

"The park provides the only habitat in the world for Cain's reed-bent grass, Rugel's ragwort, and Jordan's red-cheeked salamander.

"Within the park are over seven hundred miles of streams offering scenic beauty and housing a diversity of aquatic life.

"Almost 95 percent of the 516,000 acres in the park is forested, with about 25 percent of the park forest never having been disturbed."

The park preserves a unique collection of log buildings, such as those found in Cades Cove, and it maintains seventy-five historic structures depicting various aspects of pioneer life. I myself have been a regular visitor to the park for more than six decades now and have yet to see it all. It's unlike any other place in the world! See "Virtual Tennessee" for website information.

Over 10,000 species of flora and fauna have been counted in the GSMNP so far. On one of my visits naturalists were counting beetles like this fellow here.

Q&A

Q. Harcourt A. Morgan was elected to the Tennessee Agricultural Hall of Fame in 1951, in part because of his research on what two types of insects?
A. Boll weevil and cattle tick.

Q. What is the smallest of Tennessee's ducks?
A. The green-winged teal.

Q. What birds are nicknamed "fish hawks"?
A. Ospreys, which live in nests around Tennessee lakes and rivers.

Q. What natural formation in Tennessee is thirty-two miles long but undetectable from the air?
A. Cumberland Caverns, near McMinnville, the largest cave in the southeastern United States and among the largest in the world. There are daily guided tours.

Q. To restore the eastern wild turkey to its previous numbers, the Tennessee Wildlife Resource Agency (TWRA) uses what procedure?
A. Hacking, which involves capturing turkeys in one area and releasing them in another.

Q. What state park is found in the center of a bustling downtown area?
A. Nashville's Bicentennial Mall, the only state park in Tennessee that's located in a city.

Q. Augustin Gattinger, who moved to Nashville from Germany as a young man, not only practiced medicine but also wrote what book on plant life in Tennessee, now regarded as a classic in its field?
A. Tennessee Flora.

Q. Each February, the city of Grand Junction sponsors what canine event that draws contestants from across the nation?
A. National Field Trials, held at the Ames Plantation.

Q. What is the Tennessee state fossil?
A. Pteratrigonia (scabrotrigonia) thoracica, which resembles a mussel. It was first dug up in Coon Creek, McNairy County.

Q. What plateau is so large that to get to Middle Tennessee early settlers traveled through Kentucky to go around it?
A. Cumberland Plateau.

Q. What is the state game bird?
A. The bobwhite quail.

Q. What is the state wildflower?
A. Passionflower.

Q. What are Tennessee's two state insects?
A. The firefly and ladybug.

Q. Thomas Sharpe Spencer, who arrived in Middle Tennessee in 1776 and was one of the earliest white settlers, spent one winter in the shelter of what kind of hollow tree?
A. A large sycamore tree, in Bledsoe County.

Q. What is the official state animal?
A. Raccoon.

Q. What is the name of the largest species of woodpecker still in existence, which nests in Tennessee?
A. Pileated woodpecker, with a height of about eighteen inches.

No Problems with Mosquitoes Here

Every evening in the balmy months, you can go by Nickajack Cave Refuge outside Chattanooga and at dusk watch as tens of thousands of bats fly out for their supper of mosquitoes and other pests.

The Tennessee Aquarium, Where You Can See the Water Creatures of the World

The Tennessee Aquarium in Chattanooga is the largest freshwater aquarium in the world, but there's much more to it than that. There are also huge saltwater tanks full of various kinds of sharks, stingrays, and other ocean-going creatures. All in all, a total of over nine thousand aquatic animals from around the world are under one enormous roof. Some tanks, for example, have exhibits of creatures from such varied places as the Amazon River in South America, the Volga River in Russia, and the Congo River in Africa. You can also view such animals as the Goliath bird-eating tarantula, the emperor scorpion, and the rhinoceros pit viper.

At the Tennessee Aquarium you can find such diverse aquatic creatures as river otters from the Louisiana bayou and red Oscars from the Amazon River

When you go, make sure you are there during feeding time, when divers go into the tanks to hand-feed sharks, rays, and moray eels.

This May Be the Strangest Kitchen in the World!

Here's just a sampling of the kind of monthly grocery list needed for the kitchen at the Tennessee Aquarium to prepare food for its denizens:

35,000 crickets
33,300 worms
1,200 pounds of restaurant-quality seafood
150 rats
300 mice

An Island... Built by a Gunboat!

In 1910 a Spanish-American War gunboat headed up the Mississippi River and weighed anchor offshore at Memphis, waiting for high water to make the river more navigable. Sand, gravel, and other debris began to deposit against the hull, and months later, after the gunboat raised anchor and left, what came to be known as Mud Island continued to grow.

Over a half century later, the people of Memphis decided to make good use of the fifty-two-acre real estate in the river by constructing a park. Among other things, it now contains a five-block-long scale model of the lower Mississippi; the River Museum containing an 1870 steamboat and part of a Union gunboat; a concert amphitheater; and swimming facilities.

Memphians certainly know how to make good use of real estate—especially when it's new real estate.

Mud Island River Park in Memphis

Justin P. Wilson Cumberland Trail State Scenic Trail State Park

In June of 1998, Governor Don Sundquist announced plans for a new, "different" kind of park in the Volunteer State. With its headquarters in Caryville, the park was first known as Cumberland Trail State Park, but was later renamed Justin P. Wilson Cumberland Trail State Scenic Trail State Park (Wilson was the Deputy Governor of Tennessee from 1996 to 2003, and is now the comptroller, but was one of the leading visionaries behind the creation of this unique park).

So, what makes this park unique in all the state? Tennessee's first and only linear park is around 220 miles long, meandering through eleven counties in Tennessee, from the Tennessee River Gorge to the Cumberland Gap National Historic Park, which is located at the Tennessee-Virginia-Kentucky border. The park contains more than 180 miles of trails, and hikers are rewarded with amazing vistas along their journey. See "Virtual Tennessee" for website information.

You Can View Three States from Here!

Cumberland Gap National Historical Park (CGNHP) is a great way to spend a day or one of those long weekends, just being in nature. This 24,000-acre piece of forested Paradise (with its headquarters just outside Middlesboro, Kentucky) was first established in 1940, but many improvements have been made since then.

The Visitor Center, for example, has displays and two short film documentaries about the park's history. Hiking enthusiasts can enjoy the many paths in the park, including Ridge Trail which runs the length of the park. Tri-State Peak rewards visitors with a splendid panoramic view of Kentucky, Virginia and Tennessee (and a large stone 3-d map explains what you're seeing).

Skylight Cave

History buffs will love walking around the restored, old structures, such as the Hensley Settlement, which was one of the original settler family's cabins.

Those who love to explore caves have their rewards, too: Skylight Cave is accessible by hiking a moderately challenging 1.4-mile trail, and Sand Cave rewards hikers with an awe-inspiring arching entrance. Gap Cave is a ranger-guided tour. There is also a campground within three miles of the park entrance which offers campers many amenities (such as firewood and hot showers in the comfort stations).

Just before press time (in 2020), I read that Blue Ridge Outdoor Magazine referred to CGNHP as "The South's best kept secret." After your visit, you will agree with them! See "Virtual Tennessee" for website information.

Q&A

Q. Crossing the state twice, what river creates the three Grand Divisions of Tennessee?
A. Tennessee.

Q. What are Tennessee's two state rocks?
A. Agate and limestone.

Q. How many miles of streams does Tennessee have within its boundaries?
A. 19,000.

Q. What U.S. senator was responsible for the legislation making the Big South Fork Area a National Recreation Area?
A. Howard H. Baker Jr.

Q. Natchez Trace State Park contains the largest tree of what species, reputed to be a world record?
A. Pecan.

Q. A blue catfish caught in the Cumberland River in June 1998 weighed in at what world record?
A. 112 pounds.

Q. What is the smallest mammal in Tennessee?
A. The short-tailed shrew.

Q. What is the largest owl found in the state?
A. The great horned owl.

Q. Both Native Americans and early Tennessee settlers used an extract from the bark of what flowering tree as a cure for fevers?
A. Dogwood.

Q. In 1820 what famous naturalist and artist visited the western Tennessee area and recorded the varieties and numbers of birds he found there?
A. John James Audubon.

Q. Roan Mountain State Park contains the world's largest stand of what kind of shrub, the stands of which early settlers called "hells"?
A. Rhododendron. If you've ever gotten lost in a rhododendron hell, you'll understand!

Q. The Memphis Zoo was home to what famous lion until he died in 1944?
A. The Metro-Goldwyn-Mayer "roaring lion."

Q. What site has the highest underground waterfall and is the deepest cave open to tourists in the United States?
A. Ruby Falls.

Q. After whom is Ruby Falls named?
A. Ruby Lambert, wife of explorer Leo Lambert, who first discovered the falls.

Q. What kinds of things are there to do at Ruby Falls?
A. There are a variety of cave tours, as well as zip-lining activities, and various events throughout the year. In 2019-2020, Ruby Falls completed a $20 million dollar expansion, which included a greater variety of dining options.

Q. In what year did Congress establish the Great Smoky Mountains National Park?
A. 1934.

Q. What continuous footpath that travels from Maine to Georgia for a total length of 2,140 miles also goes through part of Tennessee?
A. The Appalachian Trail. People who hike the "AT" in its entirety are called "thru-hikers."

Q. Herman Baggenstoss began the bulletin "Turkey Feathers, Boar Bristles and Fish Fins" that evolved into the periodical Tennessee Wildlife and now is called by what name?
A. The Tennessee Conservationist.

Q. What natural stone formation is one of the largest in the world?
A. Twin Arches, in Big South Fork National River and Recreation Area. The South Arch has a clearance of 70 feet and a span of more than 135 feet; the North Arch is somewhat smaller.

CHAPTER FOURTEEN

Speech, Food and Fascinating Cultural Tidbits

The Way Tennesseans Say It

Speech patterns and grammar usage vary within the three so-called Grand Divisions of West, Middle, and East Tennessee (which are, incidentally, represented by the three stars of the state flag). West Tennesseans speak with a more "Deep South" kind of drawl than people in the rest of the state, while in Middle Tennessee, language patterns reveal the influence of the Kentucky Bluegrass Region. East Tennesseans' speech may be the most colorful of all, because their linguistic patterns stem from old Briticisms, which have been retained due to the relative isolation of those Tennesseans in the mountainous area of the state.

If there's one thing that sets strangers apart from locals, it's the pronunciation of Appalachia. Visitors usually say "Apple-AY-cha," but the "right" way is "Appah-LATCH-a."

When you come to visit people in Tennessee, it doesn't matter what your business is. You first ask them how they are, how the family is, and maybe even how their dog is (if they don't have a pet, they're sure to be renovating their car or house, or following a particular sport). After all this is out of the way, you'll probably be asked if you'd like something to drink. It might be coffee, it might be sweet iced tea, and after the sun's setting behind the nearest sycamore tree, you might be offered something stronger. Then, and only then, is it polite to discuss the reason for your visit.

This pattern of manners is one reason northerners say things move so slowly in the South—but then, Tennesseans have a lot more fun taking their time.

Glossary to Help You Communicate with the Natives

A-fixing: getting ready to do something.

Aim: intend or plan. "I aim to chop wood tomorrow."

Book read: well educated; read up on, to study something.

Crick: something you have in your neck or back, a kind of stiffness or pain; also the pronunciation of creek, a small stream.

Poke: a container, usually a bag. "I need a poke to carry these turnip greens home in."

Put out: angry or upset, as in, "You look awful put out. What's wrong?"

Shed of: get rid of or do away with. "I'm getting shed of that coon hound tomorrow. He's no good."

Doin's: function or event; big doin's, a really important function or event.

Far piece: pronounced "fur piece;" a long distance.

Fetch: bring, as in, "Fetch me that kettle."

Frog-strangler or Gully-washer: a torrential rain.

Lollygagging: loafing or loitering. "Stop your lollygagging, we've got to get to church!"

Mess of: a lot of, as in, "That's a mess of fish you got there."

Parts: usually refers to a geographical area, as in, "He's not from these parts."

Plumb: totally or completely, as in, "You look plumb tuckered out."

Skittish: nervous or jittery. "My dog gets a little skittish in a thunder-storm."

Smack-dab: right in the middle of. (Hey, even James Taylor used this term in his song "Up on a Roof": "right smack-dab in the middle of town.")

Take a gander: look at, check out.

Tuckered out: tired.

Uppity or Biggety: someone who's being snobbish or stuck-up.

Want to Go to to Paris? You Don't Even Have to Leave Tennessee!

Just about 2 hours from the bustling city of Nashville lies the small (population approximately 11,000) village of Paris. Its lovely courthouse, pleasant parks, and quiet way of life (except during the "World's Biggest Fish Fry" every April) makes for a nice place to get away from it all. You'll have to stop for a photo-op at their own Eiffel Tower.

In 1990, engineering students commemorated that year's "Memphis in May" with a replica of the Eiffel Tower (every year the students chose a country to honor). After it was over, it was offered to the city of Paris.

Home Cookin'

No matter where you go in Tennessee, food is important. Some health-conscious, well-meaning soul might try to explain how bad some of the traditional foods are, from a health standpoint. That person might get enlightened to the fact that most Tennesseans were raised on fried catfish and hushpuppies, fried okra and cornbread with chitlins, and Lumberjack Special breakfasts. Plus, an old relative (Great-Aunt

Eloise or Great-Uncle Augustus) ate this every day of her or his life and lived to a ripe old age, never spent a day in the hospital, and died smoking a pipe to boot.

Tennesseans like their barbecue, country ham, biscuits and cornbread, sweet tea, and turnip greens and black-eyed peas with bacon drippings. You'll see food like this at all kinds of events: cemetery-decorating days, family reunions, tailgate parties, and church potlucks.

On the TV show Hee Haw, the late great Grandpa Jones would answer the question, "What's for supper?" These are the foods that most Tennesseans probably had on the table as he reeled off his menu.

The Vilest-Smelling, Sweetest-Tasting Weed in East Tennessee

Every April the people in Polk County have their Annual Ramp Festival. The ramp is a wild onion-like plant of the Allium family that grows only in the Appalachian Mountains.

For Tennesseans, that's special enough to celebrate, with craft shows, lots of live bluegrass and country music, and, of course, plenty of ramps to eat (and they're in just about everything except maybe the ice cream). President Truman was the guest of honor at the very first Ramp Festival in 1954.

Here's how you cook 'em:

Holland Reese's Ramps and Eggs

Rinse ramps with cool water until they are really clean; then chop them. Heat bacon grease until very hot in large iron skillet. Place chopped ramps in skillet and cook for 25 to 30 minutes. Add three dozen scrambled eggs, salt to taste, and heat. Serve with bacon and fried cornbread.

When Tennessee Was Host to the World

In June 1976, Nashville hosted a meeting of the entire United Nations, including ambassadors, their bodyguards, and their families. This was the only time the United Nations has ever met socially in the United States outside of New York. The meeting was all top secret until a few weeks before, with media coverage coordinated by Brooks Parker, press secretary for Governor Ray Blanton.

Food preparation to serve more than sixteen hundred was overseen by the late chef and my long-time friend, Phila Hach of Montgomery County. She served them traditional southern fare. The United Nations enjoyed mint julep frappé, Tennessee country ham, catfish and hush puppies, southern fried chicken, cornbread, green beans with ham hocks, corn on the cob, and Hach's famous southern pecan pie (see recipe below). The meal was served in Centennial Park.

Recipes You Might Want to Try

Every good cook in the Volunteer State will tell you his or her recipe for their favorite dish is the best. Here are just a few:

Phila Hach's Best Pecan Pie in the World

3 eggs
1 teaspoon vanilla
3 tablespoons melted margarine
1/2 teaspoon salt

1/2 cup sugar
1 cup Karo syrup
1 cup chopped pecans
1 unbaked pie crust

Beat eggs slightly. Add vanilla, margarine, salt, sugar, and Karo syrup. Blend well. Add chopped pecans. Pour in pie crust. Bake for 12 minutes at 375°; reduce heat to 325° and continue baking until pie is set.

Vernon Summerlin's Gar Balls and Rusty Gravy

Vernon Summerlin, former editor of Tennessee Angler Magazine, is the author of many books, including a cookbook on preparing game. This recipe works equally well with alligator gar or catfish.

2 1/2 pounds gar (or catfish), ground
1/2 cup bell peppers, ground
2 cups water
2 eggs
1 pound whole tomatoes
1 cup onions, minced
2 tablespoons salt
1 teaspoon black pepper
1/2 cup oil, plus extra for browning
1 1/2 cups flour, plus extra for dusting
Thoroughly mix all the ingredients in a large bowl. Shape into large balls, dust with flour, and brown in oil in a heavy skillet. Cook until done.

<u>Gravy</u>

3 tablespoons flour
tomato juice (enough to make desired consistency)
2 cups water

In a skillet, brown flour, tomato juice, and water. Crumble two gar/fish balls into gravy, stirring well to make heavy gravy. Add remaining gar/fish balls to gravy, being careful not to break them. Cover skillet and simmer 30 minutes. Serve gravy over hot rice. Serves around 6.

A Springtime-Only Dish

In east Tennessee, people living there will go out in early spring to look for what they call "fiddlehead ferns." These are ferns that grow wild in the forests of east Tennessee. When they first begin to sprout and just before they unfurl, they are called "fiddleheads."

Locals like to cut these fiddleheads, and when they get about a basketful, will carry them home and saute them with garlic, butter and maybe a little olive oil. To me, they taste like asparagus, and locals say it's a "powerful" spring tonic.

Everytown, Tennessee: Where You Can Eat Like a Local

Pretty much every town in Tennessee has what locals call a "meat 'n three," where you order a meat (like fried chicken or meatloaf) and three vegetables. When you're visiting, ask a local, "Where's a good meat-n-three?" and you'll get plenty of answers.

Tennessee is awash with good cooks and good restaurants that serve up local fare. One place in particular, the Museum of Appalachia in Norris, has a restaurant specializing in Southern Appalachian country cooking. And Tennessee cooking is so fantastic, that the Tennessee State Museum in Nashville had an exhibit in 2019-early 2020 called "Let's Eat: Origins and Evolutions of Tennessee Food."

Venison Sauerbraten with Gingersnap Gravy

This is my own recipe, which appeared in Vernon Summerlin's book on game cooking.

3-to-4-pound venison roast
2 red onions, diced
3 bay leaves
peppercorns
whole cloves
teaspoons salt
1 3⁄4 cups red wine vinegar (or apple cider vinegar)
cup boiling water
tablespoons bacon drippings or shortening
gingersnap cookies, crushed to make at least 3⁄4 cup
teaspoons brown sugar

Put roast in a glass bowl or crock with onions, bay leaves, peppercorns, cloves, salt, vinegar, and boiling water. Cover with a tight-fitting lid; refrigerate for at least three days. Turn the roast twice a day in the marinade.

After three days, remove meat, saving marinade. Sear roast in heavy skillet on all sides. Put in a slow electric cooker or large, heavy pot, simmer on low for around 31⁄2 hours or until meat is tender. Remove roast from the pot and keep it warm while you make the gravy.

To make gingersnap gravy, strain the simmered marinade. Add water, if needed, to make 21⁄2 cups liquid. Cover and simmer 10 minutes; then add crushed gingersnaps and brown sugar. Simmer for another 5 minutes.

Pass gravy with roast and pour over potatoes or rice, and meat.

A Little about Poke Salad

This coarse perennial herb's botanical name is Phytolacca americana, but old-timers in Tennessee call the edible green "poke sallet." It grows wild in the woods and fields and although the root is said to be poisonous, the tender green leaves and young stems are delicious when cooked tender. Some people strip the stalk on the older plants; cut it in half-inch pieces; roll it in meal, salt, and pepper; and fry it as they would okra. Whether it's called poke salad or poke sallet, it's worth a try.

Old-timer's Poke Salad

This recipe was told to me by an old Appalachian woman who said, "Honey, please don't bother folks about my name. Just give 'em the recipe." So I'm telling you just what she said:

"The trick of it is to pick the poke while it's tender . . . about a foot high, I'd say, in late April when it's the best. You pick your poke, stems and leaves, while it's young, about 2 pounds of that. After you wash it, you put it in about 2 or 3 quarts of water. Make sure it's covered with the water, and boil it till it's tender. Then take a big colander and pour the poke and water in it and drain it. Squeeze out all the moisture, as much as you can. Have you an iron skillet, that's the best, about a 10- or 12-inch skillet. Get your bacon drippings, about a half a cup of bacon drippings, and put it in there. Add your drained poke salad; break it apart with your hands as you add it. Cook it good in the grease, about 5 or 10 minutes in there.

"Break 6 eggs in a bowl, mix them with a fork, and pour that with your salt and pepper into the poke in the skillet. Cook the eggs and mix it with the poke until they're done. It's really good. You can also take the bacon and crumble it over. Some people put a little minced onion, but old-timers don't do it that way.

"We'll have this for supper with hot cornbread and fresh churned butter and sweet tea. There's nothin' better."

Tennessee Barbecue Sauce, Jack Daniel's Style

1 medium onion, finely chopped
1 clove garlic, minced
2 tablespoons vegetable oil
1 1/2 cups catsup
1/4 cup brown sugar
2 tablespoons Jack Daniel's whiskey
1 teaspoon liquid smoke
2 1/2 tablespoons cider vinegar
1/2 teaspoon dry mustard
2 drops hot pepper sauce

Sauté onion and garlic in vegetable oil until tender. Stir in the remaining ingredients and bring to a boil over medium heat. Reduce heat and simmer for 10 minutes. Makes about 2 cups. Great for chicken, pork, and beef.

Prize-Winning Cornbread

At South Pittsburg's annual National Cornbread Festival the last weekend in April, the Cornbread Cook-off usually gets around seven hundred entries. Usually one hundred thousand people attend the festivities, which include music, crafts, children's activities, and, of course, cornbread. Festival executive board member Beth Duggar gave me this winning recipe.

Reuben Casserole with Cornbread

(27-ounce) can sauerkraut, drained
2 medium tomatoes, thinly sliced
1/3 cup Thousand Island salad dressing
1/3 cup sliced black olives, drained
2 tablespoons butter or margarine
9 ounces sliced corned beef, shredded
2 cups shredded Swiss cheese
1 cup Martha White cornmeal mix
1/3 cup Martha White self-rising flour
1 teaspoon sugar
1 egg, slightly beaten
1 cup buttermilk
1/3 cup whole milk (or 2 percent)
3 tablespoons oil

Heat oven to 425°. Spread sauerkraut in ungreased cast-iron skillet. Arrange tomato slices over sauerkraut; spread with salad dressing; dot with 2 tablespoons butter and sprinkle with black olives. Top with corned beef and cheese. Bake for 15 minutes.

While casserole is baking, combine cornmeal, flour, sugar, egg, buttermilk, milk, and oil. Stir until well mixed. Remove skillet from oven. Pour cornbread mixture over baked mixture. Return to oven and bake for 15 to 20 minutes or until cornbread is golden brown.

Serve with Quick Mustard Sauce, if desired. Serves 6 to 8.

Quick Mustard Sauce

1/2 cup mayonnaise
1/2 teaspoon prepared mustard
1 teaspoon finely chopped onion
Combine all ingredients. Makes 1 cup.

Fish Camp in Centerville Catfish House Recipes

If you drive to Centerville, you'll find the Fish Camp, which in my opinion serves the best fried catfish in Tennessee. One of the cooks gave me a couple of recipes, one for catfish and one for hushpuppies.

Hushpuppies

I cup meal
1/2 cup flour
1/4 cup ground onion
1/4 cup sharp cheddar cheese, grated
1 "pony" size Budweiser
egg buttermilk

Mix that all together until it's real thick, like you would for making a cake. Let it stand for about 15 minutes. Drop the hushpuppy dough by spoonsful into hot grease, cook 'em until they're done. Drain and serve them with catfish.

Catfish

2 cups cracker meal
1 cup self-rising flour
2 tablespoons Cajun seasoning (like Tony Cachere's)
1/2 teaspoon garlic

Mix all this well and batter your catfish fillets in it. Fry 'em up in deep fat for 3 to 5 minutes, depending on thickness of the fillets. Serve with hushpuppies.

Are You Hungry Tonight? Order Barbecue.

No matter where you travel in Tennessee, even the most remote hamlet will have a barbecue stand. It's also interesting the way barbecue dishes vary depending on where in the state you travel. In East Tennessee you'll find "pulled" pork, which is pulled off the bone before serving. In Middle Tennessee you'll find primarily pulled pork and ribs. But it's in West Tennessee that the controversy of wet versus dry ribs is a big deal. "Dry" means the meat hasn't been basted with a sauce and is treated with dry seasonings. "Wet" is basted with barbecue sauces of all kinds. You'll find aficionados of pulled, wet, and dry barbecue just about everywhere.

And for true barbecue lovers, forget about barbecued chicken or beef. As one barbecue chef quipped, "If it ain't pork, it ain't barbecue."

Braggin Rights

Here are some of Tennessee's claims to fame

One of the last true grasslands: Coffee County's May Prairie.

First full admiral in the U.S. Navy: Knoxville native and Civil War hero David Glasgow Farragut, who was promoted to vice admiral in 1866 by act of Congress.

World's longest paper clip chain: measures 18.22 miles and was made by Clarksville High School students on April 18, 1999, as a fund-raiser to buy computers for an orphanage in Mexico.

World's first self-service grocery store: introduced by Clarence Saunders, who opened his first Piggly Wiggly store in Memphis in 1916.

Nation's oldest continuously run weight-for-age steeplechase: the Iroquois Steeplechase in Nashville's Percy Warner Park every May, which started back in 1941.

First American surgeon to perform a hysterectomy: Dr. Paul Fitzsimmons Eve, professor of surgery at the University of Nashville from 1851 to 1861 and from 1870 to 1877.

Most visited home in the nation, after the White House: Graceland, Elvis's palatial mansion in Memphis, which in 1991 was listed with the National Register of Historic Places.

Graceland

World's steepest railroad: Chattanooga's Incline Railway, which takes visitors to see Rock City at the top of Lookout Mountain. The incline is an adrenaline-producing 70 degrees!

Oldest registered distillery in America: Jack Daniel's in Lynchburg.

Member of the first sheep-cloning team: Erin native Dr. J. Lannett Edwards, a reproductive biologist and embryologist who for a time worked with the Scottish cloning team that produced Dolly, the cloned sheep. "If only I could clone the experience!" said the enthusiastic Dr. Edwards.

The undisputed title "pork barbecue capital of the world": claimed by Memphis.

Highest sheer-drop waterfall east of the Mississippi River: Fall Creek Falls near Cookeville (at 256 feet, for those who really need a number).

Only bridge of its kind in the United States (and one of only two in the world): the post-tensioned, segmental concrete double-arch bridge on the Natchez Trace Parkway over Highway 96, southwest of Nashville. It looks like a work of art (and an expensive one, too, at a cost of $12 million).

Postmaster general who introduced the postage stamp to the nation: Tennessean Cave Johnson, postmaster general during the administration of James K. Polk, another Tennessean.

Greatest collection of Victorian literature in America: at the Thomas Hughes Library in Rugby.

Best place to live for starting a rock band: Memphis, according to Swing magazine's 1997 nationwide survey, because "starving musicians can benefit from the low cost of living while enjoying plenty of cheap barbecued pork."

World's second-largest Eiffel Tower: in Paris, Tennessee. Built to scale at Christian Brothers University in Memphis, for Memphis in May's 1990 salute to France, the tower is sixty-five feet tall and is made of five hundred pieces of Douglas fir and six thousand steel rods.

The title "pumpkin capital of the world": claimed by Pikeville in Bledsoe County.

Worst earthquake in U.S. history: formed Reelfoot Lake in West Tennessee in 1812.

World's largest freshwater aquarium: the Tennessee Aquarium in Chattanooga. It is the height of a twelve-story building, measures 130,000 square feet in size, and holds approximately 400,00 gallons of water.

World's largest country music research center: The Country Music Foundation in Nashville.

Largest knife store in the world: Smoky Mountain Knife Works in Sevierville, which houses a knife museum and also claims to have Tennessee's largest collection of mounted heads on its walls.

World's only exact-size replica of the ancient temple the Parthenon in Athens, Greece: Nashville's Parthenon, situated in Centennial Park. In keeping with Nashville's reputation as "the Athens of the South," it was originally built to celebrate Tennessee's Centennial Exposition. Inside you'll find a forty-two-foot-tall statue of the Greek goddess Athena.

World's biggest fish fry: held every April in Paris, when they cook more than 12,500 pounds of catfish—that's well over six tons!

World's largest outdoor barbecue: the annual Irish Picnic and Homecoming, held the last weekend in July in the tiny town of McEwen (population approximately 1,500). Begun in 1854, the barbecue is hosted by St. Patrick Church and School and is attended by over 20,000 people, who eat more than 20,000 pounds of pork and 2,100 whole chickens, plus fixin's.

The title "nursery capital of the world": claimed by Warren County, which has more than four hundred nursery growers within its boundaries.

World's largest pencil: in Shelbyville, made by the city's pencil manufacturer, Sanford Corporation.

Possibly the world's oldest cooking grease still in use: in Dyer's Cafe in Bartlett. The original owner, Elmer Dyer, started using the grease in 1912 when he was cooking and serving from a covered wagon. The restaurant strains the grease twice a day, and it is so special they use a police escort whenever the twelve-gallon grease vat is moved.

Tennessee: Serious about Food

All over the Volunteer State, you'll find that wherever you go, Tennesseans are passionate about cooking and food. From Norris to Memphis, you'll find a variety of barbecues, fried catfish, country ham, desserts, and homemade biscuits that'll be sure and tickle your taste-buds. And just about every town in the state (even the smallest hamlet like Burns), will have what they call a "meat and three" (or "meat and two"), which is a special meat choice of the day with a plethora of choices of two or three vegetables.

Two of my personal favorites include Dickson's restaurant, Sisters, and Elliston Place in Nashville. When I'm visiting Lynchburg and seeing the folks at Jack Daniel's Distillery, it's a good way to wind up the day with a meal at Miss Mary Bobo's (but reservations are a requirement here). Another restaurant that's a chain, but is a favorite with many people because, regardless of which establishment you visit, Cracker Barrel Old Country Stores serves up consistently good, down-home food.

With their first restaurant established in Lebanon, Tennessee, they celebrated their 50th anniversary in 2019!

Some other restaurants that have stood the proverbial test of time include Varallo's (Nashville), which is said to be THE oldest restaurant in Tennessee, Leonard's Pit Bar-be-cue (Memphis), and Pancake Pantry (Nashville). Another restaurant that has barbecue down to a fine art is The Rendezvous in Memphis (and lot of people will say you "haven't really been to Tennessee if you haven't been here"!).

There are many food places that have retail outlets and gift shops. For example, Tripp Country Hams in Brownsville sells their delicious smoked hams and bacon out of their shop located in the front of their establishment.

The Most Prestigious Barbecue Competition on the Planet

The biggest and most prestigious barbecue competition in the world is the Championship Invitational Barbecue, hosted by Jack Daniels. As the name implies, only invited competitors are included in this high-stakes competition.

Did You Know?

J. Bush (of Bush's Beans fame) with Golden Retriever has a museum, café and general store in Dandridge.

Tying the Knot in the Volunteer State

Many historic homes in the Volunteer State are open for special events, especially weddings. Carnton Plantation in Franklin may be one of the busiest venues for vow exchanges, but other places, such as Belle Meade Plantation, Two Rivers Mansion and Riverwood Mansion (all in Nashville), are splendid backdrops for weddings and receptions. Memphis has the

Woodruff-Fontaine House, a French Victorian style mansion with lovely, manicured lawns, as a romantic setting in which to say your "I dos." Smyrna's Sam Davis Home, Rippavilla Plantation in Spring Hill, Cedar Hall in Bartlett and Crescent Bend House and Gardens in Knoxville also offer elegant and historic settings in which to make your wedding day special.

Besides historic antebellum homes, some folks like to have their weddings in even more unique settings. A variety of vineyards offer their properties for weddings and receptions. Highland Manor in Jamestown, which is Tennessee's oldest winery, is among the vineyards that offers couples a unique setting for their wedding. Or, if something a bit more rustic is something you'd like, there are several farms in Tennessee where you can tie the knot. Three of these are Crazy K Ranch in Michie, The Barn at Sycamore Farms in Arrington, and The Lily Barn in Townsend. See "Virtual Tennessee" for websites.

Want to Step Back in Time? Go Visit Tennessee's Answer to Mayberry

The once-bustling former riverboat town of Granville, just an hour's drive east of Nashville, is one place you'll want to visit. You'll feel a sense of nostalgia overwhelm you in this quiet and quaint town that's like stepping back in time. Surrounded by the Cumberland River on three sides, just about any place you look in Granville offers a scenic view. The town of Granville has, among other attractions, a general store, a homestead pioneer museum, and an antique car museum. Originally settled by Revolutionary War heroes and their families, the people of Granville still want to keep their town as if you've stepped back in time.

The Granville Pioneer Village is, on occasion, full of people dressed in period costume, weaving, blacksmithing, cooking, or doing household chores as they might have been done "back in the day." In October, Granville hosts a Scarecrow Festival—the biggest one, they say, in all of the Volunteer State. See "Virtual Tennessee" for website information.

A Dickens of a Christmas in Franklin

Every December, approximately 200 of Franklin's regular citizenry become characters from Charles Dickens' novel, A Christmas Carol. This is something you must experience for yourself: people dressed in period costume (18th century) walk the sidewalks and step into the shops of Franklin, taking on the personas of the people in Dickens' English novel. You can easily take part in this walking drama by speaking to the characters, and you never know if you'll come face-to-face with

Actor portraying Bob Marley's Ghost

Scrooge, Tiny Tim, Bob Cratchit and others. It brings the novel alive for those of us who love the story.

CHAPTER FIFTEEN

Unusual Grave, Ghost and Burial Site Stories

Andrew Jackson and the Infamous Bell Witch

The quiet village of Adams in Robertson County, near the Kentucky line, is the site of such strange hauntings and supernatural occurrences that it's the only place of its kind to be designated with a Historical Marker by the state of Tennessee. Many people, curious about the so-called "Bell Witch," explore the now-famous Bell Witch Cave. Even future President Andrew Jackson couldn't resist investigating it for himself.

There are several stories about the origins of the Bell Witch. Some say it's the ghost of a neighbor, Kate Batts, who haunted farmer John Bell and his family. Others say it's an ancient Native American ghost— maybe several. What is known for certain is that the hauntings began around 1816, when John Bell and his family first became aware of a malevolent presence. The ghost threw heavy furniture, sang to visitors, quoted Scripture to visiting ministers, and pulled the hair of and otherwise tortured John Bell's daughters.

News of the hauntings spread, and people began coming from all over the county, then the state, and even other states, to see and hear the hauntings for themselves.

Then Andrew Jackson decided to come and rid the Bell family of their unwelcome visitor. The year was 1820, and the future seventh president was at his home, the Hermitage, in Nashville. John Bell Jr. had served Jackson in the military, and Jackson had a reputation for "braving the very harrows of Hell" to help a friend.

Gathering together a contingent of friends and servants, Jackson loaded a four-horse covered wagon as if he were on one of his military campaigns and headed out. Toward the end

of their journey, a strange thing happened. Nearing the Bell farm, one of Old Hickory's companions made "slighting remarks" about the Bell Witch. Just then, the wagon wheels froze, although the weather was fine and dry, and the wagon trail was firm and level. The driver whipped the horses, which only whinnied and reared in fright.

Checking the wagon himself and finding no reason for it to be stopped in its tracks, Jackson is said to have declared, "It's the witch!" Then a voice came from nowhere: "All right, General, let the wagon move on. I'll see you tonight!" At that moment the wheels became free of their preternatural stays, and the party rolled on toward the Bell farm.

John Bell and his family welcomed the group; after supper, they all sat around the fireplace, telling stories and enjoying an after-dinner drink . . . or two. During this conversation, one of the men in the party began to brag that he was a "witch tamer" and had brought along a silver bullet for the sole purpose of killing the spirit. Just then they heard footsteps and a voice said, "All right, General, I am on hand, ready for business!"

The "witch tamer" was the one who caught the wrath of the spirit that night. He had imaginary "pins" stuck in his backside while the spirit taunted him to shoot. The spirit slapped the man's face repeatedly and finally had him running through the house and out the front door.

Finally, the entity declared, "There's another fraud in your party, General. I'll get him tomorrow night." Jackson was eager to stay and see what else the Bell Witch would do, but the rest of his group was more than ready to return to Nashville the following morning. Jackson never again sought out the Bell Witch.

When asked about his adventure, he is reported to have remarked to his friends, "I saw nothing, but I heard enough to convince me that I would rather fight the British than deal with this torment they call the Bell Witch!"

Some years following this, John Bell died, haunted to his last days by a being who wouldn't let him rest. He and his family are buried in a cemetery near the house. Today, owners of the land say the area is still haunted.

If you think you feel brave enough to go investigate this eerie phenomenon for yourself, spirit yourself over to "Virtual Tennessee" for websites.

The Enduring Lure of Nannie Taylor's Shrine

In Clarksville, just northwest of Nashville, there once lived a little girl named Nannie Taylor, the daughter of Judge Charles W. and Molly Taylor, who were wealthy and respected in the community. Born in 1881, "Little Nannie" died of pneumonia when she was only four years old.

In those days, if you had anything special done in the way of burial sculptures, it was done in France, so the grieving father sent a photo of Nannie and ordered an exact replica of her to be created.

The statue was intricately carved in marble, even down to Nannie's little teeth, delicate dimpled hands, and the lace on her pantaloons. Frozen in time, Nannie's sculpted image stood in Greenwood Cemetery until 1996, when her statue was stolen. The Taylor family appealed for its return, and the story of the search for Nannie's statue made national television.

In Boston, an antiques dealer was watching the news and thought the statue looked familiar. Sure enough, he had it for sale in his shop.

The dealer drove it back to Clarksville, where there was a

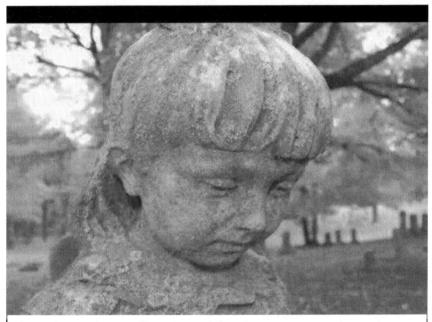

For decades, the statue of Nannie Taylor has been a sort of shrine, with visitors leaving tokens at "her" feet.

rededication ceremony, complete with a speech from the mayor. For years after its return to Greenwood Cemetery, Nannie's statue became a kind of shrine. It was often found decorated with toys, costume jewelry and knickknacks. Depending on the season, her statue might also be decorated with a Christmas tree, Easter lily or an American flag (for the Fourth of July). As time went on, visitors to Nannie's statue, perhaps hoping that she could help heal a loved one, would leave pictures of their sick family member at "her" feet.

After it received so much attention, the statue was knocked over (either accidentally or deliberately) and one arm was broken off. Now it is protected in a building near the cemetery.

Strange... but True

These Confederate Soldiers Moved to Missouri— after They Died!

In Lake County, near Reelfoot Lake, approximately seventy-five Confederate soldiers were buried in a cemetery near where they fell at the 1862 battle of Island No. 10. Several years after they were buried, the Mississippi River changed course, and the island on which the soldiers are buried is now part of Missouri.

The Mysterious Death of Meriwether Lewis

The burial site of Meriwether Lewis, the co-leader of the Lewis and Clark expedition, lies near the tiny village of Hohenwald, in Lewis County, which is named for him. At first, he was honored for his brave exploration across the American continent, but his problems began after he was made governor of the Louisiana Territory and Congress raised questions about his account-keeping. Dismayed and deeply depressed by these charges, Lewis was on his way from St Louis to Washington along the Natchez Trace to defend himself. At sunset on October 11, 1810, he reached Grinder's Stand, an inn owned by

Robert Grinder, who was away from home. Mrs. Grinder put Lewis up for the night. Sometime that evening, Lewis was shot. Some people claimed he was robbed; but he carried documents, not money. Other people speculated that he shot himself out of a sense of hopeless despair. At any rate, at daylight he was found, still conscious but fatally wounded, with a piece of his forehead blown off. He died soon after.

Captain Meriwether *Lewis*

Captain Lewis is buried where he died, and the site is a National Landmark in the Meriwether Lewis Park at mile marker 385.9 on the Natchez Trace. The grave monument is in the shape of a broken column, a symbol of a life ended before it was fully lived.

Did You Know??

In 1862 President Abraham Lincoln signed a bill creating national cemeteries "for the soldiers who shall die in service of the country." After the Civil War, recovery teams worked to disinter the remains of about 250,000 Union soldiers from makeshift burial sites. By 1870 the remains were properly reburied by the federal government in seventy-three different national cemeteries. Individual states of the old Confederacy were responsible for preparing and maintaining cemeteries for Southern soldiers.

The Largest Private Cemetery in the Nation

The small town of Franklin, and the peaceful home known as Carnton Plantation, were to become the backdrop for one of the most decisive and bloody battles of the Civil War. Carnton Plantation would also go on to become the site of the largest private cemetery in the United States because of the battle of Franklin.

Carnton Plantation was built around 1826 by Irishman Randal McGavock, a former mayor of Nashville. In 1848, his son John married Carrie Winder; they lived on the plantation, raising wheat, corn, oats, and thoroughbred horses. They had two children, Hattie and Winder.

When the battle of Franklin burst upon their peaceful world, their home became one of the forty-four in the area that became field hospitals and morgues. The McGavock children, nine-year-old Hattie and seven-year-old Winder, assisted the surgeons and helped tend the wounded. One can only guess at the atrocities their young eyes saw then: the dead were stacked, according to one account, "like cordwood" on the porch and in the yard around the house, and the wooden floor became stained with blood that is still visible today.

Their mother, Carrie, worked tirelessly with surgeons from the regiments to save whomever she could, but there were so many casualties it was impossible to treat them all. Four dead confederate generals were laid out on the back porch: Cleburne, Granbury, Strahl, and Adams. That dark day of November 30, 1864, saw more than fifteen hundred Confederates die within four hours; thousands more died in the following weeks from complications and poor hygiene.

But that was far from the end of the story. The Union dead were buried where they fell, then later claimed by friends or relatives, or reinterred in national cemeteries. Over 1,750 Confederate dead remained buries on the battlefield. Wooden headstones indicated these soldiers' names, companies, and regiments, but as time went on, the inscriptions began to fade.

Steadfast in their role as hosts, the McGavock family set aside two acres of their land and reinterred each soldier there, buried by state of origin. In her own hand, Carrie recorded the information from each original wooden marker; her list became known as the Register of the Dead. The family gave each grave a new cedar headstone, and the Register of the Dead is now the property of the Historic Carnton Association. Because of the foresight and patriotism of Carrie McGavock, the memories of those fallen soldiers will never fade.

Did You Know?

Fort Donelson National Cemetery is Tennessee's most diverse cemetery. It is the burial place of veterans of seven different wars.

The Tale of the Missing Grave

The French-Canadian fur trader Timothe Boucher de Montbrun became one of Nashville's first white settlers when his pirogue slipped along the Shauvanon River (now called the Cumberland River) in 1769.

The young man lived for a time in a cave above the river in the area known as French Lick and formed friendships with the Cherokee, Chickasaw, and Creek, who traded their furs for wares he could supply. He served in the military as a lieutenant governor in command of the Northwest Territory, after which he opened a mercantile business on Nashville's Public Square. He had anglicized his name to Demonbreun, the name of a Nashville street today, and had two wives: one in Illinois and one in Nashville.

When he died in 1826, his obituary in the November edition of the Nashville Banner & Nashville Whig read simply, "On Monday evening last, Capt. Timothy DeMumbrane, a venerable citizen of Nashville, and the first white man that ever emigrated to this vicinity. Passed away." No mention was made of the place of burial.

Timothy Demonbreun's grave has never been found. Some historians say he was buried in the old North Nashville Cemetery (near what today is Fourth Avenue North). Others say his remains were reburied in City Cemetery. Still others think his remains were never moved and are now buried in the back of what used to be a blacksmith shop on Jefferson Street. Finally, his descendants erected a marker next to that of his common-law wife in a cemetery near Ashland City. In 1996 another monument to Demonbreun was erected by the city of Nashville to commemorate its "first citizen." The 8-foot-tall, 650-pound bronze statue stands near Fort Nashborough; it was sculpted by Germantown resident Alan LeQuire.

Guarding "Our Forefathers' Bones"

In Chattanooga some gravesites that are not tourist attractions are guarded by a special patrol deputized by the Hamilton County Sheriff's office.

Ancient Native American burial places in around 600 acres of Chattanooga's Moccasin Bend were being destroyed. In the 1970s alone, more than 800 burial sites were looted or vandalized.

Alarmed by the destruction, a group of Native Americans approached the sheriff to see what could be done to stop it. The sheriff told them he did not have enough personnel for such a task as guarding the forests and fields along the Tennessee River.

Thus Cherokees Robert DeBord and Gary Williams formed their own patrol, the Native American Reserve Force of Hamilton County, and became deputized. The sheriff's office has since reported grave vandalism as nearly eliminated, and according to state archaeologists, there is no other such reserve force in the entire United States.

A "Capitol" Burial Site

Who's buried in the capitol in Nashville? Two people, to be exact. One is William Strickland, a noted Philadelphia architect who came to Nashville in 1845 to oversee construction of the building. The process was long and laborious, and Strickland even had to resort to using prisoners from the state penitentiary to save on labor expenses.

The General Assembly was able to meet in the capitol in October 1853, although construction was not yet complete. To honor Strickland's efforts, the legislators designated a burial place for Strickland at the northeast wall of the north basement portico.

Strickland died six weeks later and is entombed in the place set aside in honor of "his genius in erecting so grand a work." Also buried in the capitol is Samuel Morgan, the only member of the Capitol Commission to serve during the entire time of the building's construction.

Graveyard Trivia

Q. In what Memphis cemetery are buried fourteen Confederate generals, two governors, three US senators, and twenty-one city mayors?
A. Elmwood, on South Dudley Street

Q. Where is the mother of Sam Houston, Elizabeth Paxton Houston, buried?
A. Maryville, in the cemetery at Baker's Creek Church.

Q. What soldier credited with firing the first shot against the British in the battle of Kings Mountain is buried in the Bean-Raulston Graveyard in Marion County?
A. Captain Robert Bean.

Q. In what city cemetery do the remains of more than 20,000 early settlers, including James Robertson and Governor William Carroll, have their final resting place?
A. City Cemetery, in Nashville, at 4th Avenue South and Oak Street.

Q. How many national Cemeteries are in Tennessee?
A. Five, in Memphis, Chattanooga, Mountain Home, Knoxville, and Nashville.

Virtual Tennessee

Tennessee State Museum: www.tnmuseum.org

James K. Polk Home and Museum: www.JamesKPolk.com

President Andrew Johnson Museum and Library: www.AJMuseum.Tusculum.edu

Andrew Johnson Homestead: www.NPS.gov/ANJO

Tennessee Museum of Aviation: www.TnAirMuseum.com

Tennessee Aviation Hall of Fame: www.TnAviationHof.org

Beechcraft Heritage Museum: www.BeechcraftHM.org

Tennessee Valley Railroad Museum: www.TVrail.com

Casey Jones Village: www.CaseyJones.com

Incline Railway, Chattanooga: www.RideTheIncline.com

International Towing and Recovery Museum: https://InternationalTowingMuseum.org

Chapter 3: Prehistoric Tennessee

McClung Museum of Natural History & Culture: https://McClungMuseum.otk.edu/
Gray Fossil Site: www.gfs.HandsOn.org

The C. H. Nash Museum, aka Chucalissa Archeological Museum: https://www.memphis.edu/chucalissa/

Old   Stone   Fort   State   Archaeological   Park:
https://tnstateparks.com/parks/old-stone-fort

Chapter 15 Unusual Grave, Ghost and Burial-Site Stories

Bell Witch Fall Festival: www.BellWitchFallFestival.com

Amazing Tennessee Virtual Links

CHAPTER 1

Page 20: Elephant Sanctuary in Hoenwald, TN:
https://www.elephants.com/

CHAPTER 2

Page 23: "Politics Makes Strange Bedfellows": http://www.tipton-haynes.org/
Page 25-26: The "Unsinkable": https://titanicpigeonforge.com/
Page 27 "Bare-Faced Honest":
- Adult Camp: https://www.pleasurelakeretreat.com/
- Family Camp: https://rockhavenlodge.com/
- "Naturist" Camp: https://campnaturist.com/

Page 28-29 "Sam Houston":
https://samhoustonhistoricschoolhouse.org/
Page 32: "Strange But True": https://tnmuseum.org/
Page 33-34: "TN and The Perfect 36":
http://tnwomansmemorial.org/
Page 36-37: "Hail to the (Vertically Challenged) Chief!:
https://jameskpolk.com/
Page 38-39: Lawrence County: Aviation's Pioneer:
https://www.tnairmuseum.com/
Page 39: Shape Is Everything:
https://visitmcminnvilletn.com/experience/heritage-alliance-center-2/
Page 40-41: For Railroad Buffs: http://cowanrailroadmuseum.org/
& https://www.caseyjones.com/
Page 41: Steepest Passenger Railway:
http://www.ridetheincline.com/
Page 42: There Has To Be A Section On Trucks!:
https://internationaltowingmuseum.org/
Page 43: N&C Railroad (several websites, not sure…)

T. Jensen Lacey

- https://www.american-rails.com/ncstl.html
- http://www.ncps-576.org/
- http://ncstl.com/history/history.htm

Page 44: The Gordon Browning Museum:
https://mckenzietn.org/mckenzie-101/community/museums/
Page 45: Salue To The Military: https://www.wmarocks.com/

CHAPTER 3

Page 53-54: Dinosaurs: http://gfs.visithandson.org/
Page 54-58 : Ancient Peoples:
- McLung Museum: https://mcclungmuseum.utk.edu/
- Mound Bottom: https://www.tn.gov/environment/program-areas/arch-archaeology/state-archaeological-parks---areas/mound-bottom-state-archaeological-area.html
- C. H. Nash Museum: https://www.memphis.edu/chucalissa/
- Fort Watauga: https://tnstateparks.com/parks/sycamore-shoals
- John & Landon Carter Mansion: https://tnstateparks.com/assets/pdf/additional-content/sycamore-shoals_carter-mansion_web.pdf
- Red Clay State Park: https://tnstateparks.com/parks/red-clay
- Pinson Mounds: https://tnstateparks.com/parks/pinson-mounds

Page 57-58: Did You Know?:
- Dunbar Cave: https://tnstateparks.com/parks/dunbar-cave
- Wyatt Archaeological Museum: https://wyatt-archaeological-museum.business.site/

Page 60: Old Stone Fort: https://tnstateparks.com/parks/old-stone-fort
Page 61: "Did You Know?"-Butler Museum:
http://www.butlermuseumtn.com/

CHAPTER 4

Page 63-65: Fort Nashborough: http://www.butlermuseumtn.com/
Page 66: "Battle Of Kings Mountain"- Overmountain Victory
National Historic Trail: https://www.nps.gov/ovvi/index.htm
Page 67-69: "The Love Story That Built A House"-Rippavilla
Mansion- https://www.rippavilla.org/
Page 69-70: "Rattle and Snap":
http://www.rattleandsnapplantation.com/
**Page 70-75: Historic Homes and Sites You Can Visit
West Tennessee:**
- Alex Haley House Museum:
  https://www.alexhaleymuseum.org/
- Ames Plantation: http://www.amesplantation.org/
- Arlington Historic Post Office:
  https://www.townofarlington.org/about_arlington/arlington_chapter_of_the_apta.php
- The Buford Pusser Home and Museum:
  https://bufordpussermuseum.com/
- Casey Jones Home and Railroad Museum:
  https://www.caseyjones.com/museum/
- Chucalissa Archaeological Museum:
  https://www.memphis.edu/chucalissa/
- Robert R Church Park:
  https://downtownmemphis.com/experience-downtown/downtown-directory/?search=Robert%20Church%20Park
- Collierville Town Square and Railroad Cars:
  http://colliervilleparks.org/parks/facilities-and-rental-information/town-square
- David Crockett Cabin (Morristown):
  https://www.tnvacation.com/local/rutherford-davy-crockett-cabin-museum
- Davies Manor (Brunswick):
  http://daviesmanorplantation.org/
- Elmwood Cemetery (Memphis):
  https://www.elmwoodcemetery.org/

- Fort Pillow State Historic Area (near Garland): https://tnstateparks.com/parks/fort-pillow
- Freed House (Memphis): http://tennesseeencyclopedia.net/entries/freed-house/
- Gotten House: https://www.memphisheritage.org/nicholas-gotten-house/
- Hannum-Rhea House: no link, only an address. This is a private residence last sold in 2017.
- The Little Courthouse Museum: https://www.tnvacation.com/local/bolivar-little-courthouse
- Magevney House: https://www.memphismuseums.org/historic-houses/about/magevney-house/
- Mallory-Neely House: https://www.memphismuseums.org/historic-houses/about/mallory-neely-house/
- The Pillars: https://tennesseeencyclopedia.net/entries/the-pillars/
- Pinson Mounds State Archaeological Area: https://tnstateparks.com/parks/pinson-mounds
- Reelfoot Lake Resort Park: https://tnstateparks.com/parks/reelfoot-lake
- Shiloh National Military Park: https://www.nps.gov/shil/index.htm
- Woodruff-Fontaine House: https://www.woodruff-fontaine.org/

Page 70-75: Historic Homes and Sites You Can Visit

Middle Tennessee
- The Athenaeum (Columbia): https://historicathenaeum.com/
- Belle Meade Plantation (Nashville): https://bellemeadeplantation.com/
- Belmont Mansion (Nashville) : https://www.belmontmansion.com/

- Bowen Plantation House (Nashville) : http://www.cityofgoodlettsville.org/115/Bowen-Plantation-House
- Carnton Plantation (Franklin) : https://boft.org/carnton
- Carter House (Franklin) : https://boft.org/the-carter-house
- Cookeville Depot Museum: https://www.cookevilledepot.com/
- Cordell Hull Birthplace and Museum (near Byrdstown): https://tnstateparks.com/parks/cordell-hull-birthplace
- Cragfont (near Gallatin): https://visitsumnertn.com/place/cragfont-state-historic-site/
- Cravens House (Chattanooga): https://www.visitchattanooga.com/listing/cravens-house/903/
- Fort Donelson National Battlefield (Dover): https://www.nps.gov/fodo/index.htm
- Fort Nashborough (Nashville): https://www.nashville.gov/Parks-and-Recreation/Historic-Sites/Fort-Nashborough.aspx
- The Hermitage (Nashville): https://thehermitage.com/
- Hohenwald Depot: https://www.tnvacation.com/local/hohenwald-hohenwald-depot
- The Homeplace 1850 (near Dover): https://www.landbetweenthelakes.us/seendo/attractions/homeplace/
- James K. Polk Home: https://jameskpolk.com/
- Natchez Trace Parkway and Meriwether Lewis Monument: https://www.nps.gov/natr/learn/historyculture/exploring-the-meriwether-lewis-site.htm
- Oaklands Historic House Museum (Murfreesboro): http://www.oaklandsmansion.org/
- The Parthenon (Nashville): https://www.nashville.gov/Parks-and-Recreation/Parthenon.aspx
- Rock Castle (near Hendersonville): https://www.historicrockcastle.com/

- Sam Davis Home (near Smyrna): https://www.samdavishome.org/
- Sergeant York Home (Jamestown): http://sgtyork.org/park-and-homeplace
- Smith-Trahern Mansion (Clarksville): http://www.fceclarksville.org/
- Sparta Rock House: https://tennesseeencyclopedia.net/entries/sparta-rock-house/
- Stones River National Battlefield: https://www.nps.gov/stri/index.htm
- Tennessee State Capitol (Nashville): https://tnmuseum.org/state-capitol
- Travellers' Rest (Nashville): https://historictravellersrest.org/
- Trousdale Place (Hartsville) : https://www.trousdalecountytn.gov/
- Tulip Grove (between Nashville and Lebanon): https://thehermitage.com/learn/mansion-grounds/garden-grounds/tulip-grove/
- Wynnewood (outside Gallatin): https://visitsumnertn.com/place/wynnewood-state-historic-site/

Page 70-75: Historic Homes and Sites You Can Visit

East Tennessee
- Andrew Johnson National Historic Site (Greeneville): https://www.nps.gov/anjo/index.htm
- Armstrong-Lockett House (Crescent Bend): http://www.crescentbend.com/
- Beck Cultural Exchange Center (Knoxville): https://www.beckcenter.net/
- Blount Mansion (Knoxville): http://www.blountmansion.org/
- Burra Burra Mine Site (Ducktown) : https://ducktownbasinmuseum.com/

- Cades Cove (near Gatlinburg) : https://www.nps.gov/grsm/planyourvisit/cadescove.htm
- Davy Crockett Birthplace State Park: https://tnstateparks.com/parks/david-crockett-birthplace
- Etowah L&N Depot: https://www.cityofetowahtn.com/2186/LN-Depot
- The Exchange Place (Kingsport): https://www.exchangeplace.info/
- Fort Loudon State Historic Area: https://www.exchangeplace.info/
- James White Fort: https://www.jameswhitesfort.org/
- Mabry-Hazen House: http://www.mabryhazen.com/
- Marble Springs (near Sevierville): https://www.marblesprings.net/home
- The Netherland Inn (Kingsport): https://thenetherlandinn.com/
- Old Roane County Courthouse: https://tennesseerivervalleygeotourism.org/entries/historic-roane-county-courthouse/e0acf846-dbb6-4b1c-8c16-665e430b6977
- President Andrew Johnson Museum Library: https://ajmuseum.tusculum.edu/
- Ramsey House (Knoxville): http://www.ramseyhouse.org/
- Red Clay State Historic Park: https://tnstateparks.com/parks/red-clay
- Rhea County Courthouse and Scopes Trial Museum: https://www.rheacountyheritage.com/
- Rocky Mount (Elizabethton): https://rockymountmuseum.com/
- Sam Houston Schoolhouse: https://samhoustonhistoricschoolhouse.org/
- Samuel Doak House (Greeneville): https://doakhouse.tusculum.edu/history-of-the-doak-house-museum/
- Tipton-Haynes Historic Site: http://www.tipton-haynes.org/

Page 75: "Did You Know": https://milan.tennessee.edu/ag-museum/

CHAPTER 5

Page 80-83: Casey Jones: https://www.caseyjones.com/
Page 83-85: Alvin York: http://www.york.k12.tn.us/
Page 86-87: Ryman Auditorium: www.ryman.com
Page 87-88: Luke Lee: http://www.easttnhistory.org/museum-east-tennessee-history
Page 97-99: Dinah Shore: Jail Museum http://www.winchester-tn.com/things-to-do/attractions/old-jail-museum/ & Russian American Museum Brooklyn, NY: http://russianheritagemuseum.com/en/RHM_Dinah_Shore/
Page 101-102: Samuel L Jackson, Civil Rights Museum Memphis: https://www.civilrightsmuseum.org/
Chattanooga History Center: https://chattanoogahistory.com/

Page 104-105: First Man-Made Tunnel. Harpeth River SP: https://tnstateparks.com/parks/harpeth-river & the forge http://tennesseeencyclopedia.net/entries/patterson-forge-narrows-harpeth-state-historical-area/
Page 105-106: Sequoyah Birthplace Museum: http://www.sequoyahmuseum.org/

CHAPTER 6

Page 110-112: The Scopes Festival : https://www.scopesfestival.com/
Page 113: Museum of Appalachia: https://www.museumofappalachia.org/
Page 116: Great Smoky Mountain Heritage Center in Townsend: https://www.gsmheritagecenter.org/
Page 116-118: Ramsey House: http://www.ramseyhouse.org/
Page 118-119: "A World War II Tale" Atomic Heritage Foundation: https://www.atomicheritage.org/location/oak-ridge-tn & Manhattan Project National Historic Park https://www.nps.gov/mapr/index.htm
Page 119: "Itching for Justice" Sevier County Circuit Court: https://www.seviercountytn.org/

Page 120-122: a Moonshine Story https://olesmoky.com/
Page 122-124: A Moonshine Glossary
- The Museum of East Tennessee History in Knoxville: http://www.easttnhistory.org/museum-east-tennessee-history
- Ole Smoky Moonshine- https://olesmoky.com/
- The Louvin Brother's Museum at The Smoke House in Monteagle: https://www.thesmokehouse.com/
- Tennessee Whiskey Tours in Nashville: https://tennesseewhiskeytours.com/

Page 125: Jonesboro https://www.storytellingcenter.net/festival/
Page 126-128: The Melungeons https://childrensmuseumofoakridge.org/

CHAPTER 7

Page 137-138: The Farm- https://thefarmcommunity.com/
Page 139-140: Reverend Sam Jones, The Ryman: www.ryman.com
Page 141: The Museum Center at 5 Points- http://www.museumcenter.org/
Page 142: Southern Gospel Museum- https://www.sgma.org/ James D Vaughan Museum- https://www.lawrenceburgtn.gov/230/James-D-Vaughn-Gospel-Music-Museum
Page 142-143: Bible Museum in Collierville- https://www.biblemuseumonthesquare.org/
Page 143: He Wore Out Some Horses! Living Heritage Museum- https://www.livingheritagemuseum.org/
Page 143-144: Wonders of Creation Museum- https://visitcreation.org/item/wonders-of-creation-center-lewisburg-tn/
Page 145-146: Historic Rugby- https://www.historicrugby.org/

CHAPTER 8

Page 149-153: Football Time In TN: Tennessee Radio Hall of Fame-http://tennesseeradiohalloffame.wildapricot.org/ Tennessee Sports Hall of Fame http://tshf.net/ and the Knoxville Sports Hall of

Fame (can't find any website!), Bridgestone Arena
https://www.bridgestonearena.com/
Page 159: "Walk In The Clouds" Gatlinburg Skybridge-
https://www.gatlinburgskylift.com/skybridge
Page 160: "Hit The Links" Fairfield Glade Course-
https://fairfieldglade.cc/golf Bear Trace Course-
https://tnstateparks.com/golf/course/bear-trace-at-cumberland-mountain/
Page 160: "Did You Know?" Geico Bassmaster Classic-
https://www.bassmaster.com/tournaments/2019-bassmaster-classic-presented-dicks-sporting-goods
Page 161: "Did You Know?" Hills & Hollers H.O.G. Rally:
https://press.tnvacation.com/press-releases/johnson-city-announced-2019-site-hills-hollers-harley-owners-group-rally
Page 161-163: Bristol Speedway:
https://www.bristolmotorspeedway.com/

CHAPTER 9

Page 171: "Did You Know?" Chickamauga and Chattanooga Military Park: https://www.nps.gov/chch/index.htm
Page 172: Immerse Yourself In Civil War Sites
- Tennessee State Museum-https://tnmuseum.org/
- Carnton Plantation-https://boft.org/carnton
- The Carter House-https://boft.org/the-carter-house
- Chickamauga National Military Park-https://www.nps.gov/chch/index.htm
- Stones River National Battlefield-https://www.nps.gov/stri/index.htm
- Lotz House Museum- https://www.lotzhouse.com/
- Shiloh National Military Park-https://www.nps.gov/shil/index.htm
- Travellers Rest- https://historictravellersrest.org/
- Belle Meade Plantation- https://bellemeadeplantation.com/
- Monthaven Arts and Cultural Center-https://monthavenartsandculturalcenter.com/
- Belmont Mansion- https://www.belmontmansion.com/

- Fort Negley Park- https://www.nashville.gov/Parks-and-Recreation/Historic-Sites/Fort-Negley.aspx
- East Tennessee Historical Society and Museum- http://www.easttnhistory.org/
- Fort Pillow State Historic Park- https://tnstateparks.com/parks/fort-pillow
- Johnsonville State Historic Park- https://tnstateparks.com/parks/johnsonville
- Abraham Lincoln Library and Museum- https://www.lmunet.edu/abraham-lincoln-library-and-museum/index.php
- The Mabry-Hazen House- http://www.mabryhazen.com/
- Dickson-Williams Mansion- http://www.mainstreetgreeneville.org/
- Farragut Folklife Museum- http://townoffarragut.org/186/Farragut-Museum
- Slave Haven Underground Railroad Museum- http://slavehavenmemphis.com/
- Sam Davis Museum and Hanging Site- https://www.tnvacation.com/local/pulaski-sam-davis-museum
- Emerald Hill (Clarksville)- https://www.visitclarksvilletn.com/plan/trip-ideas/historic-sites/

Page 177: "Headless Corpse" Carter House- https://boft.org/the-carter-house
Page 179: "Waterloo Teeth" Customs House Museum and Cultural Center- https://customshousemuseum.org/
Page 179-180: Headquarters for Both Armies-Cravens House http://www.aboutnorthgeorgia.com/ang/Cravens_House
Page 182: "Did You Know?" Mitchell Museum- https://www.tullahomanews.com/living/museum-houses-tullahomas-history/article_af962f0f-491c-5d9f-9252-73f1cc937589.html
Tullahoma Confederate Cemetery-

https://www.tnvacation.com/civil-war/place/4496/maplewood-
confederate-cemetery/
Page 182-184: "County That Left Tennessee" Scott County
Museum in Huntsville- https://www.scottcountymuseum.com/
Page 186: "Soldier Who Fought For Love" Pink Palace Museum in
Memphis- https://www.memphismuseums.org/
Page 186: Nathan Bedford Forrest State Park-
https://tnstateparks.com/parks/nathan-bedford-forrest
Page 187-188: Battle of Fort Sanders, Bethel Cemetery-
http://www.mabryhazen.com/bethel-cemetery

CHAPTER 10

Page 197: Green McAdoo Cultural Center,
http://www.greenmcadoo.org/
Page 198: Cherokee Removal Memorial Park,
https://tennesseerivervalleygeotourism.org/entries/cherokee-
removal-memorial-park-at-historic-blythe-ferry/d2a64d12-f649-
427c-b415-26363b2a0df9
Page 200: American Baptist College, Griggs Hall-
https://civilrightstrail.com/attraction/griggs-hall-american-baptist-
college/
Page 200-201: "Counter Culture" Woolworth on 5th-
https://woolworthonfifth.com/
Page 201: Nashvilles' Civil Rights Room-
https://library.nashville.org/research/civil-rights-room

CHAPTER 11

Page 203-204: Chattanooga Choo Choo-
https://www.choochoo.com/
Page 206-208: Adolph Ochs, Tennessee Newspaper and Printing
Museum- https://rogersvilletnmainstreet.com/tennessee-newspaper-
and-printing-museum/
Page 208-210: Opryland Hotel-
https://www.marriott.com/hotels/travel/bnago-gaylord-opryland-
resort-and-convention-center/?scid=bb1a189a-fec3-4d19-a255-
54ba596febe2&y_source=1_OTcyOTYzLTcxNS1sb2NhdGlvbi5nb
29nbGVfd2Vic2l0ZV9vdmVycmlkZQ%3D%3D

Page 211-212: Belmont Belle, Belmont Mansion-
https://www.belmontmansion.com/
Page 213 : Opry Mills- https://www.simon.com/mall/opry-mills
Page 213-214: The World's Fair, Sun Sphere-
https://www.visitknoxville.com/listings/sunsphere/567/
Page 218: Strange But True, Nickajack Dam-
https://www.tva.com/energy/our-power-
system/hydroelectric/nickajack
Page 219: "Something Brewed" Big River Grille and Brewing-
https://www.bigrivergrille.com/
Page 220-221: City of Alcoa- https://www.cityofalcoa-tn.gov/
Page 221: Slave Who Created His Own Fate, TN State Museum-
https://tnmuseum.org/
Page 222-223: Entrepreneurial "Spirits", Dickel-
https://www.georgedickel.com/distillery-tour-information
Jack Daniels- https://www.jackdaniels.com/en-us/visit-distillery
Page 223-224: Hatch Show Prints-
https://hatchshowprint.com/tours/
Page 225-227: Black Patch War, Museum of Tobacco Art-
Page 227: "Did You Know" Lodge Cast Iron, National Cornbread
Festival-
http://nationalcornbread.com/entertainment/tour/#:~:text=Lodge%20
Manufacturing%20opens%20its%20doors,Cast%20Iron%20cookwa
re%20is%20made.
Page 228: "Sweet Business" Martin's Honey House-
https://martinshoney.com/

CHAPTER 12

Page 230: Gibson Guitars Factory- https://www.gibson.com/
Page 231: Birthplace of Rock N' Roll, Sun Studio-
https://www.sunstudio.com/visit
Page 232-233: "Strange But True" W. C. Handy Boyhood Home-
https://www.wchandymuseum.org/
Page 236-237: The Boy Who Didn't Get His Wish, Graceland-
https://www.graceland.com/mansion
Page 237-238: "Guess Who", Roy Acuff Union Museum &
Library- https://www.historicunioncounty.com/event/union-county-

historical-society?fbclid=IwAR1cjfE7Zn8Ekvu-
r1mP3QIzaaYhKpX9VCpN7cq2_nwUNisYW9kHxdEwU_c
Page 241-243: Grand Ole Opry- https://www.opry.com/tours/
Page 249-250 : "Twice In A Lifetime", Memphis Music Hall of
Fame- https://memphismusichalloffame.com/
Page 253: "Did You Know" Blake Shelton Restaurants, Ole Red
Nashville- https://olered.com/nashville/
Ole Red Gatlinburg- https://olered.com/gatlinburg/
Page 253-254: Johnny and June Cash Retreat-
https://www.storytellershideawayfarm.com/
Page 254: Hatch Show Prints (again),
https://hatchshowprint.com/tours/
Page 255-256: "Tennessee's Got Drama", Tennessee Theatre-
https://www.tennesseetheatre.com/
Nashville's Shakespeare Festival- https://www.nashvilleshakes.org/
Page 256-257: Carnegie Museum In Jackson-
https://jacksoncarnegie.com/
Page 257-258: John Estes, West Tennessee Delta Heritage Center/
Tina Turner Museum-
https://www.tnvacation.com/local/brownsville-west-tennessee-delta-
heritage-center
Page 258-260: "One Coal Miner's Daughter", Country Music Hall
of Fame- https://countrymusichalloffame.org/ Loretta Lynn Home
and Museum-
https://www.lorettalynnranch.net/main/musuems/coal-
miner%E2%80%99s-daughter-museum/
Page 264: "Pretty Women Don't Need Money"-
https://www.musicianshalloffame.com/
Page 269-271: Bessie Smith, Bessie Smith Cultural Center-
http://www.bessiesmithcc.org/
Page 273-274: "She Couldn't Act, But…" Minnie Pearl Museum-
https://countrymusichalloffame.org/artist/minnie-pearl/

CHAPTER 13

Page 283-285: Reelfoot Lake-
https://tnstateparks.com/parks/reelfoot-lake

Page 285: Sandhill Crane Festival-
https://www.tnvacation.com/local/birchwood-tennessee-sandhill-crane-festival
Page 286-287: Elephant Sanctuary in Hoenwald, TN:
https://www.elephants.com/
Page 287: "Did You Know", The Lost Sea- https://thelostsea.com/
Page 288-289: "A Gem of A Tale" Birdsong pearl farm-
http://www.tennesseeriverpearls.com/
Page 292-293: Tiger Haven- http://www.tigerhaven.org/index.asp
Page 296-298: Great Smoky Mountain NP-
https://www.nps.gov/grsm/index.htm
Page 301: Tennessee Aquarium- https://tnaqua.org/
Page 302: Mud Island-
https://www.memphisriverparks.org/parks/mud-island/
Page 303-304 : Justin P. Wilson Cumberland Trail State Scenic
Trail State Park- https://tnstateparks.com/parks/cumberland-trail
Page 304-305: "You Can View Three States From Here!",
Cumberland Gap National Historical Park-
https://www.nps.gov/cuga/index.htm

CHAPTER 14

Page 328-329: Tying The Knot In Tennessee
- Carnton Plantation in Franklin- https://boft.org/carnton
- Belle Meade Plantation- https://bellemeadeplantation.com/
- Two Rivers Mansion- https://www.nashville.gov/Parks-and-Recreation/Historic-Sites/Two-Rivers-Mansion.aspx
- Riverwood Mansion- https://www.riverwoodmansion.com/
- Woodruff-Fontaine House- https://www.woodruff-fontaine.org/
- Sam Davis Home- https://www.samdavishome.org/
- Rippavilla Plantation- https://www.rippavilla.org/
- Cedar Hall- https://www.evergroveestates.com/cedar-hall
- Crescent Bend House and Gardens-
http://www.crescentbend.com/
- Highland Manor- https://www.highlandmanorwinery.com/
- Crazy K Ranch- http://www.crazykranch.com/

- The Barn at Sycamore Farms- https://sycamorefarmsevents.com/
- The Lily Barn- https://www.lilybarn.com/

Page 329-330: "Tennessee's Answer to Mayberry" Granville Pioneer Village- https://www.granvilletn.com/pioneer-village

CHAPTER 15

Page 331-334: The Bell Witch Cave- https://www.bellwitchcave.com/

INDEX

T. Jensen Lacey

Tennessee State Museum (Nashville), 44, 50, 106, 172, 198, 221, 317
Tennessee State Prison, 7
Tennessee Supreme Court, 112
Tennessee Titans (football), 151-152
Tennessee Valley Authority, 218-219, 221
Tennessee Valley Railroad Museum (Chattanooga), 40
Tennessee Walking Horse Breeders' Association, 291
Texas, Republic of, 29
"Third Coast," Tennessee known as, 233
Thomas, Benjamin, 216
Thompson, Fred, actor and politician, 95-96
Tiger Haven (Kingsport), 292-293
Tigrett, Isaac, 256
Tillis, Mel, 247
Tillman, Floyd, 242
Titanic, movie, 85
Titanic Museum (Pigeon Forge), 25-27
Tobacco, 225-227
Tootsie's Orchid Lounge, 275-276
Touch 'Em All (Garth Brooks' charity), 268
Townsend, 116, 128
Trace, Creek, 187
Trade, town of, 61
Travellers Rest, 174
Troost, Gerald, 43
Truman, Harry S., 312
Tubb, Ernest, 259
Tullahoma, 39, 182
Tunnel, first man-made, see Bell, John
Turner, Ike, 231, 266
Turner, Tina, 257-258

Turner, Tina, Museum (Nutbush), 258
Twitty, Conway, 275

U2, 231
Underground Railroad, 176, 184
Union Gospel Tabernacle (Nashville), 141
United Nations, 314
University of Tennessee, football at, 149-150

Van Buren, Martin, 36
Van Leer, 243
Varney, Jim, 91
Velazquez, Loreta, 186
Volunteers (Vols), 149-150
Vonore, 106

Walker, James, 32-33
Walker, William, "Gray-eyed man of destiny," 15
Walking Tall (movie), 94
Waltrip, Darrell, 162
War of the Roses, 34-35
Ward, John, "Voice of the Vols," 149-151
Ward, Nancy, 65-66
Warren County, "the Round County," 39
Wartrace, 291
Wear, Samuel, 117
Wedding venues in Tennessee, 329-330
Weems, Ward, 149
Wells, Kitty, 242
Wells-Barnett, Ida B., 90
West Tennessee Delta Heritage Center (Brownsville), 259
Whiskey, see Moonshine
Whitehead, Joseph, 26
Wilder, john, 35
Williams, Hank, Sr. & Jr., 261
Williams, Lucinda, 249

Biography for T. Jensen Lacey

Lacey has been a writer for 55 years—since she was able to hold a pencil. Her specialties are history and travel writing. Lacey is author of 18 published books and has contributed to 17 anthologies; most of these are consistently on the New York Times Bestselling <u>Chicken Soup for the Soul</u> books.

For approximately 20 years, Lacey was a military correspondent for The Catholic News Service, where she covered the activities of the 101st Airborne Division (Screaming Eagles).

Lacey is also a freelance journalist and has published more than 800 articles for newspapers and magazines. She has interviewed such notables as actress Patricia Neal, Dolly Parton, Archie Manning and General David Petraeus. Her articles have appeared in all kinds of publications worldwide; here in the U.S., her work has appeared in International Wood Trade, Southern Living and Vanderbilt Magazine.

Lacey is available for editing, speaking engagements and book-signings.

Made in the USA
Columbia, SC
26 February 2024

32300223R00231